C000228539

DATELINE: PURGATORY

DATELINE: PURGATORY

Examining the Case that Sentenced Darlie Routier to Death

Kathy Cruz

With a Foreword by Joyce Ann Brown

TCU Press
Fort Worth, Texas

Copyright © 2015 by Kathy Cruz

Library of Congress Cataloging-in-Publication Data

Cruz, Kathy, author.
 Dateline purgatory : examining the case that sentenced Darlie Routier to death / Kathy Cruz.
   pages cm
 ISBN 978-0-87565-610-6 (alk. paper)
1. Murder--Investigation--Texas--Rowlett. 2. Routier, Darlie, 1970- 3. Routier, Devon, 1989-1996. 4. Routier, Damon, 1991-1996. 5. Children--Crimes against--Texas--Rowlett. 6. Trials (Murder)--Texas. I. Title.
 HV6534.R625C78 2015
 364.152'3092--dc23

                          2014046413

Cover photo courtesy Texas Department of Criminal Justice

The excerpt from "Sabine River Blues" on page XIII is courtesy Document Records Ltd.

The excerpt "Everything here is so clear you can see it" in Chapter 10 is from
"Grazing in the Grass"
Words by Harry Elston
Music by Philemon Hou
© 1968 (Renewed) CHERIO CORP.
All Rights Reserved
Reprinted by Permission of Hal Leonard Corporation

The excerpt from the Craig Watkins interview in Chapter 21 is courtesy of CBS News/*60 Minutes*

TCU Press
TCU Box 298300
Fort Worth, Texas 76129
817.257.7822
www.prs.tcu.edu
To order books: 1.800.826.8911

Designed by fusion29.com

To Howard Swindle, who would have continued seeking the truth
about Darlie Routier if he had lived.
To Stryker and Jake, of whom I couldn't be more proud.
To Jerry Tidwell, a publisher with the vision to see beyond the
boundaries of his newspaper's circulation.
To Tommy Thomason, my mentor and "brother."
To Tracie James Dipple, a friend when I needed one.
To justice.

CONTENTS

CONTENTS

Imperiled Justice

Exonerations Are Proof of Problems in Our Courtrooms

Before I was prosecuted in 1980 by the Dallas County District Attorney's Office for a robbery and murder I did not commit, I, like many others, believed that only the guilty went to prison. I was so naïve—and so wrong.

Words cannot describe what it is like to have one's freedom unjustly ripped from them by a justice system that we are told is the best in the world. Hundreds of exonerations—some for those who have served time on death row—have finally proven what people like me have known for a long, long time: our justice system is flawed.

I lost nine years, five months, and twenty-four days of freedom because Dallas prosecutors pursued me even though they knew I was not the Joyce Ann Brown responsible for the crime. I was blessed. Michael Morton served twenty-five years before he was finally exonerated and the man who prosecuted him held accountable. Because the state got it wrong, the true killer who took the life of Christine Morton is believed to have killed again.

What happened to me and to Michael Morton could happen to you—or to someone you love. I fear that it may have happened to Darlie Routier. I, and many others, have long been troubled by this case. The reasons are many. I always believed Routier's case was so obviously egregious that surely someone would come to her aid, much like Centurion Ministries rescued me from a life behind bars. That has not yet happened—even though Dallas County created the first Conviction Integrity Unit in the nation.

Though several books have been written about the Routier case, they were published shortly after the young mother's conviction, when public opinion was strongly against her. Many things have come to light since she was rushed to trial with stunning speed. The case is worthy of review.

I am living proof of what can happen when one is in the crosshairs of an overly ambitious prosecutor. I am living proof that justice cannot always be found inside a courtroom. I am living proof that the system sometimes gets it wrong. But at least I am living. If the state of Texas gets its way, the same will not hold true for Darlie Routier.

JOYCE ANN BROWN
Wrongfully convicted in Dallas County in 1980,
exonerated in 1989

Perdition

per-di-tion. 1. a. Loss of the soul; eternal damnation

Barbara Davis was on a roll. Her third book was fresh off the presses, and there was little doubt more true-crime books were in the talented author's future. *Precious Angels: A True Story of Two Slain Children and a Mother Convicted of Murder* might prove to be her most lucrative project. After all, the case of "Dallas's Susan Smith" had captured the nation's attention.

Seats in the courtroom at the Kerr County Courthouse had been prime real estate during the capital murder trial of Rowlett homemaker Darlie Routier, accused in the brutal stabbing deaths of her two young sons, but Davis had a seat in the courtroom for the entire five weeks of the trial. A helpful bailiff made sure none of the local looky-loos eager for a juicy story to tell their friends claimed the seat of the author who penned true tales of chilling crimes.

Before writing *Precious Angels*, Davis had written *Stalked: A True Story* and *Suffer the Little Children*. She had sold a movie to ABC. Few writers of true crime had the kind of perspective Davis brought to the keyboard. She had spent more than a decade working for criminal defense attorneys and another decade in the Tarrant County Criminal District Attorney's Office in Fort Worth. She had been a legal secretary for prosecutors in Criminal District Court Number 3, a victims advocate, and a court coordinator for a felony court judge. She had always been on the side of justice and thought prosecutors were, too.

But shortly after *Precious Angels* was published, Davis received a phone call from someone inside the Dallas County District Attorney's Office. The writer was told there were some things she needed to see. The Deep Throat source was leaving the DA's office, and wanted the author whose book praised the work of the Dallas prosecutors to know the truth about what had been done to Darlie Routier.

A secret meeting was arranged. It was there the author says she was confronted with evidence of cover-ups by the DA's office, witness manipulation, suppressed evidence, perjured testimony, and photographs of the blonde housewife's injuries that were entered into evidence, but never published to the jury—a key distinction. "The more I learned and the more I learned, the sicker I got," Davis said almost seventeen years after Routier was sent to Texas's death row. "The final decision for me was the pictures. I cried for days."

As Davis concluded that Darlie Routier had not killed her children, she was hit with another realization: she would no longer feel pride about the book she had dedicated to the Dallas prosecutorial team. Since that meeting, Davis's keyboard has been silenced. She has not written another book since *Precious Angels*. She cut short her own promising career and locked herself into a mental prison of shame and remorse that is perhaps as real as the cell on death row inhabited by Darlie Routier.

Davis feels she deserves the crippling pain of her recently diagnosed degenerative spinal disease because of the role she played in convincing the public that Routier butchered her children. She has searched her soul to determine whether she cared more about selling books than she did the truth. "It became my biggest shame," she says of *Precious Angels* on an autumn night when the pain had released its grip long enough for her to talk about the case that haunts her.

In the years since Routier was sent to a prison unit in Gatesville to await execution, the true-crime author has suffered tragedy. One year after *Precious Angels* was published, her own son, Troy, was shot and killed in a SWAT team no-knock drug raid in the Tarrant County suburb of North Richland Hills. Davis, who was in another room of the house when two bullets from an officer's gun ripped through her son's chest, was arrested on a drug possession charge. It would later be determined the officers were acting on false information. Like Darlie, Davis was locked in a jail cell while grieving the loss of her son.

Eventually, humbled and broken, the talented writer with a once-promising career retreated with her husband to a small Texas town. But her conscience, and the reality of what sometimes happens in Texas courtrooms, has followed her. In a phone conversation with a reporter at a community newspaper a couple hundred miles from the secluded home that has afforded her no refuge, the sixty-one-year-old Davis says: "I know Texas justice. Truth is not the bottom line. Winning is the bottom line."

The author says she will never be free so long as the woman she once vili-fied is behind bars. Routier's ultimate death by lethal injection will be difficult for her to bear. "This case," she says before hanging up, "will bother me until the day I die."

A sliver of autumn moon, a fraction of its potential, has risen over the Sabine River that flows not far from Davis's country home. Its deep, dark waters, spanning more than five hundred miles in Texas and Louisiana, were memorialized by singer Alger "Texas" Alexander in "Sabine River Blues."

I am leavin', sweet Mama, don't you want to go? 'Cause my house is hainted [sic] *and I can't stay there no more.*

ACKNOWLEDGMENTS

I would like to express my gratitude to Courtney Fillmore, a Texas Christian University student and daughter of a lawyer, who arranged my interview with experienced court reporter Suzi Kelly.

I would like to thank my selfless coworker Nancy Pricer, who transcribed recorded interviews and flagged the trial transcript with Post-it notes so that I could more easily find what I needed.

I am grateful to Stephen Cooper, Darlie Kee, and especially Darlie Routier for putting their trust in me, even though they had no reason to do so.

I am thankful to those within the legal profession who had the courage to speak out about this troubling conviction.

Lastly, I appreciate those who are willing to view this case dispassionately, with a fresh perspective and an open mind.

PART I

Silver Bullet

I don't know what these dreams are telling me,
I only know that I am not yet ready to leave my wonderful life here.
Time will tell the story.

. . . .

— DIARY ENTRY OF DARLIE LYNN ROUTIER
SEPTEMBER 7, 1995, NINE MONTHS BEFORE SHE WAS ARRESTED
IN THE KILLINGS OF HER CHILDREN.

"Time Will Tell the Story"

— WAYLON JENNINGS

CHAPTER 1

6-6-6

"Rowlett 9-1-1, what is your emergency?"

It was 2:31 a.m. on June 6, 1996, when a Rowlett emergency dispatcher was jolted to high alert by a hysterical, breathless woman on the other end of the line. "Somebody came in here—they broke in—they just stabbed me and my children!" For five minutes and forty-four seconds, "Operator #1" had a tiger by the tail.

"Oh my God—my babies are dead! . . . some man . . . came in . . . stabbed my babies . . . stabbed me . . . I woke up . . . I was fighting . . . he ran out through the garage . . . threw the knife down . . . my babies are dying . . . they're dead . . . oh my God . . ."

The dispatcher tried to calm Darlie Routier enough to get a grip on what had happened even as she was dispatching units to 5801 Eagle Drive. During the call, other voices joined the fray. The 911 transcript would include Darlie, Operator #1, Operator #2, radio traffic from cops speeding to the scene, and Darlie's husband, Darin.

Darin Routier would tell police he had been sleeping upstairs with the couple's baby, Drake, who was almost eight months old, when he was awakened by his wife's screams. When he went to bed a short time earlier, Darlie had been on a downstairs sofa, where she planned to sleep near Devon and Damon. The little boys had made pallets on the floor in front of the television.

As Darlie stayed on the line with emergency dispatch, Darin performed CPR on six-year-old Devon. He could hear air escaping through the knife wounds in the boy's lungs as quickly as he breathed it into them. The little boy, whose birthday party invitations had just gone out in the mail, would never see seven. He was dead on the family's living room floor, four knife wounds in his torso. Damon survived just long enough for a Rowlett police officer to witness him taking his last breath.

On a nearby countertop, a cluster of Darlie's jewelry sat untouched. Blood was everywhere. It was on the white carpet. It was on the furniture and on Darlie's pillow. It was on the glass coffee table and the linoleum floor leading from the kitchen to the laundry room. It had turned Darlie's Victoria's Secret nightshirt from white to crimson, pouring from a slash across her throat. She had other wounds as well, including a gash in her right arm that went to the bone and would require stitches. Drake and the family's Pomeranian, Domain, were unharmed.

Paramedics lifted the twenty-six-year-old blonde onto a gurney and placed her inside the second ambulance to arrive at the scene. One paramedic cut away Routier's nightshirt and another started a saline IV. Her blood pressure was taken and it was good—140 over 80. There were no indications that her body had gone into shock. Within minutes, medics slammed the ambulance doors shut to begin the frantic drive to Baylor Hospital in Dallas. Darlie and Darin would later state that although she was not wearing underpants when she was treated by the EMTs, she had been wearing panties under her nightshirt when she had settled in for the night.

Damon, too, would be rushed to Baylor by ambulance. Unlike his mother, however, he would not be rushed into surgery. Instead, the boy's lifeless body was zipped into a body bag and taken to the hospital's morgue. Devon's body was still in Rowlett, on the living room floor, the horror of his death being captured by a crime scene photographer.

In the nearby suburb of Plano, a ringing phone heralded the end of Darlie Kee's peaceful sleep, both on that night and for years to come. She had just been with her daughter and grandsons the night before. They had eaten pizza, and she and Darlie had drunk wine and tried on clothes in Darlie's big walk-in closet as they talked about the upcoming wedding of Darlie's younger sister, Dana. Kee rushed to her daughter's home to find it cordoned off by yellow crime scene tape, the shapes of police officers and investigators silhouetted in the yellow light that spilled from the open doorway.

A surgeon stitched together the gash in Darlie's throat, where her necklace had been imbedded. It was not clear whether the necklace had been imbedded by the knife, by Darlie holding a towel to her neck, or by the bandage placed on the wound by a paramedic. Later, two nicks would be found on it.

Before the sun would rise on another hot day in Texas, crime scene investigator James Cron would arrive at the Routier home after having been awakened by a call from a Rowlett 911 dispatcher. Cron, who had retired several years earlier from the Dallas County Sheriff's Department, was a hired gun who provided training to law enforcement and assisted with criminal investigations. Despite the bloody chaos that spanned several rooms, Cron would later tell a jury he had determined within minutes that the crime was an inside job. He made the determination without interviewing Darin or Darlie Routier, and before a sock containing spots of both boys' blood was found seventy-five yards down the alley.

Darlie remained in the hospital for two days. Lying in the hospital bed, medicated and stitched, she was questioned by a lead investigator who took no written notes. More questioning awaited her upon her release. Both Darin and Darlie made themselves available to police. They answered questions and provided written statements, seeing no need for legal representation. The interviews caused the couple to be late for the viewing of the boys' bodies at the funeral home.

A few days after the slain children were buried in a shared coffin at Rest Haven Memorial Park, Darlie, Darin, and other family members and friends held a graveside memorial service. Then they dried their tears and celebrated Devon's birthday with balloons and Silly String. The Silly String had been a favorite plaything of the little boy, and it had been purchased as a birthday gift before his murder. A television news camera captured a shorts-clad, gum-chewing Darlie smiling and spraying Silly String on the fresh grave of her murdered children.

Four days later, after another round of questioning by a police department that had little experience with homicides, Darlie Routier was arrested for capital murder. Kee learned of her daughter's arrest on a television news report. When she arrived at the Rowlett Police Department, she saw officers high-fiving each other. For Kee, the devastation brought by June 6, 1996—6-6-6—had just entered a new dimension. Kee remembers how her daughter had emerged from one of the sessions with investigators and climbed, like a lost child, onto her waiting mother's lap.

"They're helping us, Mom," she had said.

CHAPTER 2

Lone Ranger

It is late on a Friday afternoon in September when I scoot into a booth at the Fuddruckers restaurant off Interstate 20 in the Fort Worth suburb of Benbrook. I am there to meet a man I'll call "Derrick," a licensed private investigator. We had agreed to split the distance—I traveling from the *Hood County News* offices in Granbury, about thirty-five miles southwest of Fort Worth; he driving from his office in Arlington. I have just settled in with a Coke when Derrick calls on my cell phone to say he is stuck in traffic.

The restaurant is empty except for employees preparing for the Friday night dinner rush. I sit in solitude, taking in the cheerful retro décor and the smells of fresh-baked brownies and cookies displayed temptingly in a glass case. An employee replenishes a ketchup dispenser a few feet away as I reflect on the course of events that have put me in a restaurant booth in Benbrook instead of heading home for the weekend.

It had all started with a random thought on a Sunday afternoon months earlier, in April. I had been sitting at my kitchen table, working on my laptop when, out of the blue, came a thought about Darlie Routier. I haven't stopped thinking about her since that day. I had never met Darlie, but my former husband, Howard Swindle, had met Darlie and her mother back in 1996, when the justice system's net had first entangled the family. At that time Howard had been projects editor for the *Dallas Morning News*. He spearheaded the newspaper's investigative projects and had come to believe the jury might have convicted Darlie on little more than character judgments. That feeling grew when, five years after Routier's conviction, her husband Darin admitted that, just before the attacks, he had sought help to stage a burglary of the family's home as part of an insurance scam.

In making its case against Darlie Routier, Rowlett police claimed there was no evidence of an intruder, and that all of the signs pointed to Darlie as the perpetrator. Police said she gave varying accounts, verbally and in writing. In one version, she said there had been no struggle between her and the intruder. In other versions, she either said she fought him on the couch or in the kitchen. She had claimed she was first awakened when Damon poked her on the shoulder and called out to her, but she also claimed that she was awakened by the intruder.

Investigators believed that after committing such a bloody crime, the intruder should have been bloody himself, yet the only blood trail was Darlie's. There were signs that she had washed away blood at the kitchen sink, they said. Shards of a shattered wine glass that allegedly was knocked from a wine rack as she pursued the intruder through the kitchen lay *on top* of her blood rather than under, indicating she had left the trail of blood before the glass was broken. If she had pursued the intruder after the glass was broken, she likely would have had cuts or marks on her feet, police said, but the soles of her feet were not marred. Darlie's bloodstains on the kitchen floor were determined to be "low velocity" stains, indicating that she had been moving slowly—a seeming contradiction to her claims of having pursued her attacker.

There were indications that items in the home had been moved to point to a struggle, yet the lack of damage indicated "a proprietary interest" in the items, according to the state's *Statement of Facts*. The glass top of a coffee table was knocked off its base, but not broken. The vase of flowers that had been atop the coffee table was knocked over, but neither the vase nor the flowers were broken or bloody. The shade of a nearby floor lamp was askew, but the lamp was still standing. As with the flower arrangement, the lamp was not damaged or bloodstained. Police found it curious that a burglar would leave expensive jewelry lying in plain sight.

Bloodstains on and beneath a vacuum cleaner in the kitchen indicated to police that it had been used as part of the staging. A window screen in the garage, where Darlie claimed the intruder had gone after fleeing through the kitchen and utility room, was cut, but investigators determined the screen had been cut from the inside. A fiber found on a bread knife taken from a butcher block in the kitchen was determined to be consistent with the material in the cut window screen. The windowsill had a thick layer of dust that was undisturbed, as was the mulch in the flower bed outside the window. The backyard's gate was difficult to open and close, yet there were no scuff marks indicating it had been kicked by a fleeing intruder.

The first officer on the scene claimed that Darlie did nothing to help Damon, who was still alive, even though the officer instructed her several times to render aid to her son. Drops of both boys' blood were found on Darlie's nightshirt. According to the state's *Statement of Facts:* "Some of the stains were consistent with appellant swinging the bloody knife up over her shoulder, and others were consistent with her swinging it down and into the boys' bodies." The document detailing facts of the case also states: "The deep penetrating wounds to the boys' vital organs indicated that the boys were the focus of the attack and that the attack was personal and motivated by anger. In stark contrast to the boys' wounds, appellant suffered only superficial cuts that avoided vital areas and could have been self-inflicted."

Medical staff at Baylor Hospital testified that during Darlie's two-day hospital stay, she had a flat affect and showed little emotion over the loss of her sons. They said they saw no sign of the severe bruising on her arms that Rowlett police photographed two days after her release, and that there should have been signs of the developing bruises during her hospital stay.

Investigators would discover that Darin and Darlie had gotten behind on their mortgage payment, as well as on a credit card payment. Business was down at Testnec, Darin's computer business. Two days before the murders, he was turned down for a $5,000 bank loan that he claimed was to pay for a vacation. When investigators confronted Darlie about a cryptic and seemingly incriminating diary entry she made a month before the murders, she said the reference was to a halfhearted plan to kill herself, not her children. Both she and Darin said that she had experienced some postpartum depression after Drake's birth, but that the depression had lifted. The case against Darlie Routier seemed damning. A jury in Kerrville bought into the state's theory. So, too, did most of the media and the public. But in the years since Darlie was convicted and sent to death row, there have been nagging doubts about her guilt. The quality and extent of the small town police department's investigation continue to be questioned. The prosecutors who tried the case have been criticized for bringing character judgments into the courtroom, and Darlie's star-quality lead defense attorney has been accused of not having adequately defended her. At least one juror regrets the guilty verdict.

Adding to the feelings of unease is that Routier does not fit the mold of mothers who killed their children. History has shown that they ultimately confess, but Darlie Routier has not. Years after her conviction, she continues to maintain her innocence. Though testimony about bloodstain evidence at the crime scene played a significant role in Darlie's conviction, the reliability of bloodstain pattern analysis has since been called into question. So, too, has the credibility of "experts" whose testimony may depend on which side is signing their paychecks.

As a Fuddruckers employee takes a tray of chocolate chip cookies out of the oven, I think back to the day in 1996 when I drove from our home in Richardson to the Routier's house on Eagle Drive in Rowlett, after taking my own two little boys to "Mother's Day Out" at our church. I didn't know why I felt compelled to go there. Now here I was, sixteen years later, having made another drive because of Darlie Routier.

Darlie had been on death row for two and a half years when, in the summer of 1999, my husband and I moved our family from the suburb north of Dallas to the lake community of Granbury, in Hood County. He died of cancer in the summer of 2004, not long after we divorced. In 2007, I went back to newspaper work, taking a job at the *Hood County News*. Working at a community newspaper was a far cry from my more glamorous days of working as a reporter for the *Dallas Morning News*, but my love of reporting was not diminished.

It had been in June 2012—after thoughts of Darlie had disturbed my sleep and my concentration—that I sent her a message through the prison system's JPay e-mail. Weeks passed. Then one day, as I sat working with my back to the opening of my cubicle, an arm reached over my shoulder with an envelope in the outstretched hand. "Mail for you." In the upper left-hand corner of the envelope, in feminine script, was the name "Routier." It had been four years since Texas's most infamous female death-row inmate had consented to a media interview, but she agreed to meet with me for two reasons: my former husband had treated her kindly; and my e-mail had mentioned the month of April. I would later learn that the month of April held spiritual significance for her, and this played a role in why she agreed to meet with me.

The prison system scheduled our interview for a Tuesday afternoon in August—perfect timing for the hour-and-a-half drive, since we put the Wednesday issue to bed by midmorning. The drive from Granbury to Gatesville took me through Glen Rose—"Dinosaur Valley"—where one of my former *Dallas Morning News* colleagues was running a community newspaper and shaking things up in a town where news coverage had seemed stuck in the Stone Age. I passed through Hico, former stomping grounds of Billy the Kid and, legend has it, the Ku Klux Klan, turning left by the Koffee Kup to head down the two-lane highway to Hamilton. Turning left on the town square, I passed the offices of the *Hamilton Herald-News*. Years earlier, the editor at the tiny newspaper had dispatched a reporter to interview the mother of a local boy who had left to pursue a career in journalism in the big city and had just won a Pulitzer Prize. Two more would follow for Howard Swindle, then the projects editor at the largest newspaper in the Southwest.

Though the state of Texas is vast, my journey to Darlie Routier happened to take me past Weiser Street, where my mother-in-law had lived. Storm's Hamburgers on the corner appeared untouched by the years. From Hamilton it is thirty miles to Gatesville, where the Mountain View prison unit sits just off the highway. The street leading into the prison complex is named, oddly enough, Ransom Road.

I parked where instructed, near a tower with an armed guard. Eventually, a guard came for me. She searched my vehicle and even looked under the hood. At a guard station by the gate, I placed my notebook, pens, camera, and recorder into a tray for inspection. The guard removed the batteries from the camera, and then put them back in. She waved a wand over my body, and asked me to remove my shoes so that the soles of my feet could be checked. She escorted me through two gates and down a sidewalk toward a building. We went inside through the lobby, then through the doors of the cinder block visitation room, where inmates and visitors talk through barriers of wire and bulletproof glass. Darlie saw me before I saw her. "Hey!" rang a friendly voice.

I rounded the corner of the enclosure and there was Darlie Routier. Her hair is now a soft brown instead of bleached blonde, but she still looks like the woman featured long ago on evening news reports and true-crime shows. We talked for two hours. I relayed a message from her mother, with whom I had been communicating, since Darlie had provided her cell phone number in her letter to me. The message was that she had not yet spoken to Derrick, but expected to do so soon. I had assumed Derrick was a relative or a family friend. Darlie didn't explain his identity, but hinted she viewed him as a possible answer to prayer. She said she had begun praying in March "for certain things to happen." April, she said, brought indications that maybe God had been listening. Her mother would later explain that Derrick was a licensed private investigator who had written to Darlie in April, offering to work pro bono on her case. Between my communications with mother and daughter, it became clear that Routier thought both Derrick and I might be part of God's response to her pleas for relief. Had I not mentioned in my e-mail that I had begun thinking of Darlie in April, it is likely she would not have met with me. If nothing else, the timing of my message was a stroke of luck.

During our talk at Mountain View, Darlie went back in time to the summer of 1996. "It was just an ordinary day," she said, reflecting on June 5—the last normal day her family would experience. "I had talked to my dad that day because we were fixin' to fly [to Pennsylvania] for my grandparents' fiftieth anniversary. Devon's birthday was planned that week. Invitations were sent out. Presents were bought." Within minutes, under a Texas moon, everything changed. "People are not as safe and secure as they want to think," Darlie said, the scar on her throat visible above the collar of her white prison jumpsuit. "If this could happen to me, it could happen to anybody else."

Only once during our interview did her eyes fill with tears. It was when she was talking about Drake, just under eight months old when his brothers were killed in the downstairs living room. Now, he was about to start his junior year in a high school in Lubbock. His seventeenth birthday would be in October. "I used to dream of walking out of prison and running to him and picking him up," Darlie said. "But now, he's going to be picking *me* up. He's six-two."

When our interview was over, Darlie remained in her chair behind glass and cinder block, patiently waiting for someone to come for her. I expected her eyes to follow me, as if wishing she could leave, too, but they did not. She seemed far more at peace than I could ever imagine. A guard escorted me outside, into the sunshine. I was keenly aware that I was free to go. As I turned the key in the ignition, the air conditioner blasted through the searing Texas heat as if trying to force me to shake off the numbness that had enveloped me.

Groundskeepers in carts motored on to their next task, driving past the visitors' parking area where Darlie's family and friends have made regular pilgrimages for so many years now. Guards stood watch in towers. Others walked to or from their vehicles on the staff parking lot. From one wafted the mournful voice of Waylon Jennings, singing about a beloved woman who deserved a better life.

Two things happened after that day. One was that I began writing a series of newspaper articles about the Routier case that were made available to hundreds of other community newspapers through the Texas Center for Community Journalism. If Darlie is indeed innocent, I reasoned, then what happened to her could happen to anyone, whether they live in Galveston or Glen Rose, Houston or Hamilton. The other thing that happened was that I bought a

Waylon Jennings CD. It was to become the sound track of my journey back in time, to when a killer claimed the lives of little Devon and Damon Routier, and the Texas justice system claimed their mother.

At Fudduckers, my reflections are interrupted by movement in my peripheral vision. A strapping, handsome man in a black shirt and a black cowboy hat strides confidently to my booth, looking like a cowboy who has just dismounted a white horse to rescue a damsel in distress. Derrick has arrived. A couple hours later, on the drive back home, an e-mail appears on my iPhone from the Innocence Project in New York. The e-mail announces that Damon Thibodeaux has just become the nation's three hundredth DNA exoneration and the eighteenth exoneree to have served time on death row. Thibodeaux had been convicted of the rape and murder of his fourteen-year-old step-cousin.

The timing of the message makes me wonder whether it is an omen indicating Derrick might indeed uncover previously hidden facts that could shed light on the controversial Darlie Routier case. After all, it has happened now with hundreds of other inmates who spent years—decades, even—behind bars. But the tall investigator with the tall promises leaves Darlie Routier's life almost as quickly as he came into it. Darlie's appellate team would soon come to view him as a little too insistent on gaining access to their attractive client on death row. It is not the first time a man has tried to meet Darlie with promises to save her.

I press on with the series, though the stories will not involve a colorful cowboy hero. Of the two April connections that Darlie Routier had hoped might be an answer to prayer, the one that fell by the wayside was the one that seemed to hold the most promise of exposing any hidden truths. Time will tell the story.

CHAPTER 3

Young Love in Purgatory, Colorado

Lubbock, Texas, May 1985: two star-crossed young lovers meet at the Western Sizzlin restaurant on Indiana Drive. Their meeting isn't by accident. Darlie Kee, a waitress at the popular steak chain, had told her hardworking cowork-er, Darin Routier, that her pretty fifteen-year-old daughter (and namesake) would be joining her and other family members for a Mother's Day lunch.

"I talked Darlie into coming to the restaurant with me and her sisters to eat. I told Darin she was coming," says Kee, who met me for the first time on an August Sunday at another steak restaurant in Mesquite, just east of Dallas. She had met me halfway so that I wouldn't have to drive to Wills Point, where she now lives with her husband, Bob. She jokes that their union is her "third and final marriage."

At the Western Sizzlin, Kee found not only a source of income to help support her three young daughters, but deep and lasting friendships. She and the other waitresses wore knee-length black skirts, red polka-dot shirts and, on one occasion, butter. "Once, we were working a late shift and about to close. We employees had to make butter balls to put in cups for the cheese rolls, and we had to clean all the condiment dishes. Someone was goofing around and we ended up having a butter fight. Even the cooks got involved. By the time we left, everything was all clean and shiny, but during the drive home, I was still fishing butter out of my hair.

"The girls—Joanie, Trish, Candy, Karen, and Margie—we'd get together for birthdays and for drinks after work. I remember sharing a few Blue Ha-waiians with about four other straws in the fishbowl glass. We were great at karaoke that night. It was a big family there. I am still friends with a few of the other women to this day. We covered for each other when we were sick, and gave up shifts for those who really needed the money that week. We partied

Darlie Kee, Darlie Routier's mother.
Photo by the author.

together and cried together. We went through divorces, separations, and marriages together.

"Every Mother's Day, there was a line that stretched out the door. When Darin saw me and Darlie that Mother's Day in 1985, he joined us in line, and that was it. They were together from that moment on."

The couple believed, as most young people did, that their future was full of promise. At an early age both had proven themselves to be responsible and hard working. Darlie became employed at just fifteen, first at McDonald's, then at Lubbock's other Western Sizzlin restaurant, on Slide Road. After she met Darin, who was the head cook at the Indiana Drive location, she transferred there.

"Darlie went everywhere with Darin. They were very responsible teens. They paid for their vehicles and insurance and most of their clothes. Darlie Lynn got grounded when she did something wrong, like stay out late with Darin. And Darin got an earful from parents on both sides. One or the other set of parents knew where they were most of the time. I am not saying they didn't go to parties, or that they didn't test their limits at times.

"Darlie and Darin were just madly in love. No one was going to stop that. He told me that he was going to marry her. I believed in young love, and our only requirements were that they finish school. I loved Darin like my son, and his family felt the same way about Darlie. Sarilda (Darin's mother) and I both married young. I believe Sarilda was fifteen and Lenny was seventeen. My

Teenagers Darin Routier and Darlie Peck smile for the camera in a photo booth. *Photo courtesy Darlie Kee.*

folks were seventeen and nineteen, and were married sixty-one years. That's just how the world was. Darin's parents went skiing a lot. When Darlie was sixteen and Darin was a senior, they all went on a ski trip to Purgatory, Colorado. Darlie came home with a ring and lots of bruises from learning to ski.

"Darin graduated from high school and went to work for Cuplex (a computer company) in the Dallas area. Darlie later moved to Dallas to be with him. They married in August 1988, at Sarilda's and Lenny's house. They paid for most of the wedding. Darlie got a beautiful dress at an obscene low price while shopping with Sarilda on New Year's Day. Times were hard financially for most families, but I remember giving them my utility money to use for a honeymoon. I could always pick up extra shifts and pay the late fee, right?

"They went on their honeymoon, and she gave up her birth control. Devon was born on June 14, 1989. I cannot tell you how much that baby was wanted and loved. He was the only grandchild. I was not allowed in the delivery room, nor was Sarilda, because they didn't allow anyone but the father back then. Sarilda and I were there in the waiting room, crying, when Darin came out with the news of Devon's birth. He was born in Baylor Hospital. I had a new man in my life.

"I had moved to Dallas with Darlie's sisters by that time, and we were close to Darin and Darlie from then on. I loved Devon so much. I used to call Darlie and tell her I was coming to get him for a day or so. I had him in the pool with me when he was three months old. I have nine grandchildren today, and I include Devon and Damon in that number.

Happier days: Damon and Devon Routier pose for the camera atop a pile of hay. *Photo courtesy Darlie Kee.*

"For a long time, it was just Devon and Damon. They were inseparable. I remember them loading up their wagon with used toys and going door to door, trying to sell them. It was a garage sale on wheels. They ended up donating the toys to a children's charity. Devon was the older brother and Damon hung on his every word. We took groups of kids to the dollar movie. We went camping together.

"Darlie loved her sisters, and they spent days at a time with her. We shared every holiday either at her house, Sarilda's house, or my house. If we weren't at Darlie's and Darin's for a Dallas Cowboys game, we were swimming at my pool or going to company parties together or shopping together. Someone stole that from us. Someone stole that from Darin and Darlie and from Devon's and Damon's younger brother, Drake. The prosecutors from Dallas didn't know my family, and they still don't. In my view, there were some involved in the case who lied and destroyed Darlie's and Darin's marriage, and they did it for the sake of their careers.

"I miss Devon and Damon every day. Darlie and I talk about them almost every visit. We have all these memories. We cry together and laugh together and miss them together. I had a close relationship with Darlie when she was growing up, and I have it with her now, through glass. No one can take that from us.

"The abuse of Darlie Lynn is more than a tragedy. They have attacked a family that will not back down, even if the abuse carries us to death's door. Darlie is not just beautiful on the outside, but on the inside as well. She would never hurt any living being. It is that simple. The state of Texas got it wrong, and I hate that my family is having to live through this. What do you do for your child? The same thing I am doing for Darlie and for the rest of my family: fight like hell, and show the world the truth about Darlie Routier.

"This is very, very hard. At times, I just want to cry and let myself become immersed in missing my grandsons and my daughter while hopefully finding the strength to see tomorrow as another day. No one knows what it is like to see all my children go through hell, to see Darin destroyed and Sarilda and Lenny changed forever.

"The killer or killers of Devon and Damon have probably killed again, and no one seems to care. Those who were involved in what happened to Darlie—their karma is right around the corner, I hope. No one should be attacked this way. No parent should have this fight on their hands. But how do you fight Satan?"

CHAPTER 4

Innocence Lost

In the Lubbock offices of the Innocence Project of Texas (IPTX), law students from the Texas Tech University School of Law have gathered to report to founder Jeff Blackburn on their research on arson convictions. The students are just a few weeks into the fall semester, and I am in the early stages of researching both the Routier case and issues that are now known to lead to wrongful convictions. Blackburn is among those who have brought such problems to light. He served on the Timothy Cole Advisory Panel, which was created by the legislature in 2009 to investigate why innocent people are sometimes put behind bars.

The advisory panel was named for former Texas Tech student Timothy Cole, who was wrongfully convicted of raping fellow student Michele Mallin in 1985. Cole was sentenced to twenty-five years in prison. On December 2, 1999—fourteen years into his sentence—Cole died in prison of an asthma-related heart attack after being forced to work in the fields. In 2007, another inmate—Jerry Wayne Johnson—confessed to raping Mallin, and Mallin acknowledged that she had been mistaken when she claimed Cole had been her attacker. Blackburn and IPTX worked with Mallin and Cole's family to clear his name. In 2010, then-Governor Rick Perry granted Cole the state's first posthumous pardon. Today, a thirteen-foot bronze and granite statue of Cole stands on 19th Street in Lubbock. The memorial is the first of its kind to honor a wrongfully convicted person.

Blackburn, an Amarillo criminal defense attorney with a passion for civil rights cases, represented thirty-eight people in the Panhandle town of Tulia who were arrested in a 1999 drug sting based solely on the testimony of one police officer with a checkered history. A total of forty-six arrests in the sting made up nearly half of Tulia's adult black population. Blackburn's work with the National Association for the Advancement of Colored People (NAACP) Legal Defense Fund to correct the injustice captured the attention

The power of DNA: This cart, marked Dallas DNA, is full of files that are kept in the storeroom of the Innocence Project of Texas's Lubbock office. At the time this book went to press, DNA testing had resulted in 27 exonerations from Dallas County. Total exonerations from Dallas County numbered 52, and the number nationwide was 1,536. *Photo by the author.*

of Hollywood, but the film featuring Billy Bob Thornton as Blackburn and Halle Berry as an attorney with the NAACP never materialized.

On this afternoon in the IPTX offices near Texas Tech, the focus is on the groundbreaking partnership forged between IPTX, the State Fire Marshal's Office, and the Forensic Science Commission. Said to be the first such partnership in the nation, the review of arson convictions is based on concerns over flawed science and on the cases of Cameron Todd Willingham and Ernest Willis. In terms of what was presented as evidence at their trials, the men's cases were very similar. Yet in 2004, Willingham was executed, and Willis was exonerated.

Seated around a conference table in a back room at the IPTX offices, Blackburn takes a particular interest in an arson case being reviewed by two female students. They tell him that the arson "expert" who helped put a man in prison paid one hundred dollars for his certificate. "Girls, I think you're on to something with this," Blackburn tells them.

Darin and Darlie Routier pose for a formal portrait
prior to 6-6-6. *Photo courtesy Darlie Kee.*

Blackburn wraps up the two-hour class with a brief lecture about why the current justice system should never be trusted. "People should be very, very afraid. From the minute we're born, we're told that America is the greatest place in the world. But all it takes is a cop that doesn't like you."

At 5:00 p.m., as the students gather their things to leave, Blackburn invites them to join him at a local bar for a beer. Nick Vilbas, IPTX's young, tattooed executive director, locks up the office and rides his bicycle to join them. I do not tag along with the group because I am due to meet Sarilda Routier, Darin Routier's mother, at a local restaurant.

As Blackburn goes one way and I go another, I reflect upon his lecture and the state's questionable theory and time line in the Darlie Routier case. Blackburn had advised the future lawyers to think carefully about alleged scenarios painted by forensic experts, law enforcement, and prosecutors. "If it's not probable, then it's probably not true," he said. "Play the movie in your head."

How likely is it, I wonder, that a young wife and mother with no prior history of violence or mental problems would stab her children when her husband was within earshot upstairs? Why would she kill two of her children,

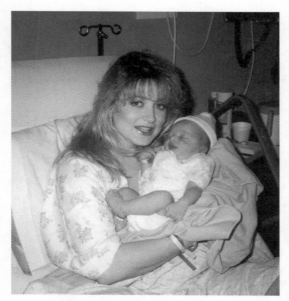

Darlie Routier holds newborn Damon.
Photo courtesy Darlie Kee.

but not all three? Why would she spare the child that required the most of her time and attention? What are the chances that Routier cut her arm to the bone and slashed her own throat? How likely is it that Routier stabbed her children, staged the crime scene, and deposited the bloodstained sock seventy-five yards down the alley in the brief span of minutes allotted by the state's time line? According to courtroom testimony, Damon would have lived only minutes after being stabbed. His blood was on the sock, which meant that the sock was deposited down the alley after he was attacked. Since there was no blood trail, Darlie would have had to inflict her own injuries *after* depositing the sock. Her 911 call lasted five minutes and forty-four seconds; she hung up only after the first responders arrived. And at that point, Damon was still alive.

These questions and doubts have plagued others in the years since Routier's conviction. In November 2008, US District Judge Royal Furgeson of the US District Court Western District of Texas signed an order granting Darlie Routier the right to do additional DNA testing. On page sixteen of the eighteen-page document, Furgeson wrote:"While petitioner has not identified with specificity precisely how the test results in question might fully exonerate her, the theory underlying the prosecution's case against petitioner is as convoluted and counterintuitive as that of any death penalty case to come before this court."

* * *

Sarilda Routier, dressed elegantly in a black top and slacks, arrives ten minutes late at Stella's restaurant on 50th Street in Lubbock. She had been delayed saying goodbye to her grandson, Drake, who has recently begun his junior year in high school. Sarilda has been both a surrogate mother and grandmother to the teen since his mother was sent to death row when he was a year old.

At a corner table at Stella's, Sarilda paints a picture of Darlie that is far different from the picture Dallas County prosecutors presented to the public. Darlie, she said, was a doting mother and, as room mother for son Devon's first grade class, bought treats for every student. The Routier house in Rowlett had been a favorite hangout for neighborhood kids, she said, because Darlie made sure the freezer was stocked with Popsicles.

She said that in June 1996, when Darlie lay in the intensive care unit at Baylor Hospital in Dallas with a slash across her throat and stitches in her arm, she lifted her daughter-in-law's hospital gown and saw a mass of black bruises. "I said, 'Darlie, my gosh, look at those bruises all over you!' I said, 'What happened?' She said, 'Well, I guess when he stabbed me, it bled under my skin.' She was fighting him like a tiger."

The jury didn't buy Darlie's claim that she had struggled with an unknown intruder who had fled through the utility room. They believed what prosecutors Greg Davis and Toby Shook said had happened to Devon and his little brother, Damon.

Sarilda thinks back on how naïve the family was back then—back before Darlie was arrested and charged with murder. Back when they had more faith in the system. "The police were putting on this big show of feeling sorry for her," she said. "They played us like a harp, and we sang to the tune. I'm sure they had big laughs over how they played us, and how we fell for it."

Referring to her son and the month when life changed forever, Sarilda says: "He says he can feel June coming."

Drake is well adjusted and a towering six feet two inches tall, his grandmother tells me. He likes girls, and they like him. He thinks the mothers of his friends love him for his personality—which is largely true—but Sarilda knows there is another reason. They all know he is the son of Darlie Routier.

Sarilda Routier, Darin Routier's mother.
Photo by the author.

The sisterhood of mothers has stepped in to fill the void.

When Drake returns from visits to the Mountain View prison unit in Gatesville, he is very quiet, Sarilda says. On this night, in the glow of a candle, she recounts the boy's demeanor when he recently returned from a visit with the mother he is never allowed to embrace.

"I said, 'Well, how's Mother?'

"'Beautiful,' was his one-word reply.

"When you have God in your life, you're not aware of how much you're carried," Sarilda says, as the wait staff at Stella's clean the dining room that is now empty except for our candlelit table in the corner. "God picks you up and puts you back down." Blackburn at IPTX had spoken about God, but in a different way. "People want to believe that God is in Heaven, and that they're not going to get swept up off the street and that nothing bad is going to happen to them."

Before leaving Stella's, where she had spent the last three and a half hours reliving painful memories, Sarilda shares her belief that angels were present when her grandsons breathed their last on 6-6-6. God allowed evil to prevail, Sarilda says, for a bigger, as-yet-to-be-revealed purpose. Before walking out the door and into darkness, she bows her head in prayer. The parking lot is nearly empty, though a few shadowy figures are silhouetted near a car in the distance. From behind the roofline of a darkened church, veins of lightning split the nighttime sky.

CHAPTER 5

Aunt Sandy's Notebooks

Sandy Aitken is inside the Walmart in Azle on a September afternoon when her cell phone rings. She and her husband, Robert, are shopping before getting on the road to go to the bedside of Sandy's ailing father in Houston. The voice on the other end of Sandy's phone is mine. I had tracked her down after Darlie Kee encouraged me to find Darin Routier's Aunt Sandy, because she had been the only family member allowed inside the Kerrville courtroom during Darlie's trial. Aunt Sandy, Darlie Kee said, had filled notebook after notebook with handwritten notes that documented the now-deceased state district judge Mark Tolle falling asleep—or at least appearing to fall asleep—numerous times as Darlie was on trial for her life.

Darlie Kee hasn't spoken to Aunt Sandy in years, and doesn't know where to find her. "Call Sarilda," she instructs me. "She'll give you her number." I call Darin's mother, as instructed, and she gives me Sandy's cell phone number. I soon discovered that Sandy lives in Springtown, just on the other side of Weatherford—only about an hour's drive from my office.

I feel apprehensive as I explain to this stranger on the other end of the line who I am, how I got her number, and why I am calling. The line remains silent for several seconds. Then Sandy speaks. The notes had been packed away for years, she tells me, but in an uncanny coincidence she had come across them, buried inside her kitchen hutch, just two days earlier. She had exhumed the papers and set them by the dining room table. She said she would be happy to share them with me.

* * *

The turn onto Carter Road from FM-51 North, about eleven miles from the Parker County Courthouse, is like passing through a time portal. On this day in early October, the rolling fields and meadows are no longer a parched

Family ties: Darin Routier's aunt, Sandy Aitken, and her husband, Robert, believe strongly in Darlie's innocence. Both believe the crime was connected to Darin's attempts to stage a home burglary as part of an insurance scam. When Sandy agreed with Waco businessman Brian Pardo's determination that Darin was likely involved, there was a rift in the family. *Photo by the author.*

summer brown, but have not yet exploded into autumn's brilliant colors. For a brief window of time, it is God's green country. The two-lane, winding road affords a view of frisky goats and lazy cows. Near the turn that leads to Aunt Sandy's house, a rooster bravely traverses the worse-for-wear country road, his head jerking forward and back as if he is propelling himself through sheer perseverance.

It is on an offshoot of Carter Road that Sandy and her husband live with their three dogs. Their home is spotless, with cozy furniture and an antique-style radio sitting on the kitchen island. "Church in the Wildwood" is playing when I come to call.

Sandy and her husband Robert take seats at the kitchen table to talk about the woman Sandy's nephew, Darin, married back in 1988. Sandy hasn't seen her in more than a decade. Premature triplet grandbabies and other happenings in a busy life eventually made it too difficult to travel all the way to women's death row in Gatesville.

But it all comes flooding back on this Tuesday afternoon, as Sandy spreads the papers that have been tucked away for years inside the kitchen hutch. The conversation involving harsh realities and modern-day crimes clashes with the guileless country decor. Robert tells me that what happened to Darlie "affects the whole family." He says: "For years, every time I would pass a cop, I would start to shake. I would think, 'If he pulls me over, am I going to jail?'"

Sandy and her husband had rushed to Baylor Hospital in Dallas on June 6, 1996, arriving hours after Darlie was brought out of surgery. Little Damon was in another part of the hospital, in a body bag. In less than two weeks, Rowlett police would arrest Darlie, claiming she had murdered her children, sliced her own throat, and beat herself with a blunt object to cause the massive bruising that appeared on her arms.

"Darlie's beautiful. Beautiful women don't mangle themselves," says Sandy. "Beautiful women will take sleeping pills. Even in death, they want to look good. But I don't think Darlie was vain. Darlie was just a regular girl."

When Darlie made collect calls to Aunt Sandy from the Lew Sterrett Justice Center, Sandy promised her that God would take care of her. She kept telling Darlie that right up to the time a jury in Kerrville pronounced her guilty and she was whisked off to death row.

During the month-long trial in Kerrville, Sandy sat in the courtroom every day. "Sandy, you slipped under their radar," lead defense attorney Doug Mulder would tell her, referring to prosecutors having banished from the courtroom other family members who were set to testify.

At first, Sandy jotted notes in a spiral notebook as a way to distract herself from what she felt was an atmosphere hostile to Darlie and her family. But then she began recording the proceedings in earnest, as fast as her fingers could move the pen. Mulder, she said, would always tell her how much her note taking annoyed the Dallas County prosecutors.

When serious problems later arose with court reporter Sandra Halsey, no one turned to Sandy for help in reconstructing the trial transcript, which was found to contain a multitude of errors. Sandy, after all, was not an official court reporter. Her notes could not be mistaken for a professional record of the proceedings that took place in the Kerr County Courthouse those weeks in early 1997. They're handwritten, and are sometimes interrupted with pleas for God's help. There are notations that have nothing to do with witness testimony, like this one on page 156: "Serious sleeping from judge."

"I had never been inside of a courtroom. I had never been to a trial," says Sandy. "But I thought as long as there's a good leader, you're going to be okay. As long as the one who's there to keep things in order is okay, then surely this whole thing will be okay." But presiding judge Mark Tolle, according to Sandy's notes, appeared to fall asleep sixteen times as Darlie Routier was on trial for her life.

Before driving out to see Sandy—a meeting that was delayed several times because of her father's illness—I had begun checking with legal experts, asking their opinions as to whether a judge falling asleep on the bench is worthy of concern. Brian Stull believes so. The senior staff attorney for the American Civil Liberties Union's (ACLU) Capital Punishment Project says judges play a "crucial" role in trial proceedings because they have to "constantly be making decisions" as evidence is presented in court. "There wouldn't be a baseball game without an umpire, so how can anyone agree with a death sentence in a trial where, effectively, you have no judge?" he tells me. "You have all these constitutional rights and all these statutory rights—and the judge cannot guarantee that the trial goes fairly if the judge is asleep."

Adding this to the court reporter's error-riddled trial transcript, an observer might find reason to question the validity of Routier's trial. "I think the court reporter/judge sleeping is a really bad combination," Stull says. "One of the things that concerns me about this case is that the notes seem to reflect that this [the judge sleeping] is happening repeatedly throughout the trial. Each time it happens, it just increases the concern and makes it less likely that she [Sandy] was mistaken. The more it happened, the more I think anyone would be concerned."

On some of Sandy's notations about the judge sleeping, she wrote the time at which he appeared to nod off. On page 105, it was at 4:45 p.m.; on page 108, it was 9:15 a.m.; on page 111, it was 9:40 a.m.; on page 121, it was 2:00 p.m.; and on page 155, it was 1:35 p.m. On page 48, she wrote this: "Judge is sleeping again. What a job."

There were two such notations on page 138, written as Rowlett Police Lieutenant James Walling was testifying about his handling of bloody crime scene evidence, some of which he said he put in his car. The trial defense team had been concerned because inexperienced police officers had placed bloody items in the same evidence bags, thus raising the possibility that blood transfers had occurred. Transfers would have compromised the integrity of any blood spatter interpretation. In the midst of Walling's testimony on that very topic, Sandy wrote this: "Judge seriously sleeping." She underlined the words twice.

Darlie mentioned Tolle's tendency to nod off in one of her letters to me, as

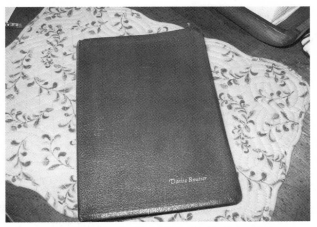

A testament to faith: Sandy Aitken is keeping Darlie Routier's embossed Bible in hopes that Darlie can someday reclaim it as a free woman. *Photo by the author.*

well. "I wouldn't say Judge Tolle slept through 'much' of the trial, but he did fall asleep several times and comments were made about it," she wrote. "One time is unacceptable. This was a capital murder case!"

Sandy and the reporters covering the highly publicized trial were not the only ones scribbling away in the courtroom. At the defense table, Darlie was, too. During breaks, members of the defense team would slip Sandy the notes Darlie wrote to her as witness after witness pushed her ever closer to the execution chamber. "I will never turn from God," was how she ended one letter, in girlish, looped cursive.

Darlie's blue Bible, with her name embossed on a corner of the cover, lies among the notes and memories of Darlie that are strewn on the kitchen table at Aunt Sandy's and Uncle Robert's house. Darlie, Sandy says, gave it to her to keep until she can someday reclaim it.

The trial was "the biggest farce I have ever seen in my life." Darlie, Sandy says, was judged on things that had nothing to do with whether she had committed murder. I think back to my first interview with Darlie two months earlier, at the Mountain View prison unit in Gatesville. She had spoken of the judgments that had been levied against her when her life hung in the balance. "At the time, I was called materialistic. I dyed my hair blonde. I liked to shop. I had a boob job. I'm like, okay, if that is the criteria for a murderer, then ninety

27

percent of the women in Dallas would be [killers]. It really hurt, because I felt like I had to really defend myself for those things. I was twenty-six years old. Of course I liked to wear nice clothes and do my hair, but that stuff didn't matter to me. Anybody that was around me will tell you the same thing.

"Darin and I, before we ever started making money, we were practically poor. We lived in a little apartment, no furniture hardly, just barely making it. But we were so happy. We were so happy."

The autumn light is a golden hue as I head back toward the entrance to the time portal, back to current-day Granbury, where there will be a city council meeting to cover that evening. A dog lopes up a long driveway. A woman in a shirt the color of pumpkins maneuvers a riding lawn mower. The plucky rooster is again in the road, where it doesn't belong. Its head thrusts forward and back, forward and back, as if it trusts sheer perseverance to get it safely over perilous terrain to the other side.

CHAPTER 6

Crimefighter

It is a rainy Saturday in May—Memorial Day weekend. Towering pine trees along Interstate 20 indicate that after three and a half hours on the road, my destination is finally near. I am in Northeast Texas, near Tyler (the "Rose Capital of the World") and the piney woods of Tyler State Park. In the outlying community of Lindale, I take the US 69 exit, pulling into the parking lot of a combination Dairy Queen/Chevron station/convenience store.

At first, I don't recognize the man standing outside DQ's doors as former FBI special agent Lloyd Harrell. The man who had been known to the Dallas press as "Crimefighter" had been hired to join Darlie Routier's defense team as a licensed private investigator. After retiring from the FBI, Harrell had operated his own investigation company. He'd known lead defense attorney Doug Mulder since the early 1970s, when Mulder was a prosecutor working for Dallas County District Attorney Henry Wade. Mulder and a team of FBI agents that included Harrell had prosecuted the men responsible for kidnapping the daughter-in-law of Joe Dealey, then president of the *Dallas Morning News*. Mulder and Harrell would go on to work other cases together through the years. It was no surprise that when the prosecutor-turned-defense-attorney was hired to represent Darlie Routier, he picked Harrell to be part of the rescue team.

On this rainy day in May, no one would guess the glamorous past of the gray-haired man dressed in shorts, a tan H&H Argentina Outfitters ball cap, and a white T-shirt that says "Bimini Big Game Club." We settle into a booth by windows that provide unglamorous views of gas pumps and the interstate. A little more than a year earlier, two elderly women in a Mercury sedan had pulled up to one of the pumps and then proceeded to plow through the front of the store. After the mishap, they'd waited on their ride at this DQ.

Haunted: Although almost two decades
have passed since he worked as an
investigator for Darlie Routier's trial
defense team, retired FBI special
agent Lloyd Harrell, known to many
as Crimefighter, continues to have
sleepless nights over the case. He is
convinced Routier is innocent.
Photo courtesy Lloyd Harrell.

I am not as prepared for the meeting as I would have liked. For the past ten days, I have helped to cover the aftermath of a tornado that took six lives in Hood County. It had been one of sixteen that night in the North Texas area. Workdays had been long. Rest had been short. I had tossed clothing into a suitcase, thrown notebooks and a digital recorder onto the front passenger seat of the Nissan Altima I had purchased two weeks earlier, and hit the highway with a this-will-just-have-to-be-good-enough attitude. I had purchased the new car for two reasons: my Ford Escape had 121,000 miles on it; and Darlie Routier. I needed reliable wheels if I was going to pursue—sometimes on dark, lonely highways—a story I had come to accept was not going to let me go.

In the booth at the Dairy Queen, I spend the next four and a half hours listening to why this former FBI special agent views the case of a naïve young housewife with a slit throat as the most unfair criminal trial he has ever seen. Though Darlie Routier was accused of murdering two of her sons, she was tried only in the death of Damon. This was so that prosecutors could have a second bite at the apple by charging her in Devon's death if the jury acquitted her the first time around. As I sit listening to Crimefighter, I pay no mind to diners that come and go, though they probably view us as a curiosity. In the center of the table is the digital recorder, standing upright in its stand. I am scribbling notes. Crimefighter has brought a folder of memos he had written for the defense team, back when the Dallas County DA's noose was tightening around Darlie Routier's neck. Anyone eavesdropping may have heard references to murdered children and unfairness within the justice system. They may have heard terms such as "lyin' son of a bitch" and "prosecutor's whore." It is perhaps fitting that my interview with the mince-no-words former G-man takes place in a fast-food restaurant that serves a burger called the FlameThrower.

Practically from the moment my jeans hit the seat of the booth at Dairy Queen, I feel overwhelmed by Crimefighter. I struggle to absorb the issues raised in memos he is reading rapid-fire and with thoughts that tumble from his brain like candy rattling down the slot of a coin-operated machine. I realize he talks this way for two reasons: He's an intelligent man whose mind never sleeps, and he's been waiting almost two decades for someone to ask him about Darlie Routier.

One of Crimefighter's memos to the defense team lawyers contained a prediction: that lead police investigator James Patterson and investigator Chris Frosch would take the Fifth against self-incrimination when questioned on the stand by the defense. The two investigators had helped plant a hidden recording device near the Routier boys' gravesite—an act that Harrell believes violated federal law, because anyone at a gravesite has a reasonable expectation of privacy. The recording was likely one of the reasons the two key players in the Routier investigation were not on the prosecution's witness list. Another reason may well have been their lack of experience in investigating crimes of this magnitude. Prosecutors likely feared the seasoned defense attorney and former prosecutor known as "Mad Dog Mulder" might chew up and spit out the small-town police officers, significantly weakening the state's case in the eyes of the jury.

Harrell's prediction was borne out. Lead investigator Patterson and his colleague Frosch both took the Fifth on the witness stand. The defense was shut out: no further questions permitted. Defense attorney John Hagler, chosen for the team because of his expertise as an appellate lawyer, immediately moved for a mistrial. Judge Tolle struck his motion down.

The team was stunned. Others in the legal profession have been equally shocked that no mistrial was granted. According to Crimefighter, the late William Wayne Justice, US district judge for the Eastern District of Texas and a senior US district judge for the US District Court for the Western District of Texas, was flabbergasted when the story was relayed to him about what had happened in the Kerr County courtroom. "I told him about the investigators taking the Fifth on the stand and Tolle not granting a mistrial, and he said, 'Crimefighter, you're kidding me.' He said, 'In my courtroom, that case would be reversed and remanded in twenty seconds. That's the most ridiculous, obscene thing—that someone is given the death penalty behind the Fifth amendment [taken by] the lead detective on a substantive issue.'" Crimefighter tells me Darlie's appellate team (which does not include Hagler) has never raised the issue on appeal.

Appellate lawyer Stephen Cooper disagrees with Harrell's viewpoint on the matter. He says prosecutors used other witnesses in presenting their case, and did not have to rely on the testimony of Patterson and Frosch. However, Crimefighter believes Patterson and Frosch taking the Fifth deprived Darlie of her Sixth Amendment right to face her accuser. Patterson had signed the criminal complaint. He was her accuser. In Harrell's view, the matter goes to the heart of *Brady v. Maryland* (1963),which requires any exculpatory evidence be made known. In the case of Officers Patterson and Frosch, the defense team wouldn't know what exculpatory evidence might be revealed through their testimony, because the defense team was not allowed to question them after they took the Fifth. "And yet, it's never been raised on appeal because no one seems to understand the significance," says the frustrated PI.

Crimefighter says Patterson's pre-Fifth testimony gave hints about how the defense could have attacked the credibility of the investigation. Among other issues, there are serious questions of a contaminated crime scene. Patterson acknowledged to court-appointed defense lawyer Wayne Huff that David Waddell, the first officer to arrive, walked through the crime scene to make sure an intruder was not in the garage. And a blonde hair found in the cut window screen in the garage was assumed to be Routier's—until tests determined that it belonged to a Rowlett police officer.

For Crimefighter, the greatest travesty of justice he has ever seen started with a prosecution theory that, in his view, was weaker than watered-down

Kool-Aid. But the jury drank that Kool-Aid nonetheless. "This is the only crime I've ever seen where a motive was not identified that was attributable to the accused," he says, as a family sits down with their burgers at a nearby table. In pretrial testimony, Patterson acknowledged that no motive had been established in the case against Routier. "We're not sure of a motive, no," he said in response to Huff's question. The state, however, is not required to present a motive as part of its case.

Crimefighter continues about the claims later made by prosecutors at trial: "Materialism is not a motive. This is an outgrowth of the Susan Smith murder case, and that's grasping at the wind. They tried to make her look bad in front of the jury because they didn't like her as a person—but that didn't prove she had killed her kids."

As for the "staging" of the crime scene, he says this: "Darlie never walks through the proscenium." The proscenium is the arch around a stage. If Darlie had truly been acting, he says, she would have walked onto the stage by including in her story to police the items she had used in the staging of the crime scene.

"All the stuff that is supposedly part of the staging, she never used them in her first dealings with the police. That should have been a clue. She doesn't say, 'I stepped on the broken wine glass that [the intruder] knocked from the rack,' or 'We knocked over the vacuum cleaner,' or 'When we struggled, we turned the coffee table over.' She never says any of those things. If you talk to her and try to get her to use the stage, she doesn't. That's because that's not what happened. If you took the time to stage a crime scene, you're going to refer to the things that you used in the staging. It's going to be in the initial statement to police. And never once does she walk through the proscenium."

Harrell acknowledges that Routier spoke about some of the items that were allegedly used in the staging when she testified at trial, but said her remarks were in response to questions that were posed to her about the items. The PI explains that when a perpetrator attempts to stage a crime scene, he or she typically refers to items in the staging in their first statements to law enforcement—even in a call to 911. They immediately refer to props used in the staging in an attempt to convince officers of their story at the outset.

In the 911 call, Darlie tells the operator that someone came in, stabbed her, stabbed her children, that she was fighting, that the intruder ran out through the garage, and that he threw the knife down. "So does she, at this point, enter the proscenium?" Crimefighter poses. "Was she using the stage, or simply relating an actual event? The stabbings of her babies are obviously not part of the staging. Every fact she relates [on the 911 call] is supported by evidence found at the scene, except for definitive proof of an intruder. Darlie told Officer Waddell that the man ran into the garage, but she does not say he left through the *window* in the garage. It is important to note that there is a blood transfer smear that has been identified as a fingerprint on the kitchen side of the utility room door frame. This fingerprint has not been identified. If the intruder had blood on his hands—and everyone agrees that is a certainty—he could have touched the door frame on his way out. It is possible that it was Darlie who touched the door frame. We know she was there from the drops of blood found there. However, Darlie did not say in the 911 call, or any time later, that she touched the door, nor did she say she saw the intruder touch the door as he fled, using the blood smear as a prop to support her story.

"James Cron, the crime scene investigator brought in by the Rowlett police, made a determination that the crime scene had been staged, partly because of the cut window screen in the garage, the layer of dust on the window sill, and the fact that mulch under the window was undisturbed. He also said he has never known an assailant to arm the victim with a weapon, which the intruder in this case did by dropping the knife. Cron assumed that all home invaders remove window screens, rather than cut them. The window was low to the ground. In a courtroom demonstration at trial, Detective Frosch—who was about the same height and build as the intruder, according to Darlie's description—was able to pass through the window, leaving the dust undisturbed, but he did leave a fingerprint in the place where an unidentified latent print was lifted. As for the mulch, there was no mulch directly under the garage window. There was concrete there. And as for the knife, which was determined to belong to the Routiers—why would an intruder want to flee with a large, bloody knife—tying himself to the scene of the crime?"

Crimefighter also addresses Darlie's use of the word "they," even though she claimed to have seen only one intruder. Police used it against her to indicate inconsistencies in her story and to prove up their theory of a staged crime scene. "The use of the plural pronoun is extremely common when victims report to police details of a crime committed by an unknown perpetrator. If one concocts a story, they will have made up their mind beforehand how many individuals were present and, if their story is that the crime was committed by one perpetrator, they will likely use only the singular pronoun."

There were a number of items that were claimed to be part of the staging, including: the broken wine glass; the cut window screen; the overturned coffee table, vase of flowers, and vacuum cleaner; a bloody outline on the carpet near the sofa of the knife that Darlie claimed the intruder dropped as he fled through the kitchen and utility room; and the sock found down the alley. Says Crimefighter:"One would think that if she planned the crime, concocted a story, and set the scene with the props, she would begin to use the stage and props at her first opportunity. But she didn't. Officer Waddell claimed at the trial that Darlie did not follow his instructions to help Damon, but in a previous hearing he testified that she laid a towel on Damon's back. The towel drawer was near the kitchen sink, where police claimed she had tried to wash away blood evidence, and wet towels were found on the floor.

"The 911 call was Darlie's first opportunity to enter the stage. The second opportunity was when she was questioned at Baylor Hospital by Patterson and Frosch, minutes after coming out of surgery. She had been given a shot of Demerol and had undergone an hour and a half of anesthesia. The interview lasted between forty minutes and an hour. She did not mention items that were supposedly used in the staging. On one hand, her lack of memory could be attributed to the medication and anesthesia. But it could also be argued that the drugs could have acted as a truth serum, causing her to say incriminating things if she was the person responsible for the crime.

"The third time she could have entered the stage was on June 8, when she was discharged from the hospital and taken by Rowlett police to the police station, where she was interviewed for about three hours. She left the hospital thinking she was going to go to the funeral home, where a viewing was to be held later that day for the boys. She asked to delay the interview and written statement until after the viewing, but Patterson insisted that she go first to the station. She was told to write down everything she thought was important. At the time, what she considered most important was her sons' viewing. Her written statement is the first time she mentions the wine glass breaking. However, at that point, Darin had already told police that he was awakened by the sound of breaking glass and Darlie screaming."

In Crimefighter's opinion, the Rowlett Police Department's notion that Darlie committed the crime is ridiculous. "She didn't cut her own throat," he says. "If you believe that, I'm nineteen feet tall. She was done for the money."

"The money" was a six-figure life insurance policy of which Darin would have been the beneficiary. Five years after his wife was sent to death row, Darin admitted in an affidavit to trying to find someone to burglarize the family's home as part of an insurance scam shortly before the murders. There are some who believe the claim was nothing more than an attempt to help Darlie in her appeals. But those involved in Darlie Routier's trial defense and appeals, as well as family members and friends, claim the burglary plot is true, and that Darin had done it before with the "theft" of a vehicle.

The fact that Testnec, Darin's business that provided testing for computer parts, had not been bringing in as much money as in years past was used by prosecutors to show motive for the boys' murders. Darin and Darlie claimed their financial situation was not as serious as prosecutors made it out to be.

Crimefighter says he has always suspected the perpetrator was Darin, and that he killed the boys because they woke up when their mother was attacked. However, a common opinion among those who have talked with me about the case is that, while Darin likely intended to commit insurance fraud, he did not intend for his children to be murdered in the process. Crimefighter sees merit in that theory as well.

Some theorize that whoever broke into the house that night believed the family had already left for Pennsylvania. Neither Darlie's Pathfinder nor Darin's Jaguar was parked in the driveway that night. The Pathfinder was parked in front of the house, but the troublesome, ten-year-old Jaguar, which Darin had managed several times to repair on his own, had broken down and he had left it on a customer's parking lot. The cut garage window screen was in the back of the house, near the empty driveway.

Crimefighter has a hypothesis to explain Darlie's hazy memory, how she could have "slept" through the attacks on her children and why a sock from the Routier house was found several houses down the alley, with traces of both boys' blood. He did not think of the possible explanation until it was too late. The trial was over, and Darlie was on death row. The investigator believes the attacker rendered Darlie unconscious by using ether or xylene—organic, colorless solvents that leave no residue. Darlie would have instinctively begun fighting if a cloth—or a sock—had been placed over her mouth. It would explain the black bruises that would later appear on her arms, why her memories of the struggle are sketchy, and why she complained at Baylor Hospital of painful sores inside her mouth. Family and friends who visited Routier in the ICU claim that she did, indeed, have sores inside her mouth.

"She interviews as if she were waking up from an anesthetic. It's hazy. It's always been the same thing—she wakes up in a cloud. She's awakened by Da-

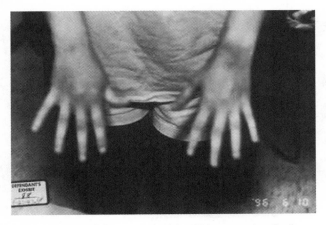

Signs of a struggle? The severe bruising that appeared on Darlie Routier's arms and hands were indicative of a struggle, according to former FBI special agent Lloyd Harrell. He believes a likely scenario is that a cloth—or the sock that was later found down the alley—was soaked in ether or xylene and then placed over the sleeping mother's mouth to render her unconscious. Darlie would have instinctively begun struggling, which would explain the bruising that later appeared on her arms, Harrell says. *Photo courtesy Rowlett Police Department.*

mon, and nothing makes sense to her. She doesn't know what's going on. She sees a guy at the end of the couch. She has no clarity whatsoever. Listen to the 911 call. She's just starting to come out of it."

Harrell admits, however, that he is puzzled about Darlie's statement to the 911 operator about having touched the bloody knife. When the dispatcher tells Darlie not to touch it, she says that she has already picked it up. "We could have gotten the prints, maybe," she says. Prosecutors used that statement against her, claiming that no mother would have been focused on fingerprints as her children lay dead or dying. "I can't explain it," he says of the statement.

Darlie would later tell me the urge to pick up the knife was instinctive, particularly since she was confused and unsure of what was happening. She said the urge is so instinctive that law enforcement officers are trained to not act on that instinct when they see evidence at a crime scene.

In Crimefighter's view, the sock not only likely holds the key to why Darlie's memory has been unclear, but also is strong evidence to indicate she did

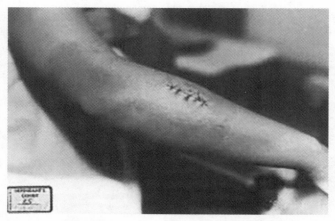

The gash on Darlie Routier's arm cut to the bone, and required stitches.
Lloyd Harrell believes the injuries were clearly defensive wounds. The
state, however, claimed the wounds were self-inflicted.
Photo courtesy Rowlett Police Department.

not stage the crime scene. "In three separate interviews, she fails to mention
or suggest that the sock exists. She never made a statement that the intruder
held a sock over her mouth, or that he had a sock in his hand as he fled. If she
placed the sock as a prop to a concocted story—and it would have been a good
prop—she never mentions it. It is interesting to note that neither did Cron or
Alan Brantley, of the FBI's profiling unit. They both know the sock does not
fit with their theory and conclusions that Darlie staged the crime scene."

I ask Crimefighter about the availability of ether and xylene. He says
both were quite easy to obtain back in 1996. They were used for auto parts,
specifically carburetors and brake parts, and also in building computer hard
drives.

* * *

It is after 9:00 p.m. when I hit the road again, this time for Waco. I will
be meeting the next day with attorney Walter "Skip" Reaves. He is one of two
vice presidents of the Innocence Project of Texas, and he represented Cameron Todd Willingham in the death-row inmate's appeals. Reaves has had
no involvement in the Darlie Routier case either through personal pro bono

work or through IPTX. Unlike the better-funded national Innocence Project in New York, the Texas organization does not take on death penalty cases because death-row inmates have resources available to assist in their appeals. According to founder and chief counsel Jeff Blackburn, IPTX instead uses its limited financial resources to push for legislative changes that will help prevent wrongful convictions in the future. Though Reaves had no role in the Routier case, other work has pitted him against prosecutor Greg Davis and blood spatter expert Tom Bevel, whose damning testimony in the Routier case was not adequately challenged by the defense, in some people's opinion. Reaves is a fan of neither Davis nor Bevel.

The drive to Waco is as long as the drive to Tyler was earlier today. SH 31 from Smith County to McLennan County is a dark, mostly desolate highway that takes me through Athens and Cameron Willingham's former home of Corsicana.

A full moon stays stubbornly, insistently, just over my left shoulder the entire way. Alone with my thoughts, I reflect upon Crimefighter's comment about having spent years "howling at the moon" over the troublesome case that refuses to give him peace. When the sun goes down, a blonde woman and two bloody children pay him a call, appearing from the shadows.

Over my shoulder, gossamer clouds appear to nudge the moon, like a child persistently poking its mother's shoulder, insistent that attention be paid. "*Mommy.*" I think of Darlie's claims that she first became conscious that night when five-year-old Damon, mortally wounded and with just minutes to live, poked her on the shoulder. "*Mommy.*"

The clock on my iPhone clicks midnight as the car's headlights illuminate a sign telling me that I am now entering McLennan County. Greg Davis's territory. At this point, the former Dallas County prosecutor is working as an assistant district attorney for McLennan County. Drawing closer to Waco, where I hope to find a motel room that I had not had time to reserve, I turn up the volume on the well-worn Waylon Jennings CD. The lights of the Baylor University campus and Interstate 35 appear through my windshield as "Just to Satisfy You" begins to play.

CHAPTER 7

Mayday

On Sunday morning, the clouds have cleared and skies are sunny. I check out of Room 128 at the Comfort Suites off I-35 and head to West, seventeen miles north of Waco. I am to meet Skip Reaves at what remains of his home. The house was destroyed more than a month earlier, on April 17, in an ammonium nitrate explosion at the West Fertilizer Company just a few blocks away. The blast obliterated the neighborhood at precisely 7:50:38 p.m. central daylight time. According to the *Dallas Morning News*, fifteen people were killed, more than three hundred were injured, and scores of buildings were damaged or destroyed. Aside from attending Catholic Mass and going to lunch with me, Reaves plans to spend the day sifting through rubble for salvageable belongings. It is noon when I gingerly steer my car through a small opening between the barricades on Grady Calvery Drive. As I enter the residential neighborhood, I see that each street has similar barricades, with small openings. The message is mixed: Enter, but don't enter. The barricades are meant to deter the morbidly curious, but not those who belong there.

I turn onto the street where Reaves lives and suck in my breath at the sight of the first house on the right. There are obvious signs of damage all around, but most stunning is a crack across the bricks at the front of the house. At the center of the crack, the bricks bow outward—a testament to how a tremendous, unstoppable force can tear apart a home.

At the end of the street, on the left of the cul-de-sac, is a house with an open front door. Much of the roof is gone. I walk to the door and stand for a few seconds, silently watching the man inside. Skip Reaves has changed out of his church clothes and into clothing more appropriate for sorting through the ruination of one's life. He is standing on the spot where he was knocked off his couch when the explosion raised his roof and then set it back down again.

I think of Routier and Willingham and the interest in justice that Reaves and I share as I pause unnoticed in his doorway. As he stands in the pile of debris, I see an expression cross Reaves's face as if he is wondering where to begin. He looks up and notices me. As we head to lunch, Reaves uses a screwdriver to lock the front door. Against what, I don't know. Climbing into my front passenger seat, he gazes through the window at the devastation of the home he had shared with the wife who died of cancer three years earlier. "The funny thing," he says, "is that my roses have never looked better."

I assume he's joking, but he's not. The shower of fertilizer, he explains, resulted in brilliantly colored flowers blooming throughout a neighborhood that now otherwise looks like a war zone. We drive through the heart of the destruction to Nora's Sausage House, where we each order the chicken-fried steak lunch special. We talk about Reaves's belief that the current prosecutorial system allows forensic experts to hold great sway over juries, even though some of their theories may be more full of holes than the houses that surround the West Fertilizer Company. "Experiments are sometimes conducted by police officers who, if they made C's in science, probably did pretty good," Reaves tells me.

The Waco lawyer has been an appellate attorney for former Fort Worth cop Warren Horinek, who was accused of fatally shooting his wife. Horinek went on trial in Tarrant County in August 1996, while Darlie Routier was in a jail cell at the Lew Sterrett Justice Center in Dallas. Even though problems with alcohol led to Horinek leaving the force and there were claims he was abusive to his wife, the main players in the investigation of Bonnie Horinek's death believed Warren Horinek's story that it was she who pulled the trigger. The Tarrant County Criminal District Attorney's Office believed the evidence supported Warren Horinek's version of events, and refused to seek an indictment. But Bonnie's parents believed otherwise. They hired an attorney to circumvent the Tarrant County DA, and the attorney convinced a grand jury to issue an indictment against Horinek. He was taken to trial on circumstantial evidence.

According to the *Texas Observer* and CNN, the jury foreman said the jurors were going to acquit Horinek—until they heard from the state's final witness. The jury sentenced Horinek to thirty years in prison, the media reports said, because of the testimony of a lone forensic expert: Tom Bevel. Blood spatter specialist Anita Zannin of Syracuse University told CNN that she was troubled that Bevel was the only forensic specialist whose testimony was introduced.

At the time I meet with Reaves, I have already communicated with Bevel about his work in both the Routier and Horinek cases. He stood by his con-clusions in both cases. Bevel believes specks of blood on Horinek's T-shirt prove he was in the bedroom that night when the fatal shot was fired—not in another room, as Horinek has claimed. But others, such as Reaves, believe the specks of blood got there when Horinek was frantically administering CPR to his dying wife. Her moans can be heard in the recording of the 911 call in which her husband is pleading for help. "My opinion of [Bevel] is that he tends to, at least in some cases I've seen, frame his testimony in favor of the state," Reaves says. "And in my view he frequently testifies about stuff way beyond the area of his expertise—if he *has* an area of expertise."

In the tavern atmosphere of Nora's, Reaves tells me he is the court-ap-pointed lawyer for a mentally challenged black man accused of killing his wife. It's a death penalty case, and he will be facing Greg Davis in court. (The prose-cutor prevails in the end, and Carnell Petetan Jr. becomes the twentieth person Davis sends to death row.)

"He's a very effective and competent prosecutor—there's no doubt about that," Reaves says of Davis. "I think he also does anything and everything he can to get not only a conviction, but a death sentence. I think he feels absolute-ly no guilt. I think he's convinced that he's doing the right thing."

I tell Reaves that a representative of the ACLU had expressed alarm when I mentioned the number of people Davis had put on death row, as reported by the *Waco Tribune*. Reaves says it is a number that many people may find admi-rable. "For people who support the death penalty, that's probably something pretty positive. When I'm called to account for my life, that's sure not the first thing I want to come out of my mouth—'Look at me, I got twenty people killed.'"

After dropping Reaves back at the house that is no longer a house, I head back to Waco. Taking the Fourth Street exit to the courthouse and Reaves's office across the street, I pull into a parking lot and sit for a moment gazing at the courthouse, with its long, imposing set of steps and its dome with a statue of the Greek goddess Themis, a symbol of justice. I think of how Reaves had tried to stop the 2004 execution of Cameron Todd Willingham, a man he believed innocent. Arson investigators had not only told the jury that Willing-ham had set the fire that killed his children in 1991, they also told the panel he poured an accelerant in the shape of a pentagram as part of a satanic ritual.

Prosecutors had claimed the thirty-six-year-old Willingham started the fire to hide evidence of child abuse, but no evidence was found that any abuse had occurred. Willingham's wife, Stacy, denied he had ever abused the children and said their girls were "spoiled rotten." Arson expert Craig Beyler wrote in a report for the Texas Forensic Science Commission that investigators in the Willingham case had relied on "folklore" and "myths" when making their arson determination. Years after the state jammed a needle into Willingham's arm in the execution chamber, the Texas Forensic Science Commission admitted what Reaves had essentially proved while Willingham was still alive: the arson claims were based on junk science.

Sitting in my car on a parking lot across the street from the McLennan County Courthouse, I am struck by the realization that those with law degrees are no different from anyone else. Lawyers are not all-knowing or infallible. Even among themselves, they often have radically different opinions about whether a defendant is guilty or innocent. One of Reaves's cohorts with the Innocence Project of Texas, Mike Ware, was the lawyer hired by Bonnie Horinek's family to seek an indictment against Warren. Ware would later tell me he staunchly believes in Horinek's guilt, though his colleague Reaves believes the opposite.

Hundreds of DNA exonerations have proven that truth does not always prevail in courtrooms. Crimefighter and Reaves—one retired, one still in the trenches—are both tormented by a justice system they know sometimes gets it wrong. As I put the Altima in gear, I realize that the first image I had of Reaves was a true reflection of his essence. Whether in his personal life or his professional one, he is a straightforward man who stands in the center of destruction, wondering how in the world to fix it.

CHAPTER 8

Rainy Day Woman

In Room 210 at the Comfort Suites in Rowlett, a TV weatherman tells me what I already know from peeking out the window at the bluish-gray clouds over Lake Ray Hubbard: the first day of June will likely bring rain showers. It is Saturday, and once again I am spending a weekend on the road in pursuit of the Darlie Routier story.

I had said nothing to coworkers the day before when slipping out the side door by my cubicle at 3:00 p.m. The tinted windows of the Silver Bullet, the rather unoriginal name I was calling my new Altima, had hidden the change of clothes hanging in the backseat. I headed up Highway 377 to Interstate 30 in Fort Worth, which would take me, in rush-hour traffic, through Dallas and then to Rowlett.

Melanie Waits, a friend of Darlie's, had warned me that she lives off the beaten path, so it seemed wise to locate her country home the evening before our meeting. Besides, since her home in Royse City is not far from Rowlett, I wanted to go by 5801 Eagle Drive and the Rowlett Police Department.

The house once owned by Darin and Darlie sits on a corner, where Eagle Drive curves. This affords an easy view of the short driveway in back and the infamous garage where Routier had supposedly slashed a window screen when she staged the crime scene. A maroon speedboat sits under a carport that has not withstood the ravages of time. It is leaning and needing repair. A green refuse container for recyclables sits by the fence that encloses the backyard. The street seems shockingly narrow, the front yard surprisingly small. Funny how scenes depicted in crime scene photos can appear quite different in real life.

Across the street from the house where the Routier boys were murdered is a home with a "For Sale" sign and a utility truck parked at the curb. A landscaper at another house sweeps a blower across freshly mowed grass. A man jogs past. Even though the Darlie Routier case, to this day, elicits strong opinions as to her guilt or innocence, there is no hint on this Friday afternoon that this neighborhood has an infamous history well known to true-crime buffs. Life, from all appearances, has gone on.

I drive past 5801 a couple of times, then quickly head back up Linda Vista to Dalrock Road. I don't want to raise suspicion, like the black car some neighbors reported seeing shortly before the Routier boys were slain. I also don't want to give neighbors the impression that another gawker has come to gape at the house whose history they might prefer to forget.

I drive to the Rowlett Police Department, which is farther away than I had assumed. I pass a Rowlett police car, and glance nervously in the rearview mirror. Stopping at a RaceTrac convenience store, I lower my head when walking past a Rowlett cop who is holding a cup of coffee. Getting back into the Altima and fastening the seat belt, I realize I am being silly. I have no cause to believe anything sinister about the Rowlett Police Department, and its officers have no reason to hone in on me. But that was pretty much what Darlie had said when Melanie and her husband Kenneth warned her that the police department's investigation seemed to be taking a disturbing turn. "You're crazy," she had told them.

After finding the Rowlett Police Department, where Darlie Kee said she had seen cops high-fiving each other after her daughter's arrest, I head to Royse City. It seems I cannot avoid law enforcement. I turn by the Rockwall Police Department, and drive past the Rockwall County Sheriff's Office. "Don't screw up without us," trumpets a billboard for auto insurance featuring the image of a sheepish man.

Turning off Highway 276, I navigate the Silver Bullet through a spiderweb of country roads to locate the home of Melanie and Kenneth, passing white fences and green pastures where horses and cows graze. The sun is lowering, bathing the picturesque country scenes in golden light. A collie lying in the grass gazes at me, feeling no threat from my presence. A bird swoops low near the windshield, then soars heavenward.

The rural area is populated by the moneyed and the not-so-much. It is far enough off of main roads that residents might opt to do without if they forget to buy milk at the store. The road becomes rough. Melanie's house is in a cul-de-sac, to the left. It is behind a fence decorated with Texas longhorns and stars that pay homage to the Lone Star State. The house on the Waitses' ten-acre parcel of land is two stories and has dormers. The driveway is long. I quickly turn back the way I came. I had merely wanted to locate the address, not violate the family's privacy.

It is nearing 9:00 p.m., daylight saving time. The summer sun is finally dipping, and so is my energy. A cottontail seems to cast me an understanding look before darting into the brush. Since I have again embarked on a road trip with no hotel reservation, I am anxious to get back to a more populated area. At a T-bone in the road, I turn left when I should have turned right and so become ensnared in the web of country roads because I forgot to use my GPS. Sunlight surrenders to darkness before I can get my bearings. Finally, the lights of I-30 appear in the distance.

I cross the dark waters of Lake Ray Hubbard, making my way to the Comfort Suites I spotted earlier. It is 10:30 p.m. Again taking the Dalrock exit, I look through the windshield to the other side of the intersection, where there is an entrance ramp onto I-30. In my mind's eye, I go back in time to the early morning hours of June 6, 1996, and see an ambulance, its lights flashing, speeding Darlie Routier to her destiny.

* * *

It is precisely 10:00 a.m. on Saturday, June 1, when I drive through the gates of the Waitses' property. Waylon is singing "Rainy Day Woman" as I make my way up the long drive. Melanie, dressed in a black sundress and flip-flops that reveal coral toenails, has come out to greet me.

We walk through the house to a covered porch by a swimming pool whose backdrop is an idyllic pond and a breathtaking tree line. In the distance, by the pond, is Melanie's twenty-two-year-old daughter, Danielle. Melanie's son, Cody, is not far from Danielle, working on a dirt-bike trail. He's twenty.

The temperature on the covered patio is pleasant for a June day in Texas. The sky is partly cloudy, not yet having decided whether to make a fool of the weatherman. We sit down for what will be a three-hour conversation about the death-row inmate Melanie loves like a sister. The family's Boston terrier, Nova, perhaps sensing we are going to be here awhile, settles in for a nap between my chair and the loveseat where Melanie is sitting. Behind Melanie a sculpture depicting the sun and its rays hangs on the wall. She sips a soft drink as we start at the beginning.

She had met Darlie in 1991 at a party in an apartment complex somewhere in the Dallas area. She can't remember now exactly where it was. The party was for a couple from Lubbock who was moving to Arizona. Darlie and Darin had met the couple when they lived in Lubbock.

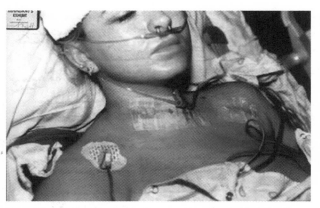

Superficial injuries? Darlie Routier spent two days in the Intensive Care Unit at Baylor Hospital in Dallas. Nurses would testify at trial that she was "whiny" and did not seem overly upset over the loss of her children. However, their shift notes tell a different story, leading some to suspect witness tampering. Despite the labeling of Routier's injuries as "superficial," the slice across her throat missed her carotid artery by 2 millimeters. The scar is still visible today. *Photo courtesy Rowlett Police Department.*

Melanie and Darlie had hit it off immediately, and spent the evening talking. Melanie took Darlie to an apartment at the complex, where a sitter was caring for one-year-old Danielle. Darlie cooed over the baby and showed Melanie photos of Devon and Damon. Devon was a little more than a year older than Danielle; Damon, five months younger. "She was bragging about them, like any mom does."

The new friends exchanged phone numbers, and began meeting for lunch. At times, the two couples would do things together. "They came out, and we went swimming. We had a hot tub and pool at our other house."

Melanie and Kenneth liked Darlie, but did not feel particularly warm toward Darin. "Darin was a braggart about everything. He bragged about how much he'd paid for stuff. And sometimes I thought he paid way too much."

Darlie was a loving mother who never raised a hand to her children, Melanie says. When their kids became old enough to start school, Melanie and Darlie became room moms for their classes. They would share ideas for class parties, and sometimes tried to outdo each other. Once, Darlie cooked and cut into small pieces two hams for a luau. "I was like, 'You cooked *two* hams and then diced them? Okay, you trumped me.'"

June 6, 1996, happened just after Devon had completed first grade and Damon had finished kindergarten. Melanie, whose birthday is June 7, was packing for a trip that she and Kenneth were taking to Mexico when a mutual friend named Michelle phoned with news that something may have happened to Darlie and the boys. "She was very distraught and upset. She said her mom had heard something about the boys. I tried to calm her down. I tried calling Darlie, but there was no answer on her home phone. I called Kenneth. At first, he was dismissive. But then he called me back and was really upset."

Soon, news of the horrific crime in Rowlett was all over the airwaves. Melanie began phoning hospitals, trying to find Darlie. "I finally tracked her down at Baylor. I went up there later that evening," she says. Darlie Kee and others were there when Melanie and Kenneth arrived. The sight of her friend was so traumatizing, it's "just kind of a blur," Melanie says. "I think sometimes your mind just kind of shuts things out. I think my mind keeps me from going too deeply. People were gathered around her bed. There were gashes on her neck and arm. Her face was really swollen. You could tell she was really drugged up. She was on a lot of pain meds. She was lethargic, just kind of out of it. She kept saying, 'My mouth hurts. My mouth hurts.' We were feeding her ice chips. We pulled down her lip and the inside of her mouth was a mess. It was all roughed up. I remember that very distinctly."

According to Amy Winslow, an advanced practice nurse (APN) and an assistant professor of nursing at Tarleton State University, intubation of a hospitalized patient can cause mouth injuries that range from simple inflammation to lesions, perforations and ulcers. Intubation is the placement of a flexible plastic tube down the windpipe to keep the airway open. "Inserting an endotracheal tube or laryngoscope sometimes can cause local trauma anywhere in the mouth, even under the lip," Winslow says.

But was Darlie intubated? Melanie isn't sure, and neither are Darin Routier and Darlie Kee. According to Winslow, whether a patient is intubated depends on the type of surgery being performed. Abdominal surgeries require intubation because the abdominal muscles and diaphragm are paralyzed, and mechanical ventilation is necessary, she says. Darlie did not have abdominal surgery. Rowlett police did not investigate whether the sores were caused by intubation or by a hand pressed hard against Darlie's mouth.

Melanie says it was Kenneth who first became suspicious of the direction the investigation was taking. "He said, 'Melanie, something's wrong.'" As police kept questioning Darlie and Darin—even making them late for the viewing of the boys' bodies at the funeral home—Melanie began to fear her husband was right.

As the air of suspicion grew thicker, the infamous Silly String incident happened. Melanie had not attended the graveside memorial service on June 14, which was followed by a birthday celebration for Devon. Considering the strain of the past eight days, her husband had advised her not to go. A television camera captured Darlie spraying Silly String on the shared grave of Devon and Damon, who had been buried, hands entwined, in a single coffin. Darlie was smiling and smacking on gum. She was arrested four days later.

The Silly String footage was later shown at Darlie's trial in Kerrville. Jury members acknowledged watching it, over and over, as they deliberated her fate. They were not influenced by arguments that Darlie had been heavily medicated, and was chewing gum because the medication had made her mouth dry. They never saw the tears that had been shed at the hour-long memorial service that preceded the birthday celebration, or heard family members advise Darlie to pull herself together so neighborhood children arriving for the birthday celebration wouldn't be further traumatized. "She couldn't win," reflects Melanie. "There were so many lies. They portrayed her as an evil, money-hungry bitch. The public only got to see half-truths. They never got to see the big picture."

At a bond hearing, Darlie was denied bond partly because of the long blonde hair found in the cut window screen in the garage. But, as later testing proved, the hair wasn't hers. It belonged to Rowlett Police Officer Sarah Jones—proof to some that cops had contaminated the crime scene. Regardless, Darlie never saw another day of freedom.

"Did you know that the bloody fingerprint on the coffee table was actually *behind* the couch where Darlie had been sleeping?" Melanie asks me. I did not. I had thought the bloody fingerprint, which had initially been described as "consistent with" that of a child, had been found on a coffee table between Darlie and the boys.

"This is what scares me," Melanie continues. "The things that they do. All the shady stuff that they have done to put her where she is and to bury the truth. They took an innocent mother who was attacked and whose children were killed—and they put her on death row. They are trying to get away with murder."

Soon after Darlie's arrest, a man from the Dallas County District Attorney's Office knocked on the door of the Waitses' home to issue subpoenas to Melanie and Kenneth. They weren't home. They were at work, at the sign shop owned by Kenneth's family in Dallas. The babysitter, not knowing who the man was, didn't answer the door. He left, but returned with a Mesquite police officer. The officer demanded the sitter open the door. She told them what a neighbor had already relayed to the man from the DA's office: Kenneth and Melanie were at work.

"The next day, [the DA representative] delivered a subpoena to Kenneth. My husband said, 'I don't appreciate you scaring my children. Give me the subpoena that you're here to serve and then get the hell out of my office.' My husband was furious. They served me at home. I just snatched [the subpoena] out of his hand and said, 'Here, you've served me. Now get the hell out.' The way they treated us—oh, my gosh. It leaves a lasting bad, bad impression of people on a power trip. They hold the cards. You're scared of what they can do. It makes you feel that you can't trust those who you are supposed to be able to trust."

It quickly became clear to Melanie that the public perception of her friend was shaped by prosecutors in the Dallas County District Attorney's Office. A judge issued a gag order preventing Darlie's friends and family from speaking to the media. It was supposed to apply to the prosecutors and investigators as well, yet unflattering and incriminating information about Darlie kept being leaked to the media.

Even some people who had been friends with the Waitses and the Routiers seemed to wonder if maybe Darlie wasn't who they thought she was. The man who had moved to Arizona with his wife, and who had since moved back, had known the Routiers since their Lubbock days, but was swayed nevertheless by the state's accusations. "He said, 'Boy, you think you know people,'" recalls Melanie. The remark angered her.

Over the years, as new friendships have developed, Melanie has stopped telling people she's friends with Darlie Routier. She grew tired of their reactions and their judgment. Just a couple of weeks prior to our meeting, she and Kenneth had met a group of friends at a restaurant that overlooks Lake Ray Hubbard. One of the men in the group made a comment about someone being "psycho, like Darlie Routier." Melanie says her husband cast her a look, as if wondering if she was going to become angered at the comment. But Melanie held her tongue and let it pass, making no mention that she is Darlie's closest friend.

She relates another story. A few years ago, Darlie's surviving son, Drake, came from Lubbock to visit his grandmother, Darlie Kee, in Wills Point, and also to spend time with the Waits family. Drake is three years younger than Cody Waits. Melanie took both boys to ride dirt bikes. "A friend of mine was out there and she was, like, 'Man, that name sounds familiar.' I finally told her: 'Well, you know, Drake Routier. He's the son of Darlie Routier.'" That revelation brought a flood of questions rooted in claims about Darlie that had been made by prosecutors. "She later called me and I was on the phone for two hours," Melanie says. "She wasn't ugly, but I got real defensive. And I thought, I'm not doing this with every friend."

Melanie feels bad about an incident prior to Darlie's trial that resulted in even more negative press about her friend. A box that held baby and childhood photos of the murdered boys was found in the attic of the Routier home after the family's possessions had been removed. Melanie had assisted Darin and Darlie Kee in that difficult task. "I think that was my fault," she says of the mementos that were accidentally left behind. "We just had so much going on. But it was as if the public blamed Darlie for it—and she was in jail!"

Melanie is fiercely loyal to Darlie, and makes pilgrimages to the Mountain View prison unit in Gatesville every few weeks. The round trip is six hours. "I love Darlie very much. She is like a sister to me. I can't explain our connection," she says.

Melanie tells me about Darlie's life on death row, but says that her friend sometimes protects her loved ones by not sharing a lot of the details. "I think she keeps a lot of that from us. Her bed is a concrete slab with a mattress about this thick." She holds her thumb and forefinger about an inch and a half apart. "Her back is always bothering her. Her pillow is a stack of magazines that she wraps in a sheet. There was a time when she had high blood pressure. The food that they are served—it's fatty, and it has so much sodium in it. It's not healthy. It's not like they get fresh fruit and vegetables. She says things like, 'When I get out, I want a little bit of everything. I want lobster. I want steak.'

"Her health is failing. I've noticed that her hands shake so bad. For a long time, that's been going on. She and Lisa [Coleman, a fellow death-row inmate] try to do a Bible study in spite of the person between them. They talk through the vents. Darlie says [the other inmate] just drives her crazy because she talks nonstop.

"She's surrounded by 'crisis' inmates. Some of them are suicidal. They'll do things like stick something in their toilets to cause flooding. Sometimes, the guards will have to teargas them, and the tear gas spreads everywhere. It makes their eyes burn and their throats hurt. They have to cover their faces with rags.

Quite often, I go in and say, 'You look exhausted,' and she'll say, 'Well, I didn't get any sleep last night.'"

The rules at Mountain View are always changing, Melanie complains. What's okay one day may not be okay the next. Letters to inmates can no longer be written on colored paper, she says, because female inmates began using the paper to dye their prison-issued bras pink. It is the only time in our conversation when she laughs. "I know Darlie can make eyeliner out of toothpaste and black ink," she says.

I ask Melanie what it was like that evening at the funeral home, when everyone was waiting for the Rowlett police to finish their questioning of Darin and Darlie so the young parents could come to the boys' viewing. No one was going to go into the room where the boys' bodies were until their parents had seen them first. Darin and Darlie were thirty-five or forty minutes late, Melanie recalls. The room suddenly grew quiet. Darin and Darlie had arrived, but they had been taken into the viewing room through another door. The sound of Darlie's screams filled the air. "Oh, my God, Darin!"

A cloud passes over Melanie's face. "June 6, 1996. 6-6-6. There was so much evil in what happened here."

* * *

We head to Rest Haven Memorial Park, which is about a fifteen-minute drive away. The sky, for the moment at least, is sunny. I follow behind Melanie, my thoughts lingering on her comment about evil. It was clear she wasn't just referring to whoever had killed Devon and Damon.

We turn on a road where a sign with an arrow indicates we are heading toward Fate. Storm clouds are rolling in again. We turn left on a two-lane highway. It is State Highway 66. Looking toward the right to check oncoming traffic, I see trees being whipped by powerful gusts of wind behind the white steeple of a Baptist church.

A short distance up the road, we turn into Rest Haven, driving under its arched entryway. I immediately recognize the statue of Jesus from a photo of a young Drake that had been posted on the Internet. Darin had snapped the photo of the little boy with his back to the camera and his arms reaching up to the effigy.

Melanie and I wind our cars slowly around the cemetery, to Devon and Damon. The scene is surreal. I see the hedge where Rowlett police investigators had placed a recorder in hopes of capturing a confession. They were accused of violating federal law in doing so. I stand on the spot where Darlie had been that day—June 14, 1996—when her teenage sister had put a can of Silly String in her hand, unknowingly sealing Darlie's fate and changing her own life forever.

The unfairness of it all angers Melanie. "I'm going to write a book, and call it *The Guide to Grieving*," she pronounces defiantly, as we stand at the headstone that bears the name Routier. "You'll open it up and the pages will be blank." Her point, of course, is that no one truly knows how they would behave in such a situation.

Despite the weather, we walk to a bench where we can sit and continue talking. We find that we are in a spiderweb. It is Melanie who sees its inhabitant suspended near my head. We move to another bench closer to the statue of Jesus, near a grave where there is a cluster of dead roses.

Melanie talks about Darlie's faith, and the forgiveness Darlie has given those who she says wrongfully convicted her. It is an absolution that Melanie thus far has been incapable of giving. "They are glorified criminals with a badge," she says bitterly. "They're no better than the criminals. They just have the state's backing."

We talk a few more minutes, then determine that we'd best head to our cars before the heavens open. As we say our goodbyes, Melanie reaches toward me to pluck something from a strand of hair. I had not escaped the spider after all.

Driving under the arch, I glance back at the statue of Jesus, stark white against the backdrop of rolling blue-gray clouds. His outstretched arms seem like a barrier against the storm that is drawing ever closer. I pull onto 66, and continue on my way.

* * *

On Monday, June 17, I receive another card and letter from Routier. It is postmarked June 10—ten days after my visit with Melanie Waits. On the card is an illustration of a fairy with flowing brunette hair and wings of blue and purple. Routier's loopy, feminine writing is inside the card and on both sides of three sheets of notepaper tucked inside. Her message says, in part:

"I talked with Mel about the visit you two had. It was very emotionally draining for her. Honestly, I am probably too emotional to be writing right now. I'm tired . . . tired of sitting in this hellhole for something I didn't do, tired of hurting from the loss of my boys, tired of seeing all the corruption within the system, tired of people and their judgment and opinions based on speculations and theories . . . and the list goes on and on. I did *not* murder Devon and Damon and I did *not* attack myself and I'm tired of how the system gets away with all its wrongdoing. Tell me where real justice and real truth is because it surely isn't in any courtroom. . . .

I think they all needed more time—2 months to prepare for a capital murder case was not enough and that judge should have been removed—period! The man nodded off during the trial a few times. . . . The entire trial was ridiculous—people cram-packed in that old courtroom like a circus.

They made me stay shackled during the entire trial—I would go back to that cell every day with bloody ankles. They eventually told me I could wear socks under the shackles, but the back of my ankles still would bleed because the shackles were so big and heavy. I could tell you so many things like that, but people are going to believe what they want. . . .

I'm sitting in hell for a crime I didn't commit and was a victim of, because I trusted all the wrong people."

I read the letter a second time, then a third. Quietly, I tuck the papers back inside the card. The fairy, dressed in purple and black stripes, watches me. Her face is unsmiling; her gaze, relentless. She is leaning across a banner with her left elbow bent and her chin propped firmly on her fist.

"Well?" she seems to be saying.

The banner bears a one-word demand.

"Believe."

CHAPTER 9

Urgent and Confidential
for Room 209

It is midafternoon on a blazing hot Friday in August when I park the Silver Bullet by the front doors of the *Hood County News* and hit the eject button on the CD player. In the trunk is a suitcase packed for another weekend on the road. I remove the Waylon Jennings disc that I have been listening to for a year now, because my coworker Nancy is coming along on this trip. I am waiting for her to finish a last-minute task before we hit the road for Fredericksburg.

The daughter of a lawyer, Nancy transcribed recorded interviews for the *Routier Revisited* newspaper series and assisted with research. She and I are to meet the next morning in Kerrville with Crimefighter and Kerrville attorney Richard Mosty, who was a member of the defense team. We are staying in Fredericksburg, thirty miles from the picturesque town where Darlie Routier's trial was held, because there is not a hotel room to be found in Kerrville. They have been snatched up by attendees of a governors' conference and by parents arriving to retrieve their children from summer camps held in the breathtaking Hill Country.

Nancy and her mother, Barbara, a sweet woman who lives in Minnesota and who sometimes sends me fan mail, at times have kept me going when I and others have questioned whether a community newspaper reporter has any business pursuing a story of this magnitude. Months earlier, at the end of the year during which the newspaper series had been published, a reader had submitted this anonymous "Sound off" to our newspaper: "It is very interesting that the story that you devoted the most space to didn't make your top ten stories of the year. Oh, maybe that's because Darlie Routier doesn't have anything to do with Hood County. A good resolution for the [*Hood County News*] would be to go back to reporting on things that matter to Hood County residents." It hurt, but I know that the person who submitted it would be desperate to grab the attention of a reporter—any reporter—if they or one of their family members perceived they were the victims of a grave injustice. Some things should matter to everyone, regardless of geography. There were some messages from readers that were positive and encouraging, such as this one sent in an e-mail: "I've been meaning to tell you that I enjoyed the Dolly Routier series. That case has always interested me."

As the air conditioning finally begins to make a dent in the oven that is my Altima, I tune the radio to a pop rock station. Nancy has shared my concerns over the Routier case, but I don't expect her to understand how or why Waylon fits into the equation. As I tuck away the CD, Nancy walks out the office doors. We toss her suitcase into the trunk, fasten our seatbelts, and set out on the long drive to Fredericksburg, where we will eat German food at the Bavarian Inn and discuss "Dolly" Routier.

*   *   *

Located seventy miles north of San Antonio, Fredericksburg is a town whose history is rich with friends and neighbors who helped each other so that all could live up to their potential—or at least, that is the message on the town's official website. It is home to the Nimitz Hotel and museum, the National Museum of the Pacific War, and dozens of shops, restaurants, and bed-and-breakfasts that make the town a popular tourist draw.

At first, it appeared that we might have the same problem with lodging in Fredericksburg that we had with Kerrville, but a few rooms had still been available at the Comfort Inn and Suites. Crimefighter, too, is staying in Fredericksburg, at the Hangar Hotel at the Gillespie County Airport. Designed to resemble a World War II hangar, the hotel is near Lady Bird Johnson Park, two miles from Main Street.

It is early afternoon on Saturday, and we have arrived back in Fredericksburg after having spent a couple of hours that morning sitting at the conference table in Mosty's office, discussing the challenges that had been faced by Darlie's defense team. After the meeting, Crimefighter asks that Nancy and I come to the Hangar Hotel so we can go through a box of documents he brought with him that he has kept since Darlie's 1997 trial. That second meeting of the day will end up lasting four and a half hours.

Immediately after Nancy and I arrive and settle into chairs by the hotel room's window, Crimefighter hands me a manila folder he had randomly pulled from the box just minutes before our arrival. "Look at that file and tell me what you see," he says. I hate situations like this because they seem like a test, and I'm always afraid I'll fail it. There are only a few papers inside the file. I begin looking at them, but nothing jumps out as being particularly significant. After a few seconds, Crimefighter says: "No, look at the back." I turn the file over and there, written in ink on the back of the manila folder, is my name and a phone number so old it takes several minutes before it finally starts to look familiar.

I look up at Crimefighter. He is standing by the box at the foot of the bed, completely perplexed.

"Do you have any idea why your name would be on that file?" he asks. I don't. "Did you ever write anything about this case?" he asks. No, I tell him. I was a stay-at-home mom back when Darlie was arrested and taken to trial.

For a moment, there is silence in the room. I look at Crimefighter, a man who seems to have so many answers to so many questions. Except for this one.

*   *   *

I am back at the Comfort Inn after a long day and dinner at Hilda's Tortillas, and the hour is late when a text lights up the screen on my iPhone. The message is from Darlie Kee, informing me that at some point during the night a fax for me will be sent to the hotel. The document being sent to me will be made public months later, but on this night Kee cautions me to keep it under wraps.

Later, I take the elevator down to the lobby to see if the fax has arrived. A desk clerk hands me a three-page document with a cover sheet that bears my name and the message: "Urgent & Confidential, Room 209." The document bears the letterhead of the DPS Austin Crime Lab and is titled *Supplemental DNA Laboratory Report*. It is dated January 11, 2013, and is addressed to the Dallas County District Attorney's Office. The "suspect" name on the report is Darlie Lynn Routier. It is the first report to come in after the Texas Court of Criminal Appeals' unanimous 2008 ruling, allowing more sophisticated genetic testing on a handful of pieces of hair and blood evidence. The court had overruled State District Judge Robert Francis's decision to deny the request after Francis concluded that retesting the items would not be enough to exonerate Routier. The panel said the judge had misinterpreted a 2001 law that permits postconviction DNA tests.

The pages contain a long list of numbered items under the heading "Evidence Description, Results of Analysis and Interpretation." Kee has drawn asterisks next to three numbered items that identify two cuttings taken from the white nightshirt that Darlie had been wearing the night her children were killed and her throat was slashed, and one cutting from the sock found down the alley. The tests took into account Darlie's DNA, as well as that of Darin, Devon, and Damon.

The findings of the DNA tests for each of the three bulleted items include the same sentence: "The DNA profile from this item is consistent with a mixture."

It would later be explained to me that a *mixture* does not refer to combined DNA of members of the Routier family. A *mixture*—found on two key pieces of evidence that helped send Darlie Routier to death row—refers to the presence of DNA from an unknown person.

CHAPTER 10

Friends of Distinction

The McDonald's restaurant at Gaston Avenue and North Washington Street near downtown Dallas is bustling when I walk in at 10:00 a.m. on a golden autumn Monday. At a booth in the back, near the restrooms, a man watches me. I give him a questioning look. He nods. Kenneth Waits and I have found each other. We had to change plans via cell phone minutes earlier, when he discovered there were no parking spots open at the Starbucks where we had originally planned to meet. I feared the same thing might happen at McDonald's, but a car backs out of a parking space just as I pull into the lot.

I am in Dallas instead of Granbury, on what typically would be a workday, because of a mission that involves killing several birds with one stone. I am attending a Dallas Bar Association luncheon, and have taken the day off in order to meet with Kenneth prior to the luncheon, and with Routier's Dallas appeals lawyer, Stephen Cooper, afterward. Coincidentally, Cooper's office is just blocks from the McDonald's where Kenneth and I are meeting. Before heading to Dallas, I had made up for the day off by writing stories about the Granbury City Council adopting a new idling ordinance, the Hood County Tea Party sponsoring a forum for local candidates, and new hours of operation for the local car-tag office. A little work over the weekend was worth it so that I could fry bigger fish on Monday.

Kenneth is the husband of Melanie Waits. He had not been home that Saturday four months earlier when I met with Melanie at the couple's home in Royse City. At the fast-food restaurant, his minimalist "Yeah, I'm him" wave tells me he is a no-nonsense guy—the kind who will tell you straight up what he thinks. He works nearby at a family-owned sign shop. Although his family owns it, he wanted us to meet at another location where there would be anonymity and no curious employees asking questions.

No one at McDonald's seems to notice the indicators that we are here for reasons other than coffee or sausage biscuits. There are no food or drink items on our table. Instead, there is the digital recorder and an open maroon leather

59

Texas Press Association folder with a yellow legal pad inside it.

I begin by telling Kenneth I had wanted to meet with him because his wife had said he was the first in the Routiers' circle to become concerned about the direction of the Rowlett Police Department's investigation. He begins to tell his story.

"I was never that close to Darin. Melanie and Darlie were close. He [Darin] was one of those people who said he paid so much for this TV, or paid so much for these skis. I don't care, you know? I have a lot of nice things, too, but you come to my house, I'm not going to start telling you how much I paid for stuff. I just don't like that."

Was Darlie the same way?

"I just put her in the same boat as him. They were pretty superficial. They just lived above their means, to me. They were always going to be in debt."

So *both* Routiers bragged about their possessions?

"That was Darin, not Darlie," he says upon further reflection. "I didn't see her without him, and vice versa. He'd talk about how much he paid for this and how much he paid for that. He's not the only person I've ever known who was that way."

"Melanie would say, 'You don't know Darlie like I do.' She and Darlie would take the kids and go wherever. Darlie took care of everybody's kids in the whole neighborhood. All the kids were at her house."

Was she a loving mother?

"Oh, yeah. She totally took care of those kids."

It was shortly before June 6, 1996, that Kenneth and Melanie had watched a made-for-TV movie called *Gone in the Night*. It was a true story about the kidnapping and murder of a seven-year-old girl named Jaclyn Dowaliby. David was Jaclyn's stepfather. Both parents were arrested and charged with the child's murder. Cynthia was acquitted by a judge on grounds of insufficient evidence. But Cynthia's husband was tried and convicted after the jury was shown photographs of a closet door with fist holes in it. It would later be proven that the damage occurred at a time when David was not yet living in the house. His conviction eventually was overturned.

Kenneth knew that in criminal cases involving child victims, investigators always look at the parents first, or at who was in the house at the time. Remembering *Gone in the Night* made him that much more convinced that Darin and Darlie were in the deadly crosshairs of law enforcement. "I just thought— they're going to go after them. That's what I said from the beginning. I said,

'They're going to go after somebody in the house first.'"

Kenneth first heard about the crime when the alarm on his clock radio went off on that June morning. He had no idea, though, that the alleged home invasion involved the Routier family until he heard another radio news report as he was driving home from work later that day. Melanie, too, was just finding out. The couple headed to Baylor Hospital as soon as Kenneth got home. It was around seven that evening when they walked into Darlie's hospital room. "She was surrounded by pictures of the kids. She was in pretty bad shape. She looked bad."

Kenneth wasted no time warning Darin. "I told Darin that night at the hospital, 'Don't talk to the police at all. Get an attoney.' And Darin's response was, 'I don't need an attorney. We didn't do anything.' There was another time later that I said, 'Are you sure you don't need an attorney?' And he said, 'No.'"

A man named Rod who worked at the sign shop had known Darin and Darlie from when the three of them lived in Lubbock. Kenneth went to him with concerns about the Routiers, and asked him to intercede. "I said, 'You know Darin better than I do.' I told him, 'Somebody needs to tell them to stop talking to the police.'"

Kenneth's sister knew the wife of well-known Dallas defense attorney Peter Lesser. Word reached Kenneth through those channels that Lesser wanted to get the same advice to the Routiers: Stop talking to the police, and get a lawyer. Lesser predicted the cops were about to arrest either Darin or Darlie. Kenneth believes the police considered Darlie the "weakest link."

"It was that night [after Lesser's prediction] that she was arrested. They [Darin and Darlie Kee] called me. They said, 'What do we do?' I said, 'You better get an attorney!' They met with Lesser, but Mama Darlie didn't like him." Darlie Kee would later tell me that she liked Lesser "very much," but felt that the family could not afford him.

Darin and Darlie Kee scraped together about $80,000, which Kenneth kept for awhile in the safe at the sign shop. Kenneth says that Darin and Darlie Kee felt that if they could get Darlie out on bond, the money spent would later be recouped through a lucrative book deal once Darlie was found not guilty. "Their goal at the time was to try to get her out on bond. That was all they were worried about. Lesser said, 'She's not getting out on bond. They need to get an attorney.'"

Kenneth felt strongly that the family needed to hire Lesser. He told Lesser the family could probably increase the $80,000 to $100,000. He said the defense lawyer told him that his retainer would be $50,000 and the rest of the money could be used "for testing."

"He said that if they don't [win it] the first time, it's such an uphill battle [to reverse it]. He said, 'You've got to win it. You've got to win it now. You've got to spend every dime you can now, not later.'

"They didn't want to do it," Kenneth says of Darin and Darlie Kee. "I remember saying, 'Are you sure you don't want to hire an attorney?' I said, 'You better make sure, because whatever decision you make, you're going to have to live with it for the rest of your life.' I think they ended up giving it [the money] to Mulder. That was when Darin met Mulder."

Initially, Darlie was given court-appointed attorneys—Doug Parks and Wayne Huff. Court-appointed attorneys are given to those who cannot afford legal representation. Though Darin and Darlie did not have the money to fund Darlie's legal representation in a costly capital murder trial, friends and family members dipped into savings, education, and retirement accounts so that Darlie could have the best lawyer money could buy.

"He [Mulder] forced himself into the picture," says Kenneth. "He contacted Darin. Then when we get to the no-bond trial, they brought in some old dude, some retired judge. He didn't care about nobody. It didn't matter what was presented, he was going to no-bond her. It was obvious. He was there just to rubber-stamp the no-bond. I told Darin, 'You keep losing. You're losing every battle.'

"That was the most ridiculous trial. The whole thing was ridiculous. They sped it up. Who goes to trial in six months on capital murder? I think the state forced it to be fast-tracked. I don't think Darlie's team did much to slow it down, either. Shoot. DWI cases take longer than that. You can get a speeding ticket to take six months, if you want."

Kenneth says Darlie's family members were fine with a speedy trial. Their reasoning was that the sooner the trial was over, the sooner they'd have her home. They were convinced the jury would find her not guilty. Kenneth's warnings about rushing the trial fell on deaf ears. "I finally backed out. I said, 'Y'all won't listen to anybody but yourselves. I'm done.'"

Before Mulder entered the picture, Dallas County Assistant District Attorney Greg Davis phoned Lesser, asking if he was going to represent Routier. Davis was aware that her family had met with him. The attorney told him that there had been no move to hire him. "It was the next day they decided to go for capital punishment," Kenneth says.

"They wouldn't listen to anybody. They wouldn't take advice. They listened to Parks and Huff and people like that for six months. All they were thinking about was getting her out. They didn't think *what if she didn't get out?* They were like, the quicker we get to trial, the quicker she gets out. How do we get her out quick for less money?"

Several months after the murders, Kenneth was able to get inside the Routier house. "It was just a mess. The carpet was ripped up. Lots of the furniture was gone. Parts of the linoleum were ripped up." He says he was anxious to go inside the house again because he knew there were things in Darlie's arrest affidavit that were wrong. For instance, Kenneth felt sure that the garage window was low to the ground—so low that someone could easily step through the window without touching the sill. "I couldn't wait to go to the house. I remember thinking, 'I don't think they have dirt there [under the garage window]. I don't think that that window is impossible to crawl through without disturbing the dirt [on the sill]. I can do it, and I'm a big guy.' It's about six inches off the ground. It's a big window, and it's almost on the ground.

"I knew they weren't telling the truth. It was a bunch of half-truths. Yeah, no dirt was disturbed in the flower beds, but there's no dirt under the window. There's no way you can walk in there and have this figured out, I don't care who you are. If they'll lie at that level, they'll lie at any level. Getting somebody arrested really isn't that hard to do. I don't think people understand. But I do."

I ask Kenneth about that evening at the funeral home, when Darin and Darlie arrived late for the boys' viewing because they were at the Rowlett police station, answering more questions. "This is the stuff [police] do that nobody knows. It's the way they break you down. They make you late for your own kids' viewing." He describes waiting with Melanie and others outside the viewing room. The door was closed. Darin and Darlie were taken through another door into the room where their sons' bodies lay.

Did he hear Darlie cry out? I ask, remembering what Melanie had said.

"That's how we knew they were in there," says Kenneth. "I can't describe it. It was just a wailing. I did hear her wail out. It was really loud. I was like, 'Oh, wow. I knew it was going to be bad.'"

We talk about the infamous Silly String incident at the gravesite. Kenneth is angry that a family member invited a television news crew to the cemetery. And he's angry at prosecutors for showing the Silly String footage to a jury. It is proof of nothing, he says. "It wasn't just the Silly String; it was the smacking of the gum," he says, referring to the devastating effect the footage had on the public's perception of Darlie. Darin and Darlie were heavily medicated. "Loopy," he says.

"They were so naïve. And what pisses me off is that people like me were trying to tell them, 'Y'all need to back up. Don't go to the police every time they call you. Why do you think they say, "Everything you say can and will be used against you?" When they say that, you need to shut up.'"

I ask him what he thinks of Greg Davis. Does he think Davis intentionally prosecuted a woman he knew to be innocent, or does he believe Davis truly believed in her guilt? "He's just a person that's able to talk himself into believing anything that he wants to believe. I don't think in his mind he thinks she's innocent. But, still, he wanted to win a case. They have to take whatever is brought to them, unless they're going to start butting heads with the police and the detectives. This was too big. It was too high profile."

I ask him about the sock from the Routier house that was found down the alley containing small drops of the boys' blood. "It doesn't make sense that she took it down there. We all know that," he says.

He says it also doesn't make sense that Darlie was as obsessed over her appearance as prosecutors claimed, yet was willing to cut her own throat to stage a crime scene. "I think [the intruders] thought they killed her, truthfully. That [necklace] saved her life. It pushed her artery back. The wound was more than superficial. She still has the scar today. It was deep because it's a big scar. If she was going to kill herself, she's not going to cut anywhere near her face. I do remember one of the nurses saying, 'Yeah, these wounds on her arms are defensive wounds.' One arm was sewn up."

Does he think Darin was involved?

"I've always questioned Darin's business practices. Maybe he got involved with the wrong person somewhere. I don't know how you make that much money testing electronic boards. But I don't know. I don't know the business. I've said from the beginning it was a personal attack. And they used a weapon that was in the house. Anybody who watches true-crime shows knows that you don't walk in with your own weapon because that can be easier to trace to you than something that's in the house."

Kenneth sees little hope at this point. "She's never going to get out of this," he says of Darlie. "I don't see her ever getting out of it, I really don't. As bad as I know it's wrong, that's just what it is. I don't know why they went after her the way they did. It was like, no matter who did it, somebody had to pay for it."

There have been times when Kenneth has thought of putting his foot down and telling his wife not to continue with her regular visits to women's death row. But he knows better than to try. And he knows that there will probably come a time when she will be making a drive to Huntsville to watch through a window as her friend takes her last breath, strapped to a gurney with a warden at her head and a chaplain at her feet. "I don't think she should [witness the execution], but what am I going to do, tell her no? The longer it takes, the easier it will probably be. At some point, Darlie will be better off. It will be better than rotting away in there. But it will be hard on Melanie.

"If I could come up with any reason to believe Darlie did it, it would be fine with me. This happens. People do snap and do things that you wouldn't expect them to do. But my opinion isn't based on the fact that I know Darlie so well that I know she couldn't do it. My opinion is based on what I saw and the facts of the case."

Melanie has told Kenneth she would have to see a video of her friend committing the heinous crime to ever believe she did it. "I just need evidence— and it's not there," Kenneth says. "My opinion has nothing to do with personal affection for Darlie or Darin. I know she didn't do it. I've seen too much and been too close to it. It was a complete railroad, top to bottom."

It is almost time for me to head to the luncheon at the Belo Mansion in downtown Dallas. Kenneth circles back to something he had mentioned earlier in our eighty-minute conversation: his feeling that he is partly to blame for Routier being on death row. "The only thing that I regret is not having pushed more, but what could I do? Darlie would call the house from jail back then. She'd call and I'd answer. It'd be a three-dollar collect call; we got those all the time. I wish I had just convinced Darlie that she needed to take control of it. I wish she could have talked to Lesser. I was encouraging Darin, and Melanie was talking to Mama Darlie. I think we were so afraid about Darlie's mental state. You would have to get her to set all that emotion aside long enough to tell her, 'This is the real deal now. The kids aren't coming back. This is the real deal now.'"

For a few seconds, there is a pause in our conversation, as if we've been carrying something heavy and need to set it down. There is a cacophony of cheerful noise in the red-and-yellow land of Happy Meals, but Kenneth and I are not smiling. For the first time, I notice how loudly music from bygone eras is playing over the speaker system. As the two of us sit looking at each other in silence, The Friends of Distinction begin singing "Grazing in the Grass."

Everything here is so clear, you can see it.

CHAPTER 11

A Poisoned Pen

It is 8:30 p.m., and a witch is screaming at me to put away my cell phone. The woman in a witch costume has singled me out for playful abuse as I stand in line at Hangman's House of Horrors in Fort Worth. The popular Halloween-season attraction that has raised millions for charity is celebrating its twenty-fifth and final season under the leadership of its founder. The theme this year is "Unhappily Ever After." The poster features a maniacal Pinocchio.

Finding out whether any dedicated volunteers hailed from Hood County had turned out to be a good idea. A top assistant lives in the Hood County community of Lipan. This means I have a hook for a story and a valid reason to visit the haunted house that sits just off Interstate 30 near Cowtown's skyscrapers.

Standing in line, reporter's notebook in hand, I notice that my iPhone is glowing in the autumn darkness. A text has come in from Darlie Kee. She has made contact with true-crime writer Barbara Davis, and Davis is willing to talk with me. Her text includes Davis's phone number.

Davis had sat through Routier's trial and had written *Precious Angels* with a belief that Routier was guilty of murdering her sons. Shortly after the book was published, she became convinced that the young mother had been railroaded by the justice system. During the years since Routier's conviction, Davis, a widow, had remarried and moved with her husband to a tiny East Texas community.

A few yards away, a group of schoolteachers and school librarians made up like zombies begin to dance to Michael Jackson's "Thriller," a song about evil things that lurk in the dark after midnight. I tuck my iPhone back into the pocket of my purse, happy at the thought that Davis is willing to speak with me. Since Davis had spent ten years working in the Tarrant County Criminal

District Attorney's Office in Fort Worth, I am eager to get her perspective on how the Dallas prosecutors had handled the Routier case. I knew she had dedicated her book to the prosecution team—an homage she later deeply regretted. As Michael Jackson sings about a beast preparing to strike, the glow from the cell phone fades to black. The witch beckons, and I enter a dark world of fairy tales gone awry, where childhood and mayhem collide.

* * *

The voice on the other end of the phone is barely audible. It is raspy and weak. The sound of someone in pain. True-crime author Barbara Davis is asking a favor. Could I call back later, in the evening, when maybe she'll be feeling better? We agree on 7:30 p.m. I hang up, accepting that midnight oil will be burned at the office. Since it is a Tuesday, that means the press crew will be on duty in another part of the building, so at least I won't be burning the midnight oil alone.

My cubicle is by the kitchen, not far from the bathrooms and just a couple feet from the door leading to the courtyard, where homeless kittens sometimes scavenge for food and where coworkers go for smoke breaks throughout the day. Not the best work location in the wintertime, but a good spot, I figure, if anybody ever walks through the front doors carrying a gun.

At 5:44 p.m., my muted cell phone lights up. The name "Barbara Davis" flashes on the screen. It is an hour and forty-five minutes before we are scheduled to talk, but Davis is calling early because she is feeling better. She wants to take advantage of the brief reprieve from pain to talk about Darlie Routier.

Davis has recently been diagnosed with degenerative spinal disease. It is an affliction she feels she deserves, her worried friend told me a week earlier, when I'd called and discovered Davis was in the hospital.

I ask Davis if I can call her back on a landline because it's easier for typing notes during a phone conversation. I've been asked a number of times by nervous readers phoning with sensitive news tips whether they are being recorded. I always assure them they are not. This is a community newspaper, after all, not the *New York Times*. Our phones don't even have caller ID, much less recording equipment.

Hanging up, I quickly open a blank document file on the desktop computer, kick off my shoes and adjust the chair in preparation for the phone interview. I had hoped to make a trip to visit Davis at her rural home, but she is too ill, and doctors want her to have surgery soon.

As I prepare for the phone interview, my eyes fall upon the rectangular tin rendering that has long been propped between my desk phone and computer monitor. The message on the rendering is spelled out in big white letters outlined in black: "A Productive Workplace is a Happy Workplace." The sign features an iconic still shot from the candy factory episode of the old *I Love Lucy* television series. Lucy and Ethel, their cheeks stuffed with the chocolates they had not been fast enough to wrap, stand frozen at a conveyer belt as a supervisor yells instructions to an unseen conveyer belt operator. "Speed it up a little!" trumpets the quote bubble by the supervisor's head. The funny episode was a classic, but I interpret the "speed it up" message differently on this night, as I hurry to speak to Davis during the brief time she will be free of pain. I quickly punch in the digits of Davis's phone number. It will be three and a half hours before I set down the receiver.

* * *

When Davis moved with her husband to East Texas several years after Darlie Routier was sent to death row, she left behind her life in North Richland Hills, a suburb in Tarrant County. North Richland Hills now holds painful memories for the true-crime author.

Davis had been inside a house in the 8200 block of Ulster Drive on the morning of December 15, 1999, when tactical team officers broke down the door. One of the officers shot Davis's son, Troy James Davis, twice in the chest. His death occurred just two weeks after his twenty-fifth birthday. Barbara Davis was arrested in connection with the drug possession investigation and was taken to the North Richland Hills jail. Davis had been forced to cope with her son's murder from a jail cell—the same as Darlie Routier had done.

Davis asked that I not divulge the name of the town where she lives, because she still has a protective order against those who filed the false police report that led to her son's death. She says charges against her were dropped, and no illegal drugs were found in the house.

Davis, sounding much better than she had earlier, begins to share her story: "*Precious Angels* probably hadn't been out a month before I got a call from a source in the Dallas County District Attorney's Office. They said, 'You need to come look at some stuff.' They were leaving that office, and there were some things they wanted to show me. I was through with the book and was ready to move on to something else, but I agreed to meet with them.

"They showed me statements that I had never seen before, by witnesses who said they had seen a black car.'"

Several witnesses had told Rowlett police that they had seen a suspicious black car just before the attacks. Some said that whoever was in the car appeared to be watching the Routier home. Though mention of the black car was made at Darlie's trial, Davis believes it should have been given more relevance and police should have better investigated that lead.

Davis continues: "I got to read the nurses' notes and doctors' statements for the first time. I started crying and I said, 'Oh, my God.' I've learned so much that I didn't want to know."

Davis had admired the prosecution team—Greg Davis, Toby Shook, and Sherri Wallace. She was friends with them. "Toby Shook said that his mother was a big fan of mine," she says.

Now that she is aware of Greg Davis's track record for winning death penalty convictions, the author feels even sicker about the Routier case. "The fact that he's put twenty people on death row is unbelievable. That's where you've got to stop and ask yourself: 'Is someone *that* good?' It's not an indictment, but it's definitely a question mark, in my mind. Every time I see Greg Davis on TV, I just cringe. He's a win-at-all-costs kind of guy. It's that mentality of looking out for number one. I've got to protect myself. I've got to protect my reputation. I've got to protect the state's money."

The meeting with the Deep Throat source shortly after publication of *Precious Angels* changed everything for Barbara Davis—both in terms of how she viewed the quality of the defense Darlie received and the tactics used by the prosecution. She had assumed blood spatter expert Terry Laber was not put on the stand by the defense because he had nothing with which to challenge the opinions of Tom Bevel, the state's blood spatter witness. Laber and his partner, Bart Epstein, both with the Minnesota Bureau of Criminal Apprehension, had been hired by court-appointed attorneys Doug Parks and Wayne Huff. The pair flew to Texas, where they examined evidence, met with Rowlett police investigators, and inspected the Routier home. Laber was prepared to testify about the determinations he and his partner had made—determinations that Routier had *not* staged a crime scene. Davis said Laber's absence at the trial "pretty much sealed it for me." As the trial wore on, she became convinced that Darlie Routier was guilty.

I had spoken with Laber about a year before my interview with Barbara Davis. He told me he had met with Mulder to discuss his and Epstein's findings, but it was the last time he ever heard from Routier's lead defense attorney.

"They had already paid us several thousand dollars to do the work. Having us come testify would have been a day's travel and a day of testimony—like $4,000, something like that," said Laber, whose early career had involved investigating the infamous Jeffrey MacDonald murder case. That crime, too, had involved young children who were stabbed to death as they slept.

Laber categorized as "extremely unlikely" Bevel's theory that Routier's nightshirt contained castoff blood droplets that landed, one on top of the other, as she stabbed her two sons. The expert stated that he had recommended genetic testing that might have challenged the state's theory. That testing would include, among other things: cuts on the left side of Darlie's nightshirt; wood fragments and blue fibers on the knife found on the kitchen counter; Darin Routier's bloodstained blue jeans; and the furniture, pillow, and wine rack, in order to reconstruct the location and movement of those at the crime scene. Laber also recommended testing the fingerprint brush and powder used by police at the crime scene, because it might refute the state's theory that a fiberglass rod found on the knife was consistent with the material from the cut window screen in the garage.

In an affidavit taken on July 11, 2002, Laber stated: "In my professional opinion, scientific testing of the physical evidence would have been critical to Darlie Lynn Routier's defense. Independent testing of that physical evidence was crucial to properly evaluate the State's case. There were numerous potential holes in the State's case that required testing to conform [to] or refute the State's presentation of the evidence, and to provide evidence that could well have refuted the State's forensics testimony."

Laber's recollection of his meeting with Mulder and investigator Lloyd Harrell is far different from what Mulder and Harrell told me. Both say Laber and Epstein were uncooperative and seemed resentful that Parks and Huff had been replaced. Mulder said the court-appointed lawyers still owed Laber and Epstein about $1,500 when he took over the case—and it was he who settled the debt. "I didn't think they had anything. I didn't think they brought anything to the party," Mulder had told me shortly after my discussion with Laber.

For courtroom observer Barbara Davis, Laber's absence at "the party" was a fatal error in the defense of Darlie Routier, and she blames Mulder for it. "To me, the defense didn't do their jobs properly," she says. "Mulder just seemed off his game. This wasn't the Mulder that I knew. I like to write both sides, but with the defense in this case, I just had to dig. With Terry Laber, I figured he didn't fly in and testify because he didn't have anything to counter the state's blood spatter expert, Tom Bevel, with. Tom Bevel is a good friend of mine, but I now think he got it wrong. A lot of blood spatter was based on transfer, and Tom didn't know that. I think they thought the money would be better spent somewhere else, and that was a devastating decision on Mulder's part.

"The [Silly String] tape hurt her and not having Terry Laber there to testify hurt her. Terry has no reason to lie, and I think Doug Mulder feels very defensive about this case. Have you ever heard of CYA [a slang acronym for Cover Your Ass]? He was confident he would win it, but he didn't."

Another criticism Davis has of the defense lawyers is that they didn't strongly assert that Darlie might have been rendered unconscious and thus unable to come to the aid of her children. "The defense attorneys kept saying that Darlie slept through it, she slept through it. She was *unconscious* through it. There's a huge difference. Later, when I spoke to jurors, that was a bone of contention with them."

Though Davis is critical of Mulder, she believes that his motion to move the trial back to Dallas should have been granted. "Kerrville is one of the most conservative counties in Texas. I knew the prosecution knew that, because they were just delighted that it was being moved to Kerrville. If you have a defense team like the court-appointed lawyers making bad decisions on your behalf, you're going to lose."

The railroading of Darlie Routier began with law enforcement officials who may have made little effort to investigate other possibilities once they had set their sights on the mother of the two dead boys, Davis believes. "The number one thing in this case was tunnel vision, and I think it started with the cops. The city of Rowlett was in an uproar. I had a lot of questions when I first heard about the Routier crime scene having been staged. I think what happened to Darlie is what would have happened to John and Patsy Ramsey in the JonBenét Ramsey case. I don't know why, but the police just tend to get tunnel vision."

JonBenét Ramsey was murdered on Christmas Day 1996—six months after the killings of Devon and Damon Routier. The body of the missing six-year-old beauty queen was found in the basement of the family's Boulder, Colorado, home about eight hours after police were called to aid in the frantic search. The little girl had been struck in the head and strangled. Law enforcement immediately suspected the parents, and even JonBenét's nine-year-old brother, Burke, came under suspicion. John and Patsy Ramsey would not be completely exonerated until July 2008. In late 2013, court documents that had previously been sealed showed that in 1999 a grand jury voted to indict the Ramseys, but District Attorney Alex Hunter refused to prosecute the couple because of insufficient evidence. John Ramsey reportedly stated he quickly obtained legal representation because of "what happened to that woman in Texas."

Barbara Davis criticizes crime scene investigator James Cron's "quick decision-making," determining within minutes that the crime had been staged. "I had some concerns about the fact that paramedics had been in there, but yet there was all this stuff about alleged staging. Those paramedics were trying to save lives, so they moved stuff around. I don't blame them at all, but I blame James Cron for making that decision, that the crime scene had been staged." Davis became even more worried that Cron might have made a mistake after it came to light that Darin Routier had previously committed insurance fraud and was plotting to stage a "burglary" of the family's home when the attacks took place. "When you pass your number around to a bunch of people, it can end up in the wrong hands. I think it was like what happened to the Clutter family."

She is referring to the murder case that was detailed in Truman Capote's 1966 true-crime novel *In Cold Blood*. In November 1959, Herbert Clutter, his wife, Bonnie Mae, and their children Nancy, sixteen, and Kenyon, fifteen, were murdered by Dick Hickock and Perry Smith at the family's farmhouse in Holcomb, Kansas. The family was targeted because of a false report from a prison inmate that a safe in the Clutter home contained $10,000. Both men were apprehended, tried, and executed.

Regarding the polygraph that Darin reportedly failed, Davis believes the results were due not to his being guilty of the crime, but to his feeling guilty over having possibly played a role by planning a staged burglary to collect insurance money. "I believe that Darin feels tremendous guilt because he brought that kind of element into his home. He answered truthfully that he didn't kill the boys."

In Davis's opinion, the intruder or intruders attacked Darlie—possibly with the intention of committing rape—and the boys woke up and went to the aid their mother. "And these idiots—whether they were high or had no compassion—dispensed with the boys quickly. In the process, they cut Darlie's throat. She was passed out. She wasn't asleep."

Davis believes Darlie was medicated in the Silly String footage, and was still medicated at the time her trial took place. "No one is *ever* tried in six months on a death penalty case," she says. "They pushed that trial under six months, when she was still on medication. I have never, in my history with the DA's office, seen a capital case go to trial in six months. The family wanted a speedy trial, but they didn't understand. They didn't see the terrible undercurrent. The family, they believed 100 percent in the legal system. They just handed over the keys, so to speak. They were all convinced she was going home. I've never seen so many shocked faces in all my life. I've never seen a courtroom so staggered—both families, not just hers, but Darin's, too."

Davis says she is "appalled" over so many things pertaining to the case: Mulder's performance, tactics by the prosecution, the testimony of the Baylor nurses that conflicted with their written notes, thousands of errors in the court reporter's record—and her own book, *Precious Angels*. "My book sold more than 200,000 copies, and I'm still battling with the fact that I wrote a book that convinced a lot of people that Darlie was guilty. I did it out of the belief that I was right. But I was fooled.

"I will go to my grave unsettled, not at peace—and I don't want that. God was watching me and counting on me to make a difference, and I think I screwed that up. I prayed throughout writing the book, 'God, let me get this right.' I have wondered, was He trying to tell me something and I just wasn't listening? I don't talk about Darlie a lot because all these feelings come out. But she's always on my mind. I have no dog in this fight. If anything, I've embarrassed myself.

"I feel less hope now. I fear that I am not going to live to see justice in this case. The clock is ticking. She is somewhere she is not supposed to be. I think the older I get, I get more scared because I'm afraid I'm not going to see that happen. Once you're convicted, it takes a lot to unconvict you. Most people have no clue that something like this could happen to them. If it's a circumstantial case, then it should not be a death penalty case. Darin said something that was very true. He said, 'If Darlie had died that night, then I would have been on death row for it because they would have said that nobody would have done that to themselves.'

"I question anybody who absolutely will not consider any other possibilities. We are *all* fallible. We all, at some point, are wrong about something. It shows a tremendous lack of character on their part to refuse to consider that they might have gotten it wrong. To me, standing up and saying that you're wrong or you could be wrong is a mark of character, not a mark of weakness.

"There are a lot of reasons to keep her where she is—jobs, careers, money that would have to be paid by the state if it's found to be a wrongful conviction. I don't care whose career is wrecked. She should only be there if she did it, and she didn't. There's no doubt in my mind."

Davis feels humbled by the forgiveness she has received from Darlie and her family. "The entire family is just unbelievable," she says. Davis went to the Lew Sterrett Justice Center in Dallas after Darlie had been transported from Gatesville for a court hearing. "With Darlie, I was forgiven the moment I sat down to visit her in jail. I went to the jail to ask her forgiveness when I learned the truth. I never felt anything but forgiveness from Darlie. I'm the one who can't forgive me."

Davis says that when she began speaking out on Darlie's behalf, she was stunned at the barrage of angry accusations and insults that were hurled at her then and even to this day. "They had me burning at the stake on a website the other day," she says. "I think there is something psychologically wrong with some of these people. They don't have a life, and this has become their life. I don't understand the hatred. These people have banded together and they absolutely hate anybody who thinks she didn't do this."

Davis believes the scheduling of an execution date for Darlie will bring a public outcry that will rival that of Karla Faye Tucker, who in 1998 was put to death by lethal injection for her role in a gruesome double murder. Karla Faye Tucker, who experienced a religious conversion while incarcerated, admitted her guilt and said she deserved to be punished. "The devil was in her heart. She turned to the Bible and I think she truly was converted," Davis says. "But Darlie has never said she did anything. She's not guilty. Darlie's execution will be completely different. I think it will be to the point of a riot."

It is after 9:00 p.m. when Davis finally winds down, ready to head to bed to rest in preparation for the next day's onslaught of pain. "If you can't believe that the justice system is going to get it right, then we're all vulnerable," she says, as we cap our lengthy conversation. I hang up and immediately feel discomfort in my right ear, where the phone receiver has been pressed for hours. I hit the "print" button and hear the newsroom's printer kick into gear, spitting out thirteen pages of single-spaced notes.

A member of the press crew rounds the corner of my cubicle in the otherwise deserted newsroom, startling me. They are done for the night, he says. It will be up to me to set the alarm. I gather up the pages from the printer, using a binder clip to hold them together. Davis's suffering and her bitter disappointment in the justice system cannot be contained by a single staple.

It is dark outside. I extinguish the office lights and hit a button on the control panel between the front entrance and the publisher's office. As I lock the doors behind me, I hear the alarm beginning its countdown, its beeps sounding more urgent as it approaches the point of no return. My Altima is the only vehicle remaining on the parking lot, its silhouette outlined by the moon. I punch the button to start the ignition. The glow of the dashboard in the autumn darkness seems almost sinister as I pause for a moment to reflect upon Davis's final words to me.

"This is the devil's doing."

CHAPTER 12

Family Secrets

On a day in late October, my drive on State Highway 6 takes me across the blue waters of Lake Waco, near Speegleville Park. It was at the park, on the south end of a cove, that the bodies of three teenagers—Jill Montgomery, Raylene Rice, and Kenneth Franks—were found by fishermen in July 1982. All three had been stabbed. The throats of both girls were slashed, and they had been sexually assaulted. The grisly crime was the focus of the book *Careless Whispers* by Carlton Stowers. I am driving to Waco on this day to interview a wealthy businessman who had tried to stop the execution of David Wayne Spence, one of four men charged in the attacks on the teens. One man was eventually exonerated after serving several years in prison.

The original police investigator acknowledged during Spence's appeals process that he had serious doubts about Spence's involvement. In 1993, a former Waco police lieutenant stated in an affidavit that he did not believe Spence committed the offense. Nevertheless, on April 3, 1997, the former roofer, who had a history of substance abuse problems, was executed by the state. In his final statement, Spence said to family members of the slain youths: "First of all, I want to say I speak the truth when I say I didn't kill your kids. Honestly, I have not killed anyone. I wish you could get the rage from your hearts and you could see the truth and get rid of the hatred."

Waco millionaire Brian Pardo had met Spence a few months before his execution and had initiated his own investigation into the case. He came to believe the state of Texas had an innocent man on death row. Pardo's efforts on Spence's behalf, though unsuccessful, caught the attention of producers at NBC's *Dateline*—and Sandy Aitken. When the show featured a segment in January 1998 on Pardo's investigation into the Lake Waco triple murder, Sandy was watching. She contacted Pardo and asked that he initiate an investigation into the crime that had landed her nephew's wife on death row. She believed in Darlie's innocence and was hoping Pardo might be able to find the true killer.

Pardo obliged, with the blessings of Darin's and Darlie's families. But when a polygraph was administered to Darin as part of that investigation—and he allegedly failed it—both families quickly parted ways not only with the wealthy businessman, but with Sandy. Sandy says her reason for asking for Pardo's help wasn't because she believed her nephew had been involved. But by the same token she remained open-minded when his findings implicated a family member.

"We saw the video," Sandy says, referring to secretly taped footage of the polygraph test that was done by a professional polygrapher. Part of the footage was shown in a 2007 episode of *The Wrong Man?* series on Court TV (now truTV). Retired New York City police detective Jerry Palace stated after watching the footage that the man who administered the test "did it 100 percent right." His partner on the show, retired New York City homicide detective Reggie Britt, noted that Darin "failed it miserably." The test indicated that Darin knew the identity of the killer or killers. He has always maintained that he had no part in the attacks on his family.

"We're the only ones in the family who have seen [the footage]," Sandy says, referring to herself and her husband, Robert. "We saw all of it. Brian had us come down and he played the whole thing. My family split company because of what happened. I mean, the screeching and the screaming and the stuff that went on about me . . ."

"They know we believe that Darin was the mastermind," explains Robert.

Says Sandy: "Brian spent a whole lot of money having a lot of things checked, and then on a Saturday afternoon he called my house and he said, 'I've got something to tell you. They've got the wrong parent.' I said, 'I'm not surprised'—and it's not because I don't love Darin. But it was because of all these little pieces."

After the polygraph results were made public, Darin held a news conference to denounce Pardo and to claim the test had been "rigged." The *Dallas Morning News* quoted Darin's mother, Sarilda, stating of Pardo: "I really wish he'd just leave us alone. He's not a detective. It's really sad that he's putting these things out there. Evidently, he has some other agenda than trying to find the truth. He just likes to get his name in the paper." Darlie Kee, as well, backed away from Pardo.

Waco businessman Brian Pardo, who funded
his own investigation into 6-6-6, believes
Darlie is innocent, but Darin was likely involved.
Photo courtesy Life Partners Holdings, Inc.

Sandy says that she tried to address Darin's possible complicity with Darlie when she went to visit her in prison. "She pointed her finger at me and she said, 'Think about what you're doing, Aunt Sandy.' And I said, 'I *am* thinking about it—and *you* need to think about it.'"

On the day that I make the drive to Waco, more than fifteen years have passed since Brian Pardo and a polygraph machine made all hell break loose within the family ranks of Darin and Darlie Routier. I am driving to the offices of Life Partners Holding, Incorporated, where Pardo is chief executive officer, to find out what he thinks today of the infamous case, and his own involvement in it. By the time the Silver Bullet heads back across the lake bridge toward Granbury, the digitial recorder will contain a very interesting story indeed.

* * *

From the street, one would never imagine that the offices of Life Partners Holdings, a company that purchases life insurance polices, contain replicas of Egyptian artifacts—including a sarcophagus or two. One is near the octagonal table where Pardo and I take our seats.

Pardo is gracious and well-mannered—a man of wealth who doesn't feel the need to show it. Our interview begins at 1:00 p.m. on this Friday, and will conclude at 2:45, when he must leave due to a family commitment. It's been a long time, he tells me, since he has had any true contact with Darlie, though his daughter, acting on his behalf, makes regular deposits into Darlie's commissary account.

"That's the least I can do for her," he says. "I am completely convinced that Darlie Routier is totally innocent. Our investigation determined that Darin was more than likely the guilty party. I think they [the state] have a real moral dilemma with her. I think the police and the prosecutors knew she wasn't guilty, but they thought she probably knew who was. And if you know their mindset—and I *do* know their mindset—once they decide somebody's guilty, they'll just stick with that theory. They will not say they made a mistake. And, of course, they make mistakes. They make mistakes all the time."

When Robert and Sandy came to meet with him about Darlie, he quickly became intrigued by her case, largely because even her husband's family strongly believed in her innocence. "I said, 'I will investigate this to a level that I feel is satisfactory. I don't know where it's going to lead. It's not going to cost you a dime, but you're not going to influence the outcome, either. It's going to lead wherever it leads.' And the more I got into it, the more there was to look at."

Pardo enlisted help from two men: a licensed private investigator named Richard Reyna and Longview attorney Stephen Losch, who died in 2003. Immediately, when the investigation got under way, Darin became "Mr. Helpful." "Darin, when he found out that I was going to be helping Darlie—right away he called me and offered to help. The way I read that was he was trying to control the situation and stay in the know."

Pardo already felt that Darin was odd, but he was shocked at what Darin did next. "About a week or ten days later, we get a knock at the door," Pardo said, referring to his wife and the home they share. "Nobody ever knocks at my door because the gates are closed, and they're electric gates. I've lived there since 1982, and I've never had somebody just show up at my door. I thought it was one of the grandkids or something. I went to the door and it was Darin standing there. I said, 'Darin, how did you get here?' And he said, 'I just climbed over the fence.' It didn't scare me, but it did make me real nervous. I invited him in. I didn't know he was armed, though."

At one point, the conversation turned to guns and Darin pulled from his back waistband a Model 1911 .45 Colt automatic. Pardo says he did not feel threatened, and believes Darin was simply proud of the weapon and wanted to show it off. Pardo said that at first his wife was listening to the conversation, but then Darin began talking to her and she was drawn into the discourse. "The three of us are talking and he starts going off on the size of his wife's breasts. It came out of nowhere, too." Pardo said the subject made his wife uncomfortable—a feeling that was compounded when Darin commented about the size of *her* breasts. "We're wanting him out of there," Pardo says.

Pardo reiterates that he did not feel threatened by Darin, nor did he feel Darin was attempting to be threatening. But the experience was disconcerting, made even more so by the fact that when Pardo had looked out the peephole, he saw no one there. Darin, he says, had deliberately avoided being spotted.

Losch and Reyna became more and more convinced that Darin was involved. Pardo claims there were reliable sources in law enforcement who said Darin owed drug dealers $200,000. He also asserts there were clues Darin had not been sleeping upstairs when the attacks occurred, and that a pair of bloodstained jeans the same size and brand as Darin wore were found in a stack of the boys' folded, clean laundry in the utility room.

"There was intense pressure on him," Brian Pardo said, regarding the alleged threat from drug dealers. "We think they were going in there to kill Darlie and he [Darin] was motivated mostly by the need for money. He had just taken out a life insurance policy on Darlie. Why would you take out a life insurance policy on a perfectly healthy young woman when you're having trouble making ends meet? They go out to kill her to collect the insurance. He [Darin] is already there. They attack Darlie and, in the process of attacking Darlie, the boys wake up. Now they [the attackers] are faced with a terrible decision—and they're probably high on something."

Pardo believes the alleged drug dealers abandoned their demands on Darin because the crime "became a huge deal." As for why the Routiers' Pomeranian, Domain, didn't bark during the attacks that were taking place downstairs, the businessman says it was "because Darin was down there." He explains: "I have a number of dogs living at home with me. My wife owns a rescue. It just so happens I know a lot about dogs. As long as a dog knows that you're there, they don't care. It's like TV to them. They mostly go on smell. They're used to television and all the noises around them. Darin and Darlie fought a lot. They yelled and screamed at each other a lot."

Pardo says Darlie refused to consider that her husband may have wanted her killed and may have been responsible for the murders of their children. But he says she told him that if Losch and Reyna came to that same conclusion, she would believe it. Once the pair was satisfied with their findings, they went to the prison unit to talk to Darlie. "After the meeting, [Losch] calls me. He was actually a little shaken by it. He said, 'In all my years of dealing with death-row inmates, I've never seen a scene like we saw when we went out and talked to Darlie.'"

Pardo says that Losch described an emotional breakdown by Darlie that resulted in guards escorting her back to her cell in hopes that she could get her emotions under control. Appellate lawyer Stephen Cooper would later confirm that the meltdown occurred. So, too, did Richard Reyna. Reyna says his tactic is to present his findings and then let the accused or the witness reach their own conclusion. "Before I discussed the blood on the jeans [with Darlie], I asked if she was the only one who washed and folded the clothes that day. When I was satisfied that she was the only one who folded the clothes, I pulled out the photograph of the bloody jeans and asked if she knew who would have folded the jeans and put them in between the clean, folded clothes. I also asked her if the jeans belonged to her. She studied the photograph and then said that they were Darin's pants. It was then that she totally lost control."

Reyna says the stains on the jeans were clearly blood. They were on the outside of the jeans, as well as on the inside where one might put their thumbs while pulling the pants off or on. The private investigator says that Darlie began to scream, "Damn him! Damn him!" and then began to cry uncontrollably. "To me, it was a genuine reaction," he says.

Reyna says that when he began investigating the case, he kept an open mind—even considering the possibility that Darlie or someone else might have planted the jeans in order to frame Darin. He has wondered if Darin would have even had time to put the folded jeans in the stack of clean laundry and then run upstairs. Darlie claims that Darin came running from the second floor when she began screaming.

Reyna is incredulous that the photos of the bloodstained jeans were taken by Rowlett police, yet he found no indication that the police had the blood tested or paid any particular attention to the garment's possible significance. "Nobody made any notations about it. I'm thinking, hey, guys—time out. There's a pair of pants with blood on them."

The private investigator also believes it was the height of stupidity that police and prosecutors focused on life insurance policies on the dead boys that totaled just $10,000, yet they ignored a sizable life insurance policy on Darlie of which Darin was the beneficiary. Reyna says that both Darin and Darlie told him the life insurance on Darlie was "in the area of $200,000 or more." He says that, according to Darlie, the policies on the boys had been in a dresser drawer. However, someone with the Rowlett Police Department pulled them out and photographed them as if they had been lying out, in an apparent attempt to make it seem as if she murdered her children in order to collect their life insurance. "I don't know how many times I shook my head and said out loud, 'Hey, Einsteins, the actual cost to bury these children was well over $10,000. Try doing the math again!'" Reyna says of the Rowlett cops.

Reyna says he disagrees with Pardo's belief that drugs were at the root of what happened that night. "I entertained several possibilities, and the one that made more sense to me was a staged burglary, which eventually concluded with the attack on Darlie. I have no reason to disbelieve Darin that he called the whole thing off. But it is likely that the person he spoke with was made aware of Darlie's insurance policy. The person or persons who entered the house could have decided on their own to go into the house to kill Darlie. It is logical that the intruder or intruders could then blackmail Darin into paying them from the insurance money collected from Darlie's death. The children would have recognized the intruder or intruders who attacked their mother, and both were killed as a result."

Reyna notes that Darin took the boys with him at times when he visited the local business of a man whom Darin likely approached about staging a burglary. That man has never been charged in connection to the crime at the Routier home.

Pardo says Darin went to see Darlie a few days after the emotional meeting with Losch and Reyna, "and when Losch came back the following week, she was back to not believing it again. And that's when I kind of dropped off. I said, 'Well, this woman is going to to die because she's choosing to die; she's not dying because she's guilty. Something's driving her. What's driving her, in my opinion, is a threat from Darin that if you turn me in, I'm going to kill the last child. Darlie didn't actually say that to me in so many words directly, but in so many words she did say that to me. 'I can't attack Darin because I'm too worried about the future'—that kind of statement. She said, 'I don't know why some stranger attacked us, but it wasn't me, and it wasn't Darin either.'"

Brian Pardo's statement makes me think of something Sandy had said to me. She said Darlie told her that if she ever gets another trial, she will not lie "for another member of this family ever again. I'm the one who has sat here all these years, not them."

I tell Pardo I am asking people involved in the case whether they have any regrets all these years later. He replies: "I have a regret that Darlie won't understand that she's making a horrible mistake by not saying what the truth is—and I'm convinced that Darlie knows it. She knows what the truth is. It's like, you're sorry that somebody's committing suicide, because that's exactly what Darlie's doing here. She's committing suicide and the thing is, she's not guilty. The system should be better than that. The system should not allow her to do that. They're going to kill her because she is willing to die to protect her other child."

CHAPTER 13

Burgers and Fries and Cherry Pies

The Whataburger on Junction Highway in Ingram, not far from Kerrville, does a brisk weekday lunch business. On a sunny Friday, six days before Thanksgiving, there is one corner booth still unoccupied. Charlie Samford, dressed in jeans, a plaid shirt, and a Vietnam Veteran cap, slides into the booth with an orange and white cup of iced tea and a dog-eared copy of *Media Tried, Justice Denied*, a posttrial book by Christopher Wayne Brown that Samford says opened his eyes about the woman he helped put on death row. Samford is there to talk with me about the long-ago murder trial of Darlie Routier, and his own troubled conscience.

Behind the fast-food restaurant are rolling hills dressed in the colors of fall. From Johnson City—home of Lyndon Baines Johnson—to Fredericksburg to Kerrville, banners already are hanging across main thoroughfares trumpeting Christmas in the Hill Country.

Before our interview gets under way, I hand Samford an orchid-colored greeting card with flowers on the cover containing a handwritten note from Darlie. On page two of her letter to me, she wrote: "Mr. Samford seemed like a very sincere man. Many years ago, I spoke with him on the phone—he wanted to apologize to me. I feel he is a man of courage and I have truly forgiven him." The former carpenter is silent for a moment as he takes in the words of pardon from the woman he helped sentence to death. If only he could forgive himself.

* * *

In early 1997, the trial of the Rowlett homemaker who the state claimed butchered her little boys in the early morning hours of June 6, 1996, had gone on for a month—in the dead of winter, and in a courthouse that had little or no heat because it was under renovation. "It was cold. It was just as cold in that

A juror's remorse: Charlie Samford, a member
of the jury that sentenced Darlie Routier to death,
regrets his role in the decision. *Photo by the author.*

courtroom as it was outside," Samford tells me as diners come and go. "The
judge would let us go get up and move around."

The other jurors had pretty much been convinced from the beginning
that the bleached blonde from Dallas County was guilty of the crime, Samford
recalls, and when they finally began their deliberations, they saw little need
for debate. "When we got into the jury room it was, boom—guilty. It didn't
take long," says Samford, a retired maintenance employee for Kerrville State
Hospital. The other jurors did not take it well when Samford said he wasn't
so sure that Routier had stabbed her children and then inflicted injuries on
herself to stage a crime scene. Samford said it was mostly the women on the
jury who were pushing for a guilty verdict.

At times during the trial, Samford and Routier would lock eyes. "She
looked at me—we'd catch eyes once in a while—and she'd be doing this," Samford said, shaking his head. "I can read people a little bit, and she didn't look to
me like she was guilty."

In the cold courtroom, where the jury deliberated behind locked doors,
Samford grew tired, and his resolve grew weak as the hours ticked by. "I guess

I caved in. The trial was so long, and everybody wanted to go home. I think they wanted to get it over with. I should have held out, but I didn't. That's what bothers me now—not using my own mind, and letting someone else do it for me."

When the verdict was read, Samford's eyes locked on Darlie's once again. "She was sitting there, looking like that," he said. He turns the book toward me. Its cover bears a photo of Darlie in prison garb, looking like a trapped animal.

The lunch crowd is getting thinner. A few diners look over at our booth with curious expressions. The digital recorder is sitting in the middle of the table, near Samford's iced tea.

Samford claims the jury never saw the photographs that showed the full extent of Routier's injuries—photographs he believes would have made a difference in the jury's verdict. The photos taken by Rowlett police show severe bruising on the inside of her arms and also on her hands. The lawyers from the Dallas County DA's office claimed that Darlie had beaten her own arms until they were severely bruised after she was released from the hospital and began to realize cops weren't believing her story about an intruder. Samford's not buying the prosecutors' claims now, but, of course, it's too late.

One day several years after the trial, Samford says, he dropped by the Kerrville office of defense team lawyer Richard Mosty. With all the things he had since learned about the Routier case, he regretted his role in the verdict and wanted Mosty to advise him on what he could do about it. "I thought, I'm going to give it a try. I don't have anything to lose; Darlie does."

Samford says that after he shared his remorse with Mosty, he phoned the warden's office at the Mountain View prison unit in Gatesville. The warden allowed Darlie to phone him. Samford says it was "rough," but he told Darlie what was on his heart. "I just apologized and I said, 'I hope someday I can be forgiven.'" He was forgiven that day, before Darlie hung up the phone.

On July 10, 2002, Samford signed an affidavit that he hoped would help Darlie in her appeals. The document stated: "During the trial of Mrs. Routier, the prosecution introduced a videotape taken by a news reporter showing a birthday party at the grave of Mrs. Routier's children sometime after her children had been killed. The tape showed Mrs. Routier smiling, chewing gum, and shooting Silly String. During our deliberations, I recall that we watched the videotape about eight or nine times, although I wasn't keeping count. The videotape was one of the main reasons I voted to convict Mrs. Routier of murder because I didn't know what to make of her behavior.

"After trial, I was shown another videotape that I was told was taken by police at the grave site that same day. This second videotape showed a prayer service that happened before the birthday party. Had we been shown this other tape so that we had been able to see the whole picture of what happened that day, I believe I would not have voted to convict Mrs. Routier."

The remorseful juror's change of heart captured the attention of the media, but not of the Texas justice system. In Ingram and Kerrville, the media spotlight didn't make him any friends. To this day, there are some who avoid him if their paths cross.

Samford prepares himself for when the state will set an execution date for a woman he now believes is innocent, and whom he helped condemn. "I've told myself I've done all I can do," he says.

As our two-hour interview draws to a close, I ask Samford if he has any message he would like for me to deliver to Darlie. "Yeah. When you look at her through that glass, do this." He balls his right hand into a fist and taps his chest twice, over his heart.

Before heading back to Granbury, I drive a few miles up the highway to Kerrville, where rush-hour traffic is bustling around the Kerr County Courthouse. With the holiday season getting into full swing, the site of one of the most infamous capital murder trials in recent history is festooned with signs of peace on Earth and good will toward men.

CHAPTER 14

'Til Death Do Us Part

In Greek mythology, sailors would be lured to coastlines by the angelic singing voices of beautiful sirens, only to shipwreck against the perilous rocks. The largest coffeehouse company in the world adopted the image of a mythical mermaid siren to seduce java lovers into its twenty-one thousand stores. It is 10:00 a.m. on a sunny spring Monday when Darin Routier walks under the familiar logo and through the doors of one of those coffeehouses. We are meeting at the Starbucks at 82nd and Quaker in Lubbock. He moved back to his hometown six years after the conviction of his now ex-wife, Darlie Routier.

When they had met here in Lubbock she was fifteen and he was seventeen. Darin had been immediately captivated by the blonde beauty who, like the mythical sirens, had a lovely singing voice. She was different. Some have described her as ahead of her time. She wore dresses more often than most other girls did, but seemed equally comfortable in a T-shirt and shorts.

But those breezy days were long ago—back before June 6, 1996, dashed the young couple and their families against the rocks. While few people might call Darin Routier lucky, he has managed to arrive at middle age no worse for wear. Some might call him handsome. His hair, now with a touch of salt and pepper, brushes his shoulders. The blue of his eyes is enhanced by the morning sun spilling in through the glass windows of the bustling cafe. His demeanor is laid back and friendly. I am casual and friendly, too, but my outward demeanor belies my inner thoughts. During our conversation, I silently reflect upon what others have told me about their suspicions that Darin was likely involved in what happened to his wife and children. "All roads lead to Darin," one source had told me. As our interview gets under way, I start with a simple question about what his life has been like, post 6-6-6. Do you often get recognized? I ask.

"Not too much," he says. "I've changed enough, I guess, to where people have to be at least twenty-five years old to remember. I got recognized everywhere in Dallas. People would say, 'You look familiar. Where did you go to school?' I'd play with them sometimes, too. One time this lady, she followed me all the way around the store. She said, 'I know you. I know you from somewhere. I just can't figure it out.' Finally, I said, 'You probably saw me on TV. I was on *Baywatch*.' And she said, 'Oh, yeah!' It [the crime and conviction] is not something you feel comfortable talking about with a stranger. It just opens up a two-hour conversation."

Darin says he came home to Lubbock twelve years earlier because he has a support system here. "And I was broke," he says about finally wiping the dust of Dallas County off his feet. "All we could think about was selling everything that we had to raise money for Darlie's defense. I wrote my last check to Mulder the day we went to trial—the last dime I had. It was probably another $10,000."

How much, total, did the family pay to Mulder? I ask.

"I'm not really sure what the final payment was, after family and friends pitched in. All I know is, it was about $100,000 or more. And we basically signed our rights away to any movie and book deal, and he wanted to know the worth of my business. He never came after it. We were pretty desperate to give Darlie the best defense we could give her, so we basically went for broke and spent every dime we had."

Darin says he is one of only a few people who have actually funded a capital murder trial. Most defendants are deemed indigent and have court-appointed attorneys. Darlie's friend Melanie, he says, has never been repaid the $12,000 that she and her husband donated to the defense fund.

During the trial in Kerrville, while the judge, lawyers, and state witnesses slept at night in hotel rooms, Darin bedded down near the banks of the Guadalupe River in a trailer owned by his parents. Since he was not allowed in the courtroom, and the families could not afford to fly defense witnesses in from Dallas, Darin spent much of those five weeks driving back and forth between Kerrville and Dallas, playing the role of chauffeur.

After the trial, the house on Eagle Drive went into foreclosure. Not long after that, the IRS emptied his bank accounts. When Child Protective Services took possession of baby Drake after Darlie's arrest, the court granted custody to Darin's parents, Lenny and Sarilda Routier. After Darlie was convicted and sent to death row, Darin reclaimed his sole surviving son and raised him as a single parent. "I took him to work with me and tried to give him a normal life," Darin says.

He and other family members kept the child away from the press—or at least tried to. One day when Darin took the tot to a Dallas Cowboys football game, they were spotted, even in the midst of thousands of spectators. "We were sitting in the sixtieth row back, and it was on the radio that we were there at the game. We're not famous. We're not Matthew McConaughey and Sandra Bullock. Me taking my son to a football game is not news."

Darin says that when Drake was small, he tried to explain to the boy in ways he could understand why his mother could not be with him. However, since the child was only a year old when his mother was sent to death row, his adjustment period was brief. "He doesn't know any different. Being around the family, there are stories that come up when we're talking about his brothers, talking about his mom. I think, personally, he's handled it pretty well. I've never let him use it for a crutch."

Going to see his mother has not been difficult for Drake, Darin says. "Before he was walking, he was seeing her behind glass. Their communication was her singing him a song. He never forgot what his mom sounded like. But that distance between them, in some ways their relationship could be stronger because she's not disciplining him. She's not getting him upset. But then again, she's not holding him or hugging him."

On this mild spring day, Drake is two months shy of his high school graduation. The ceremony will take place one day after the eighteenth anniversary of his brothers' deaths. It has been a significant year for Drake in other ways: he was diagnosed with leukemia eight months earlier, in the summer before the start of his senior year. His prognosis is hopeful, but he will have to undergo treatment for three years. The chemotherapy has been difficult, resulting in hospital stays that have lasted weeks. Drake was once airlifted from Texas Health Presbyterian Hospital in Kaufman to Children's Hospital in Dallas, where he was placed for a time in the intensive care unit.

The leukemia diagnosis came shortly after Drake moved from Lubbock to the home of Darlie's sister Danelle. It's not far from his grandmother's home in Wills Point.

Darin says that neither he nor his family members have ever doubted Darlie's innocence. As for the divorce that finally occurred after Darlie had been on death row for many years, he says: "It doesn't take anything away from the love I have for her, but I just have to move on. And also, financially, I needed to be separated from her because I do believe that she'll go to trial again, and I can't afford it."

Darin says he is building a house. His parents will also have a home on the property. Lenny Routier is a sometime employee of Darin's company, which manages technology for stores and other businesses. Darin has a woman in his life, but he has not remarried and does not know if he ever will.

In the years since he lost his wife and two older sons, Darin has been to several counselors. He has flashbacks, which he refers to as "nightmares," that occur during the day when he is fully awake. "I'll be driving, just thinking, and all of a sudden I start seeing Devon's eyes." The child's eyes were open and lifeless, he says, when he started CPR.

Darin disputes claims that the crime scene had been staged. I ask him about the motion-activated backyard security light that police believe would have still been on when officers arrived on the scene, had an intruder fled through the gate by the driveway. "I've heard that police said it stayed on for eighteen minutes. It was in Patricia Springer's book [*Flesh and Blood*]," he says. "It was the first series of motion lights, and it was on the side of the hot tub. As soon as you walked out there, it would turn on. You could either set them for two [minutes] or five. If you stayed real close to the house, it might not have set it off. They came through right by the fence, and the window was right there. The light might have never come on." According to Darlie Kee, the light would remain on for an extended period only if someone was standing within range of its motion sensors.

The Rowlett Police Department was so inexperienced, Darin says, "apparently, they didn't have cameras or audio in the interview room where they interviewed me and Darlie." He continues: "I'm not saying cops are bad. They're not. But it only takes a handful to not do their jobs properly, or to not be trained properly, to sway things and come up with what I call 'selective adjectives.' That's what happens in a courtroom, too. They just pull out these words. How can you describe a wound as 'superficial' when it's almost to the carotid artery? I've said over and over that if she had died, they would have come after me.

"The truth has nothing to do with what happens in the courtroom. When cops tell you that you have the right to remain silent—when they tell you that, shut up. I always felt that innocent people don't need a lawyer. But an innocent person needs a lawyer faster than a guilty one."

Darin recalls that on the day his wife was arrested, she was kept at the police station, allegedly for further questioning, while two Rowlett police officers took him back to the house for another walk-through replay. He didn't realize at the time that the officers wanted him away from the police station. When they got into the patrol car to head back, the officers told him they were going to stop at a store to buy cigars. "I was like, fine, y'all smoke cigars, I don't care. We get to the police station and I get a call from Mama Darlie. She says, 'They've got Darlie Lynn. They're arresting her.' I said, 'No, they're not. I'm right here at the police station.' And she said, 'Darin, I'm watching it on TV.' I get inside. They bring me in, lock the doors down, we walk upstairs. We go into a room and there are five cops around me. They say, 'We're arresting Darlie.' And I said, 'Oh, no. You guys got it all wrong.'"

Darin says he witnessed police officers smoking cigars to celebrate having made an arrest in the biggest crime the bedroom community had ever seen. Darin believes that the knife that was used to stab Devon was different from the knife that was used to cut Darlie and Damon—and that knife has never been found.

The ex-husband of Texas's most infamous female death-row inmate tells me what others have said: She was convicted because of Silly String and character judgments. "She was high as a kite," he says, referring to medication Darlie had taken prior to the graveside memorial service and birthday celebration. "At times like that, you're laughing one minute and you're sobbing the next. I mean, it's a roller coaster."

As for the public's judgment, he says: "We are loving, supportive people. We're good people. And if it can happen to us, it can happen to anybody."

I ask him about Waco millionaire Brian Pardo and the polygraph examination. "I think it was just a ploy. I fell into it, thinking he was actually going to do something. I think we were desperate."

I ask Darin if he thinks the attacks were related to the burglary/insurance plot. He says he believes it had more to do with maids that had been inside the home. Loose lips about the Routiers' expensive possessions may have caused the home to be targeted.

"Darin, did you have *anything* at all to do with what happened that night?" I ask. "Absolutely not," he replies. "I only know who *didn't* do it. It wasn't me or Darlie." Then he adds, "We may have to accept the fact that we may never know."

I say nothing, but think to myself that Darin is right—we may never know. If Darin was involved—either directly or indirectly—the chance to prove it may have been forever lost by a small town police department that focused immediately on Darlie.

I save for another day a question that I know must be asked, opting instead to let our conversation wind down on pleasant terms. Darin comments that the interview "was painless." On the parking lot outside Starbucks, he shakes my hand, then gives me a hug.

The question that I temporarily put on the back burner has to do with something Darin's Aunt Sandy told me. She said that, as she and her nephew's wife had drawn closer during their visits at the Lew Sterrett jail and, later, at Mountain View, Darlie Routier told her something about that night that she had not shared with police or her defense lawyers.

She had asked her husband for a divorce.

CHAPTER 15

Darkness Falls in Arkansas

It is a cold weekday in February and I am writing a story for the next *HCN* issue when Bonnie rounds the corner by my cubicle as she makes her daily rounds. "Mail for you." She hands me another letter from Texas Department of Criminal Justice (TDCJ) inmate #999220—Darlie Routier. I open it to find that Darlie has sent me a letter she had received from a male inmate in Tennessee Colony.

Darlie receives a good deal of correspondence. This is not surprising, considering her attractiveness, the made-for-TV aspects of the shocking crime for which she was sent to death row, and the lingering doubts about her guilt. The reason she paid attention to this particular letter was because the man had written to her once before—fifteen years earlier. Now, here he was again, making the same claims about an argument he overheard in the recreation yard at the Potter County jail in Amarillo in the fall of 1996.

Darlie's concern about the mysterious letter, which was written by a man serving a sentence for murder, causes me to take an unexpected detour in my reexamination of her case, but that's what often happens in this line of work. Reporters take side streets off main thoroughfares because dark characters, and the secrets they hold, can lurk in the shadows of roads less traveled. Those detours often do little more than circle back or lead to dead ends. But not always.

* * *

Here are excerpts from the letter the inmate wrote to Darlie:
"Dear Darlie:
"Listen, it's been a long time since you have heard from me. I really had no intentions of writing you again at all, but I am going to make this my last letter. . . .
"The guy who killed your kids is Timothy Harris. . . . I went off on 'Arkansas' [Timothy Harris] when he said he had to kill one of your kids be-

cause he started to run to the hallway and holler after he seen him.

"I told you back in '98 what the state was going to do to you. They didn't want to try and execute you while you're still young and pretty because it will draw a public outcry. So they will put off your date for 25 years when you get old and ugly. And they are on course of doing that. Then they will offer you this: They will tell you if you just plead guilty, they will commute your sentence to life. Then you will have to do 35 flat years before you become eligible for parole—when you're about 65. So you might as well be dead. . . . I don't know how else to help you, Darlie. There are a lot of people who want you to die."

A few days later, I get a letter from Darlie. "What if what he is saying is true?" she wrote about the message from the inmate. "Now he's contacted me again after all these years. The part in his letter where he is talking about one of my boys is so creepy, it made my stomach hurt."

As I begin to explore the man's claims, the story that will unfold can be credited to old-fashioned gumshoe investigative reporting—not mine, but someone else's. A few weeks after receiving the letters from both the inmate and Darlie, I stay late at the office because of a scheduled phone call to a Houston attorney named Quinncy McNeal. In his past life as an ABC affiliate reporter based in Green Bay, Wisconsin, Quinncy had become fascinated with the Routier case. He took a job with the Fox-owned-and-operated station in Austin in hopes of doing more reporting on the story. His bosses allowed him to travel to Dallas a few times to do some reporting on the case during the early years of Darlie's appeals. At least one of those reports was seen by the inmate who had written to Darlie in 1998. He wrote to Quinncy, making the same assertions he had made to Darlie.

In relating this story, I will refer to the inmate as "Karl," though that is not his real name. The reason for the alias is that during the course of Quinncy's investigation, he uncovered a cast of characters that he believes may have been connected to the Routier murders. Some are still alive, but have never been charged in the crime. Aliases will be given to everyone except Timothy Harris.

"In 2004, Karl saw me on the news in Austin and he wrote a letter to me," Quinncy explains. "Karl told me this story about when he was in the Potter County jail in October of 1996. I go up and see him. I'm always skeptical because many [inmates] just want someone to speak to. At the time, he was at the French Robertson Unit in Abilene."

In 1996, Karl had been at the jail in Amarillo on a federal bench warrant.

"He said he was just coming in from the recreation yard and he heard two inmates yelling and screaming very loudly about a crime they had been involved in. He remembered them talking about children—hurting children—and about using knives. It was something about a drug issue. Karl got upset. He overheard them talking about two children who were hurt and knives used and the name Darla. At that time, he didn't know anything about Darlie. He had been in jail and didn't know anything about it.

"Then in 1998, he's reading the *New Yorker* magazine about the execution of Karla Faye Tucker. The story mentions a woman in Texas named Darlie whose children were killed with knives. It hit him that the guys in the rec yard must have been talking about Darlie. He put two and two together. He told me that he remembered what they looked like. One had long hair, like Axl Rose. It was chestnut-colored. The other guy, his nickname was 'Arkansas.' He looked like a big cowboy."

Quinncy began submitting Open Records requests to get mug shots and names of every male inmate at the Potter County Jail during that time. It was a slow, tedious process. Every time he would get a mug shot, he would "snail mail" it to Karl. The inmate was never able to pin down the guy with the Axl Rose hair, but he sent one of the mug shots back to Quinncy with the message: "This is Arkansas."

Arkansas was twenty-two-year-old Timothy Gene Harris. Quinncy found confirmation that Arkansas was Harris's street name after he obtained documents through Open Records. His investigation revealed the names of people that Harris tended to hang out with. They were known to have drug problems and they had criminal rap sheets.

Quinncy began tracking down information on two of those associates, a married couple whom I'll refer to as "Dwayne" and "Karen." He came to believe that all three might have been involved in what happened at 5801 Eagle Drive in Rowlett.

Quinncy's written daily reports from that time detail conversations with Karen's two grown daughters, who spoke with him about their mother's criminal history and allegedly confronted her about Quinncy's belief that she was connected to the Rowlett crime. Karen told one of her daughters that Arkansas and two other men had gotten into a fight "about drugs" and had "left town for Dallas" in June of 1996 in a stolen white truck. "It might match the description of a white truck that Donna Dobbins told police about. See her statement in a lead sheet dated 6/7/96," Quinncy wrote in one of his daily reports.

Dobbins was one of several people who had phoned Rowlett police in the aftermath of the Routier murders with tips that included information on vehicles seen in the vicinity around the time the crime occurred.

Quinncy went to the Lubbock County jail, where Karen was incarcerated. She told him she had not gone on the trip to the Dallas area and that the details she had heard were just "hearsay." Some of the details did not seem to fit the Routier crime, but some were very similar. "Karen says that, according to the stories she'd heard, no one was supposed to be home," Quinncy related in his notes. "They broke into a home and it all went bad. Dwayne said there were some kids in the room, the fight escalated and some kids woke up. The kids were very young, Karen remembers them saying. Karen also made a point of telling me that it wouldn't have been random—that those guys would have known someone on the inside."

According to Quinncy, Karen is from Wylie, about ten minutes from Rowlett.

Quinncy categorized in his notes things that fit the Routier crime and things that didn't. Among the things that didn't were Karen's belief that the woman who was attacked had been a dancer that Arkansas had met in a bar and the home was a duplex or condo. Among the things that fit were: Karen remembered that the crime happened in June of 1996; Dwayne and another one of the men claimed to have broken into a home "and fucked some people up"; kids were inside, and in the room; no one was supposed to be home; and the victims were stabbed.

Shortly after Karl overheard the argument between Arkansas and the inmate with Axl Rose hair, Arkansas was sent to the Estelle Unit in Huntsville, where he was to participate in the state's Substance Abuse Felony Punishment, or SAFP, program. SAFP was developed as an alternative to prison for offenders with substance abuse problems. The program's three in-prison phases are followed by a three-month stay at a transitional treatment center.

Within just a few weeks of his arrival, Timothy Harris—the volatile Arkansas— was told he was being kicked out of the program because of his "threatening behavior" and "attempts to intimidate." Shortly after that decision was made, by a panel that included Harris's peer group, he attempted to hang himself in his cell with a shoelace. Clinic notes obtained by me through Open Records refer to Harris as a "rather large, slow-talking Oklahoma cowboy," and state that he asked to see a psychiatrist because he was being plagued by "bad dreams" tied to his criminal past.

Regarding Harris's suicide attempt, a doctor's notes state: "The attempt or gesture was viewed as a manipulative effort to enable the Client to avoid going to the penitentiary. The Client was subsequently remanded to the Skyview Crisis Management Unit in Rusk where he underwent a brief psychiatric admission, which did involve an evaluation and screening. Their assessment at that time was that the patient was not suicidal or homicidal. . . ."

They were wrong.

* * *

William Dale Pachta Jr. waited a few seconds for the water to warm up before stepping into the shower at the Potter County Detention Center. It was around 12:30 p.m., three days after Christmas in 1996. Inmates were allowed out of their cells for one hour each day to shower and use the phone. Pachta, a resident of Cell 21 in Pod E-16, had noticed when he walked through the day room that the other inmates in the pod were lying on their bunks, seemingly settling in for naps after having just eaten lunch. There is little else to do, after all, in a nine-by-six-foot cell.

Pachta had been in the shower for about five minutes when he heard the pod door open. He looked out to see officers sprinting into the pod toward Cell 19, where an inmate had been placed sometime after midnight after an altercation with other inmates. "I looked over toward [Cell 19] and saw the inmate who was in that cell hanging in front of the door. The officers were [yelling] for someone to get a knife and cut him down," Pachta stated in an affidavit. "I am certain that this inmate couldn't have been hanging more than five to seven minutes, as prior to me getting into the shower I saw him lying down on his bunk."

The inmate was Timothy Gene Harris, whose latest brush with the law had involved an armed robbery committed while in the company of another man and five women. Ricardo Cabrera told Amarillo police officers that he had been forced to hand over the keys to his 1986 Olds Cutlass by a man who held a knife to his throat. Upon investigation, cops had arrested Harris for the crime. He was booted back to Potter County on a bench warrant after getting kicked out of SAFP.

In Cell 19, officers cut from the metal grating above the doorway the ligature that had been fashioned out of "elastic and brown braided material," according to jail reports. The "slow-talking Oklahoma cowboy" that TDCJ officials had determined was not suicidal was laid on the floor so that officers could frantically administer CPR until paramedics arrived. Though a faint pulse initially was found, efforts to save Harris's life were to no avail. He was pronounced dead by doctors at Northwest Texas Hospital at 1:35 p.m.

In his affidavit, Sgt. Donald E. Lancaster of the Potter County Sheriff's Office stated: "The inmate's hands were tied in the front of his body, similar to a set of handcuffs, secured in front of a person. The instrument utilized appeared to be a bed sheet that had been secured very securely around each wrist."

It was an odd detail that did not go unnoticed by Dr. Randall E. Frost, a forensic pathologist at the Lubbock County Medical Examiner's Office. Frost determined that the cause of death was hanging by two cloth ligatures. "The wrist scar is consistent with the decedent's reported history of suicidal ideations, and this would support a suicidal hanging," Frost wrote in his report. "However, the history of a ligature around the wrists must be considered. Unless the ligature was tied in a manner which would allow the decedent to apply it himself, this finding is highly suspicious."

Harris's death would later be ruled a suicide. He is buried in Heavener, Oklahoma. On his tombstone, the message "Time Marches On" is etched beneath his birth date of May 7, 1974, and his date of death, December 28, 1996.

The street thug plagued by recurring nightmares died six months after the murders of Devon and Damon Routier, and just nine days before their mother was taken to trial. Autopsy photos show that the ligature mark made Arkansas's throat appear to have been slashed, just as Darlie's had been.

*   *   *

Through the TDCJ website, I look up Karl's inmate number and send him an e-mail through JPay. I don't particularly need him, since I have copies of the letters he sent to Quinncy and Darlie. I also have Amarillo police reports on Harris, thanks to Quinncy.

I had submitted my own Open Records requests for prison records that are in Harris's court file in Potter County. Those records revealed the previous suicide attempt that was not taken seriously. An Open Records request filed with the Potter County sheriff resulted in documents from the county attorney's office that included affidavits by inmates and officers, Harris's autopsy report, and autopsy photos.

Nevertheless, I e-mail Karl and he mails me a letter in reply. I make arrangements to drive to a facility in Tennessee Colony and meet with him on a day in June when I will be making a trip to San Antonio. I make these plans even though it is clear from his letter that dealing with Karl will be a dicey proposition. He and Quinncy had parted ways over Karl's efforts to persuade Quinncy to investigate his own case as well as Darlie's. I have the feeling from reading Karl's first letter to me that he might try the same thing with me.

In late April, I receive a phone call from the TDCJ's public information officer giving me a heads-up about a letter from Karl that is on its way to me. The letter had alarmed prison officials, who were aware that I was scheduled to come for an interview. I can still do the interview, the PIO says, but prison guards have had problems with Karl in the past and they are concerned about how he will behave during our meeting.

I tell the PIO that I'll pass on the face-to-face interview. A day or two later, Karl's letter arrives. It states, in part: "You lie, exaggerate and blow things out of proportion to add drama to your story. . . . I have never even met you, but I already have been able to gather enough about you as a person to know that it's people like you that's the downfall to this country. . . . You will see cause I hope to meet with you just so I can question *you*! Cause with all bullshit aside your a mortal enemy of mine. You're exactly like my mom."

Prison officials apparently do not pass on to Karl that I will not be enjoying the pleasure of his company after all. In late July, another letter from him arrives in the mail.

"So what happen? I guess I barked at you to loud and scared you. But it's expected as 99% of you authors, reporters, etc. are scary people. That's why a lot of people are starting to say your like maggots. You feed off the plights and pain and injury of people. . . . What you need to do is get your scary ass on down here and let's get Darlie's case on the road."

The tale of Arkansas certainly adds drama to the Darlie Routier story. If there is any exaggeration, it may be perpetuated by a delusional inmate who thinks that relating the tale will somehow unlock his cell door. But it's curious that Karl has been telling the same story since 1998 and, according to Quinncy, has never wavered from it.

Waco businessman Brian Pardo claims the crime that occurred at the Routier home was connected to drugs and that Darin owed a significant sum to drug suppliers. Quinncy says Arkansas and some of his partners in crime had been involved in insurance scams as well as drug use. Appellate attorney Stephen Cooper says it is true that Darin Routier had previously committed insurance fraud and was scouting for help to stage a home burglary shortly before his children were murdered. The Routier family was scheduled to fly to Pennsylvania within days of June 6, 1996, raising the question of whether an intruder or intruders could have gotten the dates wrong.

In Quinncy's view, the story of Arkansas and witnesses' claims of having seen a suspicious black car near the Routier home might be connected to the two men Darlene Potter saw in the early morning hours on 6-6-6.

In her affidavit, the Rowlett resident said she saw two men walking on the side of Dalrock Road not far from the Routier home sometime after 2 a.m. on June 6. One of the men had shoulder length, unkempt brownish hair. He was wearing a black T-shirt and, curiously, was barefoot. The other man was wearing a light-colored baseball cap, a white shirt, and blue jeans. Potter lived near where she spotted the men. She stated that about forty-five minutes after she arrived home and went to bed, she noticed a small, dark-colored car driving through the field next door.

If nothing else, Karl's story about Arkansas, the repeated mention by witnesses of a black car, and Darlene Potter's sighting of the two men are perhaps more reason to question the thoroughness of the Rowlett Police Department's investigation. If officers had taken more time to investigate, or if the Texas Rangers had been brought in to assist the inexperienced police department, might Darin's previous insurance scam and his newly hatched plot have been discovered?

"I don't believe they truly examined [Testnec's] financials at all. I think they jumped the gun," says Anne Good, a former writer for the online magazine *Justice Denied*. She says she spoke off the record with Rowlett police officers back when she was writing about the case. "The general feeling was that [Darlie] knew more than she was saying, and if they arrested her, it would put the squeeze on her and the truth would come out—and that didn't happen. Once they made that big, bold move—they can't *unarrest* her, right? Thus began the odyssey." Good adds that the officers she spoke with indicated they did come to believe in Darlie's guilt.

Like others, Good suspects that Rowlett police were under intense pressure to solve the crime quickly. "There were millions and millions tied up in development in Rowlett," she says. "It was an up-and-coming neighborhood, and Darin and Darlie bought into it early. The catalyst for this kind of intense pressure may have stemmed from the millions of dollars that were tied up in contracts. Rowlett appealed to a lot of young families. You can't have an unsolved murder of two young children and expect the town to grow in quite the same way. That kind of external pressure can change the course of an investigation when everyone's under the gun to get this solved quickly. There's a lot on the line. They couldn't have done much of an investigation *at all* in twelve days."

Of course, the chance to interrogate Arkansas is gone.

If Arkansas held any secrets about what happened on 6-6-6, he took them to his grave. At the time of this writing, Dwayne is incarcerated in a Texas prison work camp. I sent him a cryptically worded JPay e-mail about Timothy Harris and asked if he had any knowledge about a particular crime involving children that occurred in June of 1996. I wasn't particularly surprised when I didn't hear back from him. But for all his wild ramblings and veiled threats, Karl has moments of sobering clarity, as demonstrated in one of his letters to Quinncy about Darlie Routier. "You know what will happen if they find out she really didn't kill her kids? All hell is going to break loose."

PART II
The Thin Blonde Line

I am so scared. Our lawyers say things are going good.
Can't say I feel the same. I am praying and trying to remember God
has his arms wrapped around us.

. . . .

— A MESSAGE TO AUNT SANDY, WRITTEN BY DARLIE ROUTIER
IN JANUARY 1997 AS SHE SAT AT THE DEFENSE TABLE INSIDE THE
KERR COUNTY COURTHOUSE.

"I Ain't Living Long Like This"

— WAYLON JENNINGS

CHAPTER 16

A Fatal Collision

Darlie Lynn Peck was around eight or so when she moved to Texas with her mother, Darlie Kee. They moved back to Altoona, Pennsylvania, for a time, but then moved again to Texas. Darlie Lynn's aunt, Sherry Moses—four years younger than her sister, Darlie Kee—remembers how much her niece Darlie Lynn loved going to Halloween events. Once, she took her niece to a church youth event where everyone dressed in costume. The two of them arrived decked out as hobos, having raided the closet of Sherry's husband, Roger.

Sherry remembers that she and her husband took fourteen-year-old Darlie Lynn to see one of the *Friday the 13th* movies. After watching the slasher film, Roger, a practical joker, tried to scare his wife and niece. Says Sherry: "Darlie and I were standing there, waiting for him to unlock the doors of the van. My crazy husband disappeared and all of a sudden, he was under the van, grabbing at our ankles."

Pretty Darlie Lynn was quite popular, says Sherry. She recalls how a neighbor boy and a preacher's son would come to her Altoona home to swim in her pool whenever Darlie Lynn was in town for a visit. "She was very pretty, and my neighbor boy and my pastor's son were around her age. She was very popular."

Sherry says her niece had a sensitive nature from an early age. "She was the sweetest, gentlest, most giving person in the family. She was always taking in strays. She didn't even like to kill a bug. She would literally sweep up a spider and take it outside. She wouldn't kill it."

Another of Darlie Lynn's aunts, LuAnn Mauk, has similar memories of how her niece always cared about the welfare of others. LuAnn is the middle sister, younger than Darlie Kee, but older than Sherry. To illustrate how supportive her niece was even at an early age, LuAnn details the time when she

Darlie Lynn Peck's first grade school photo.
Photo courtesy Darlie Kee.

and her young daughter lived briefly with Darlie Lynn's family. It was in 1986, when Darlie Lynn was sixteen.

That summer, LuAnn loaded up her white Renault LeCar with the black racing stripe and put Altoona—and her boyfriend, Jerry—in her rearview mirror. LuAnn was moving to Lubbock, where she would live with her sister Darlie Kee and Kee's family until she could find a job and get her own place. LuAnn was tired of waiting on her boyfriend to commit and wanted to see what else life had to offer. Darlie Lynn's boyfriend, Darin, had told her that Texas men love blondes, so it was a safe bet she would soon get over Jerry Black.

LuAnn shipped her belongings to her sister's house. Darlie Kee flew to Altoona to ride with LuAnn and LuAnn's ten-year-old daughter, Melissa, to Texas. The drive in the cramped quarters of the tiny car was not particularly pleasant, especially since it was June and the car had no air conditioning. "It looked like a high-top sneaker," LuAnn laughs, referring to the little Renault.

Within two weeks of arriving in Lubbock, LuAnn got a job at Western Sizzlin, where she worked alongside Darlie, Darlie Lynn, and Darlie Lynn's boyfriend, Darin. The job was fun, the four of them joking around as they

Darlie Lynn Peck at her senior prom, 1988.
Photo courtesy Darlie Kee.

worked. It wasn't long after LuAnn started work at the restaurant that Jerry phoned. Recalls LuAnn: "Jerry said, 'I guess the only way to get you to come back here is if I fly down there and marry you.' And I said, 'What, is that a proposal?' And he said, 'I guess it is.'"

The wedding was held in Lubbock, and then LuAnn and Melissa went with Jerry back to Altoona. LuAnn's wedding dress and big Texas hair were courtesy of young Darlie Lynn. "She would go to things and she had used a real pretty white dress for a dance. It was really beautiful and that was what I got married in. I bought it off of her for fifty dollars. Darlie Lynn would do people's hair. Everybody would go to her. She knew how to set it and tease it up. That was the style."

During the couple of months that LuAnn was trying to get over Jerry, feeling he would never commit to her, Darlie Lynn provided both distractions and a sympathetic ear. "We could be silly and goofy and comfortable with each other, talking about anything. I confided in her about my feelings about Jerry and everything. Darlie Lynn, she was just always so interested and caring. She paid attention to you. She was just a sweetheart. Everybody loved her. I didn't know anybody who didn't like her."

* * *

Assistant DA Gregory Scott Davis was a teenager when he first asserted his independence, choosing a path different from the one his father had planned for him. Lyle Davis had long had a love of baseball and had encouraged his firstborn son to excel in the sport. Bruce Davis, born one year to the day after his brother, says his father was the equivalent of a "stage mom" where Greg was concerned. Though in some ways Lyle pushed his eldest son, Greg had a natural interest in competitive sports. But no matter how well Greg did, his father believed he should have done better. According to Bruce, Lyle Davis was generous when it came to material things for his sons, but "when it came to passing out praise, our dad was stingy."

In 1964, Greg's West Garland Little League team was among the top four in the state. At the championship games held in Breckenridge, eleven-year-old Bruce snapped a photo of then-governor John Connally. The photo was taken just nine months after Connally had sustained a serious gunshot wound while riding in a motorcade in downtown Dallas with President John F. Kennedy.

"I remember, back when my brother was like sixteen or so, he decided he didn't want to play [baseball]," Bruce says. "It just crushed our dad." Bruce says that Greg was left feeling disappointed as well because of his father's efforts to control him when "he wanted to be his own person."

Greg and Bruce graduated from Garland High School one year apart. Both were eleventh in their class. Their childhoods were relatively uneventful. For a time, the family attended Garland First Baptist Church, but stopped going when the boys were in their early teens. "I would say, in general, neither of my parents was very religious. We did go to church—not every Sunday, but fairly regularly until I was fourteen. We just kind of stopped. I don't know exactly what went on there. Dad just was not all that interested," relates Bruce.

Lyle Davis grew up poor, in a house that had no electricity until he was sixteen. As a young man, he earned a living as a migrant onion picker and a short-order cook. He served in World War II. Eventually, Lyle got his journeyman's license and became an electrician, working for Pennington Electric

Company for several years. In 1962, he and a couple of other men formed their own company. Around 1968, Lyle branched out on his own, forming the Davis Electric Company.

Joann Martin Davis helped her husband with the business. She had worked for years at the Resistol Hats factory, where she was secretary to the chief executive. It was good experience that later made her an asset to the family business. "They were perfect partners when it came to business," Bruce Davis says of his parents. "They disagreed on very little. They were very, very focused on making that business succeed. They did well enough to send their two sons to Southern Methodist University. My brother got a scholarship to SMU and started in the engineering program. My dad wanted my brother to join him in business. With an engineering degree, my brother could probably help him grow the business better."

But Greg stayed in the engineering program for only a year, according to his brother. Both brothers went into SMU's School of Business. Bruce would go on to have a career in IT, but Greg did not go into the corporate world. He decided he wanted to go to SMU's law school after meeting a girl who planned to pursue law, his brother says. Greg graduated from the law school in 1977 in the top 15 percent of his class, says Bruce. A few months later, after spending the summer taking it easy at his parents' home in Garland, Greg scored a job interview with Dallas County District Attorney Henry Wade.

*　*　*

It was in the summer of 1983 that Greg Davis brought a young woman named Lisa to a family lunch gathering. A few months later, in October, they married and moved into the house in Garland that Greg had built. Greg put in a swimming pool as a gift to his wife. "She came from a family in North Dallas and was used to having some really nice stuff. My brother and I, we grew up lower middle class until we were adolescents. We didn't have much of anything. So when I look at my brother's house in a nice neighborhood, with a pool, I think he's done pretty good."

In May of 1987, the couple welcomed a son, Cameron. But just a short time later, the marriage fell apart. According to Bruce, Lisa left, taking the baby with her. The couple was separated for several months before divorce proceedings were started. The divorce took two years and was bitter and costly, Bruce says.

Lisa remarried and, in 2002, moved out of state with her son and new husband. Bruce says his brother felt the loss of his son keenly, after having been able to see him regularly for several years. "He was extremely dejected and down. It was very hard on my brother. He genuinely cares about his son."

* * *

In 1988, during the time Greg Davis was coping with the loss of his marriage and separation from his son, eighteen-year-old Darlie Lynn Peck was living with Darin in Dallas and planning their wedding. Darin had moved to Dallas to attend the Video Technical Institute, which was associated with DeVry University. He landed a job as a technician at a computer chip company. In August, Darin and Darlie married in the backyard of his parents' home in Lubbock. After their honeymoon, the couple returned to Dallas, ultimately settling in the up-and-coming suburban town of Rowlett.

As the Routiers were building their electronics company and their family, Greg Davis, newly single, was building his career. He had left the Dallas County DA's office to open his own law office, but ended up going to work for a law firm, his brother says. Around 1992, he went back to work as a prosecutor in the DA's office. In a state that favors the death penalty, Greg Davis began to devote his time to the prosecution of those charged with violent crimes. The year 1996 would prove to be a career-defining year for him: by mid-2014, the *Waco Tribune-Herald* would report that he had prosecuted twenty-two death penalty cases against twenty-one defendants, putting twenty of them on death row—"likely a record among Texas prosecutors," the editorial stated. Two of the twenty were women.

Says Davis's brother, Bruce: "He is most proud of the women he has put on death row. He holds the record. He's very proud of that one."

In the aftermath of the horrific crime that occurred four years after Greg Davis returned to the DA's office, residents of Rowlett's Dalrock Heights neighborhood grew accustomed to seeing police officers, detectives, and forensics experts coming and going from the Routier house. They may have paid no particular attention the day crime scene investigator James Cron made a return visit there, or given any thought to the man accompanying him, whose course in life had led him that day to 5801 Eagle Drive. That man, Greg Davis, would send to death row the first woman Dallas County ever put there.

CHAPTER 17

Code Red

I arrive at work on a Tuesday morning in December to find that Crimefighter sent me an e-mail. Judging from the subject line ("Howling at the Moon") and the time the message crash-landed in my inbox (6:09 a.m.), I know before I open it that the former FBI man has had another turbulent night because of Darlie Routier.

For the past several days, streets and highways throughout much of North Texas have been blanketed with ice because of below-freezing temperatures and sleet that fell the previous Thursday night. During that time, the local hospital had treated seventy-three people who had fallen on the ice. Not wanting to be among them, I'd stayed inside. I watched *An Unreal Dream*, a documentary about a high-profile wrongful-conviction case that had resulted in a district judge being arrested in the very courthouse where he presided on the bench.

Michael Morton had spent twenty-five years in Texas prisons after being wrongfully convicted in the beating death of his wife, Christine. He was set free by DNA testing done on a blue bandana found not far from the family's home near Austin. Ken Anderson, who had been the Williamson County district attorney at that time, was found to have withheld exculpatory evidence that included a claim by Morton's then-three-year-old son that his father had not been home and that "a monster" had killed his mother.

CNN had aired the documentary several times. I was struck by similarities between the Morton and Routier cases: lead investigators not put on the stand; prosecution theories that seemed far-fetched; disturbing comments made by jurors that suggested a lack of understanding about how the system is supposed to work; and important pieces of evidence found yards away from the crime scenes. Amid the pines of East Texas, Crimefighter, it turns out, was watching the same documentary and having the same reaction. Thus, another restless night and an e-mail in my inbox.

"Sorry to bother you, but I have been howling at the moon about the Darlie trial and the whole issue of what I have begun to call the Courthouse Crowd and how they played into the conviction of an innocent woman: their ulterior motives, the decisions they made that benefited each individually, and how it all effected the eventual outcome of the case.

"I believe that the moment the trial was shifted to Kerrville, Darlie's fate was known to all involved. It was not possible to get a 'fair' trial in Kerr County, which is much smaller than Dallas with a much smaller jury pool that was known for its death penalty convictions. At least at that time, it was considered one of the most conservative counties in the state.

"So, why was it moved? I keep asking myself: Why would a defense lawyer of any ability allow that to happen? When Mulder was hired to replace the court-appointed team, he tried to get the venue changed back, but his motion was denied.

"I asked Mulder and others on the defense team why the family wanted to hire them at that stage in the game. They told me the family was not satisifed with the defense efforts, and they felt Darlie was being railroaded. They did not think that [court-appointed attorney Doug] Parks was fighting for Darlie, or that he believed in her innocence. They felt that he was just going through the motions.

"At that time, I believed that Darlie was guilty, and I expressed that opinion to the defense team. I never made a commitment to work on a case until I had reviewed all discovery materials that were available. The materials in Darlie's case were sent to me, and I began to read them.

"My first doubt about her guilt occurred when I studied the medical stuff that was provided by Baylor. The operative word of the trauma surgeon was 'superficial.' Because I had heard through the media that her wounds were superficial, I had assumed that the wounds were scratches—easily self-inflicted, and part of a staged crime scene and cover-up.

"It is interesting that, as I recall, this was the language used in the original criminal complaint that I believe was written to be as much a press release as a charging document. I had never seen a criminal complaint written in such a way. Usually in a proceeding, the original complaint contains very few facts. It usually just contains enough to establish probable cause, and then arrest and detention follow. A great deal of information is not available because the only 'attack' on such a document is the application for bond.

"No case of note that I can recall has ever been dismissed as a result of lack of probable cause in the criminal complaint. The reason is obvious: it will be followed up shortly by an indictment, the supporting evidence for which is secret and will come out at trial.

"The question in my mind was, why does a prosecution disclose so much in the criminal complaint? The answer was simple: to provide a press release that would influence public opinion."

The arrest warrant affidavit signed by lead investigator Jimmy Patterson is a six-page, single-spaced document chock full of damaging details, though in Harrell's opinion, the information had more to do with "editorial comments" than actual facts. It was available to the media through Open Records. Harrell suspects that Patterson may have been helped with the affidavit by the Dallas County DA's office, where prosecutors were savvy enough to realize the media would obtain the document and publish its contents. Harrell believes lead prosecutor Greg Davis would have known that the amount of detail in the affidavit would likely result in the public determining Routier to be guilty well before she was taken to trial.

"They wanted to put as much information out as possible to taint the jury pool and possible witnesses," Harrell surmises. "If you do not have true probable cause, you can make it look as if you do if you write a lengthy affidavit."

Ten days after Routier was arrested and the criminal complaint was made public, State District Judge Mark Tolle issued a gag order. The order went unchallenged by the media, perhaps because of legal costs involved in posing a challenge. Harrell suspects it was all part of a plot to control the outcome of the case and bring about a change of venue that benefited everyone except the person it was *supposed* to benefit—the defendant. "I believe it was a deliberate plan by the prosecution to besmirch Darlie's name and character, to get her arrested, to assign court-appointed attorneys who were familiar members of the Courthouse Crowd and then to get a gag order so none of the media would check into any of the facts. Why was a change of venue even necessary, since the gag order was put in place? Nothing was done to determine whether the jury pool in Dallas County had, in fact, been tainted.

"All of the stuff in the arrest affidavit would have been used in the defense's examination of Patterson at trial. He held Darlie to a different standard, alleging she had told different stories at a time when she was under stress. Yet, there were discrepancies in things *he* said, as well, that the defense was never allowed to attack because everything shut down when he took the Fifth. In my opinion, it goes to the heart of *Brady*, because the defense's questioning of Patterson could very well have revealed exculpatory evidence."

Rick Wardroup, capital resource lawyer for the Texas Criminal Defense Lawyers Association, agrees with Harrell that the criminal complaint in the Routier case is unusual, and says he has never seen an arrest warrant affidavit with so much detail. "The authorities are required to allege facts, and not conclusions, which are sufficient to show probable cause that the offense they are alleging was committed by the person they seek to arrest," Wardroup says. "It would not have been conclusory to have said that the blood patterns at the scene were inconsistent with Mrs. Routier's description of the attack and/or that she gave multiple, inconsistent statements to authorities, without going into all the specifics set out in this affidavit.

"I hesitate to assign an intent to the law enforcement officials, but since the affidavit would have been a public record, available to any news purveyor, not only the facts observed at the scene, but law enforcement's evaluation of the significance of the facts would have been there for all to see. This can sometimes be a dangerous tack, though, because if they disclose too much of their theory of the case, the defense investigation may be able to focus on one aspect that seems susceptible to being disproved. As a practical matter, unless a gag order had been entered, all of this information was probably being reported anyway. I guess the bottom line is that I think the specificity is unusual, but I don't know what advantage the state or law enforcement could have achieved by its use."

The advantage may have been that prosecutors, who did not put Patterson on their own witness list, were betting the defense would get little out of him because of the secret recording he made at the graveside. They may have known all along he would take the Fifth on the stand. Harrell, who leans toward the cynical, wonders who suggested the electronic eavesdropping to begin with.

Harrell's e-mail continues:"One of my gripes ever since I got involved was the issue of the gag order. The gag order was how Mulder got involved. Darin and Mama Darlie were hauled before the judge because they had allegedly 'violated' the order. Mulder represented them in that matter. The family believed in her innocence and wanted the media to know.

"By this time, the media had convicted Darlie because of the footage of her spraying Silly String on her sons' grave. Once the mainstream media had convicted her, everyone quit looking for any other possible perpetrator.

"The purpose of a gag order is to ensure a fair trial, to keep the jury pool from being contaminated. The gag order was not fought by the court-appointed attorneys or the media—none of them. This is when the trial plan by the Courthouse Crowd was launched. They had captured the media by the criminal complaint/press release, and now they stifled all ancillary inquiry by the media. They controlled the whole process. Why was that necessary? Because the Courthouse Crowd had to have a plan in order for all to end up benefiting.

"Greg Davis knew that his case was weak from the start. They had read the medical reports and knew they had real difficulties with the issue of 'self-inflicted' wounds. To believe that the crime scene had been staged, one must believe that Darlie's wounds were self-inflicted. This was the first thing that convinced me she was innocent. If one looks at the photographs, looks at the medical evidence, looks at the reports of the medical examiner who examined Darlie in the hospital, one had to conclude that the wounds were not self-inflicted.

"I believe that Cron made the decision that the wounds were part of the staging while Darlie was still in the recovery room. I think that part of the defense strategy was to question lead investigator James Patterson extensively about how such wounds could be self-inflicted, but the questioning was shut down when Patterson took the Fifth on the stand.

"The state also knew that the sock found down the alley was problematic because it disrupted their timeline and their theory. It did not fit. Darlie would have had to cut her throat after the sock was taken down the alley, or Darin would have had to be involved. These two things would have destroyed their entire case.

"In my heart, I believe Judge Tolle knew there were problems with the case, and he secretly desired to assist the state in his final trial of significance. In fact, it was his *only* trial of significance, and he wanted to go out with a bang—ensuring that he would be a legend as a great trial judge and securing a postretirement position as a visiting judge. If all went as planned, he would be on television—the Texas version of Judge Lance Ito from the O. J. Simpson trial.

"Tolle was a friend of Parks, and I have been told they had shared offices together prior to his election. He was the one who appointed Parks early on. Parks was part of the Courthouse Crowd and could be counted on not to go to the press or take any wild actions that would embarrass the state or the court. Tolle knew that Parks would not object to the state wanting a change of venue.

"The change of venue was necessary for Tolle to be the trial judge for the case because his retirement was to become effective Jan. 1—just a few days before the trial was to start. If the venue had remained in Dallas County, the newly elected judge, Bobby Francis, would have presided.

"I awoke early this morning, just before 3, and, as has often happened since the Darlie trial, began to howl at the moon. In the documentary, Michael Morton's trial defense lawyer, Bill Allison, said that everyone is entitled to a fair trial, and Morton did not have that. The similarites to Darlie's trial were amazing.

"While howling at the moon, I thought of the secret 'code red' order in the Marines that was detailed in the movie *A Few Good Men*. A question occurred to me: If early on in the prosecution process a gag order was put in effect, and that order went unchallenged by the media, and the order was put in place to ensure a fair trial by limiting pretrial publicity so as not to taint the jury pool—why was a change of venue even necessary? It was *not* necessary, and no effort was ever made to find out whether the jury pool had, in fact, been contaminated. It was not contested as it should have been by the court-appointed defense lawyers. They should have insisted from the get-go that the trial be held in Dallas.

"Since the gag order had been granted, why did Dallas County taxpayers have to pay the extreme costs of moving the trial to Kerrville—the entire trial team, as well as all of the witnesses, etc.?

"Mulder made an effort to return the trial to Dallas, but his motion was not granted. The denial benefited the Courthouse Crowd by keeping the trial in Kerrville. The results were predictable.

"In the documentary, a juror who served in the Morton case made a comment that the defense hadn't done anything to prove him innocent—which was very similar to a statement made by a woman who served on the jury in Darlie's case.

"I believe that comments like this highlight the difference between juries in small towns and juries in big cities like Dallas. The difference is in the psychology. A small-town juror feels intimately involved with their own security, i.e.: 'If we do not find this monster guilty, then none of us is safe.' In a large metropolitan area, however, the monster is not really among us, but rather out there in Rowlett.

"The jurors in the Michael Morton case now know that the monster in that case was the unfairness of the trial. The monster was the prosecution."

CHAPTER 18

Psycho

I am trying to hang on and be strong. I know they will try to rip me apart
on the stand, but I don't care what they do to me because the worst
has already been done to me—Devon and Damon were murdered
and that man is still out there free. . . . I am physically and mentally tired.
It is cold in here today. I am ready for this all to be over.

. . . .

—A NOTE TO AUNT SANDY, WRITTEN BY DARLIE ROUTIER
AS SHE SAT AT THE DEFENSE TABLE DURING TRIAL.

Every morning at 4:00 a.m., a chaotic din emanates from cellblocks inside the bowels of the Mountain View Unit in Gatesville, making the prison sound like a mental asylum. Female inmates—some suicidal—scream and sob. Some manage to find something with which to cut themselves. Others deliberately create bedlam by clogging toilets to cause flooding.

"Where we're living, there's no peace," Lisa Coleman tells me, she on one side of the glass and cinder block, me on the other. On the day of our interview, Coleman is one of only ten women on Texas's death row. At the time of this writing, the number has dropped to eight, and Coleman is likely to be next. Despite the chaos that greets each dawn, a calmer, softer noise radiates from a run of cells that house Coleman and four other death-row inmates, including Darlie Routier. Before the sun peeks over the horizon, the women, though in separate cells, start the day with scripture reading and prayer.

In the years since Routier arrived on death row, there has been no sign of the psychopathy claimed by then-Dallas County assistant district attorney Greg Davis. "She's a psychopath!" the lead prosecutor had told television news reporters. But is she? "She has been evaluated, and no one has said that," says Dallas attorney Stephen Cooper, a member of Routier's appellate team. For

Zealous advocate: Dallas appellate lawyer Stephen Cooper
has been on the case since shortly after Routier's conviction.
He has worked on the case pro bono for years.
Photo courtesy Stephen Cooper.

anyone else, making such inflammatory, unsubstantiated claims about another—especially in front of television cameras—might bring a lawsuit. But for a prosecutor, it might bring job security.

Darlie Kee says the claim about her daughter's alleged mental illness was made more than once, by more than one representative of the Dallas County District Attorney's Office. Coprosecutor Toby Shook referred to Routier as "a psychopath" in an on-camera interview with retired New York City police detective Jerry Palace and homicide investigator Reggie Britt for Court TV's *The Wrong Man?* series. The fact that Routier's attorney says no mental health professional has ever determined her to be a psychopath—only prosecutors have labeled her as such—raises ethical questions.

Ellen Yaroshefsky, a professor at the Benjamin N. Cardozo School of Law in New York and director of the Jacob Burns Center for Ethics in the Practice of Law, says that prosecutors referring to Routier as a psychopath with no factual basis to back it up is "outrageous." Yaroshefsky has assisted the Innocence Project, of which her Cardozo colleague, Barry Scheck, is codirector. "Particularly, a public servant who is a minister of justice should not be characterizing defendants in this manner. It is unethical to do so," Yaroshefsky said.

Powerhouse: Doug Mulder, formerly a highly successful prosecutor in the Dallas County District Attorney's Office, went on to become a sought-after defense attorney. Though his many wins include a surprise acquittal for Dallas Methodist minister Walker Railey in the attack that left Railey's wife, Peggy, comatose, Mulder's star power was not enough to acquit Darlie Routier. *Photo courtesy of the* Dallas Morning News.

According to Stephen Cooper, the Dallas County District Attorney's Office has had a long history of referring to defendants as psychopaths. That history dates back to the era of Henry Wade, the longest-serving district attorney in American history, whose star prosecutor was a young lawyer named Doug Mulder. Mulder and Cooper were destined to tangle more than once during the course of their careers. The two lawyers who have played a role in the Routier case were also involved in another high-profile case from Dallas County: Mulder was the prosecutor who convinced a jury to put Randall Dale Adams on death row for the murder of Dallas policeman Robert W. Wood. Stephen Cooper was among other appellate lawyers who helped free him.

The wrongful conviction of Randall Dale Adams would become the subject of Errol Morris's 1988 documentary film, *The Thin Blue Line*. The Texas Court of Criminal Appeals overturned Adams's conviction in 1989, citing malfeasance by Mulder and inconsistencies in witness testimony. The CCA determined that the "conviction was unfair mainly because of prosecutor Doug Mulder."

"When I first started practicing law in Dallas in 1977, one of the first cases I worked on appeal was the Randall Dale Adams case," Cooper says. "And the go-to shrink for Dallas County at that time was 'Dr. Death.'" Dr. James Grigson, known as Dr. Death, testified for the state in 167 capital murder trials, almost all of which resulted in death sentences. "He [Grigson] called Randall Dale Adams a psychopath. It's interesting that he was a psychopath when he was wholly innocent. It was [Grigson's] global description of wrongdoers. Darlie's prosecutors saying she's a psychopath is just par for the course."

The title for Morris's award-winning documentary came from a statement made by Mulder during closing arguments, that police are "the thin blue line" separating society from anarchy. Years after that case left a bad taste in Cooper's mouth, he would again find himself in a position of trying to undo damage that he blamed largely on Mulder—this time for Mulder's performance for the defense. Cooper feels that Mulder allowed the prosecution to besmirch Darlie Routier's character. He also believes Mulder did not put forth enough effort to defend his client—likely because he assumed an easy win against the state's far-fetched theory.

"The state's case is weak. I think it's reasonable that Mulder believed that and knew that," Cooper says. As far as Mulder's performance as a prosecutor goes: "We can't take anything away from him. . . . I mean, he successfully put Randall Dale Adams on death row—and he was innocent. That's good work for a prosecutor, right?" Cooper says with dry sarcasm.

The claims against Routier were made eleven months after South Carolina mother Susan Smith was convicted for the murders of her two small sons, Michael, three, and Alex, fourteen months. Smith deliberately let her 1990 Mazda Protege roll into the dark waters of John D. Long Lake with Michael and Alex inside, strapped into their car seats. A psychiatrist hired by the defense testified at trial that Smith suffered from dependent personality disorder and major depression. Smith's stepfather admitted having molested her as a child, and said that the two had engaged in consensual sex as adults.

The shocking case gained worldwide attention. Smith was even featured on the cover of *TIME* magazine with the headline "How Could She Do It?" In the wake of the trial, prosecutor Tommy Pope became a frequent speaker for state prosecutors' associations across the nation and began providing legal commentary for various national media outlets. In 2010, he was elected to South Carolina's House of Representatives. The biography on his website states: "Tommy is most often recognized for his prosecution of Susan Smith

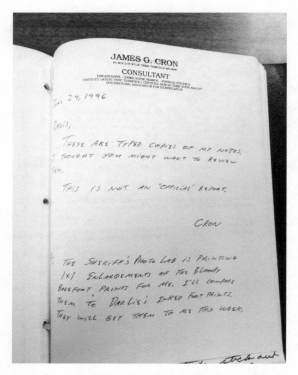

James Cron's "unofficial" report: Members of Routier's trial defense team suspect that the lack of official written reports by some of the state's witnesses was deliberate. The law allows for defense attorneys to have access to certain reports prior to trial, better enabling them to mount challenges in defense of their client. This report by James Cron is part of the Routier case file stored in the basement of the Court of Criminal Appeals in Austin. *Photo by the author.*

in Union County, South Carolina, in 1995 for the drowning death of her two children."

Could ambitions within the Dallas County District Attorney's Office be responsible for Routier being quickly blamed for her children's murders and labeled "Dallas's Susan Smith"? Barbara Davis believes that Greg Davis "knew exactly what he was doing" when he affixed such a label on Routier. "He can call Darlie a psychopath all he wants, but there has never been anything to prove that Darlie is a psychopath or has since become a psychopath. But that doesn't stop him from saying it. If there had been *any* indicators that Darlie was capable of such a thing, the families would have known it. They know her better than anyone, and they have defended her for years and years and years."

Says Lloyd Harrell: "It has always been my belief that Susan Smith played into the decision making of the Rowlett Police Department, including James Cron. I never got that feeling about Greg Davis, but [Cron] definitely had his stinger out for Darlie."

Smith allegedly had twice attempted suicide before murdering her children. In 2012, a former inmate at South Carolina's Leath Correctional Institute claimed Smith had attempted suicide again in prison. In Routier's case, prosecutors used postpartum depression and a cryptic diary entry written by Routier asking forgiveness "for what I am about to do" as proof it was she who stabbed Devon and Damon. Routier admitted having considered suicide during a time when she was suffering from postpartum depression. However, she said the depression lifted after she and Darin talked about her difficulties and after she had her first menstrual period following Drake's birth. Appellate lawyer Stephen Cooper says there was no prior history with Routier to indicate the presence of serious mental or emotional disorders, and there has been no indication since.

In the Susan Smith case, after nine days of the public frantically searching for little Michael and Alex, their mother finally cracked and confessed to murdering her children and fabricating a tale about a carjacking. She then led the police to the place her car went into the water. Routier, however, continues to adamantly deny killing her sons.

Stephen Cooper says there are "specific DSM criteria" for antisocial personality disorders. DSM is an acronym for the *Diagnostic and Statistical Manual of Mental Disorders*. To fit the state's claims that Routier is a psychopath, she would had to have experienced a brief psychotic break that served as her *only* psychotic episode. "Psychopaths don't just turn over one day, and they're all better now," Cooper says.

Yaroshefsky says making such a claim against a defendant when there is "nothing in the record" is "prohibited by the disciplinary rules of every jurisdiction." Any prosecutor committing such an infraction should be brought before a disciplinary committee, she says.

Tactics used by prosecutors have come under the spotlight in the wake of more than three hundred DNA exonerations, hundreds of other exonerations that did not involve DNA testing, and some Innocence Projects pushing for courts of inquiry to determine whether prosecutorial misconduct occurred. Those involved in Routier's defense and others who believe in her innocence suspect that prosecutors may have crossed ethical lines. A possible example is the puzzling testimony of the Baylor nurses, who painted Routier as a cold, emotionless woman, despite the fact that their shift notes seem to reflect the opposite impression.

According to Lloyd Harrell, he and defense attorney Curtis Glover tried twice to meet with the Baylor nurses prior to the trial, but they were told the nurses could not be interviewed without the hospital's attorney present. When efforts were made to arrange a meeting, the attorney was unavailable. "Each time, we were stiffed. The second time, we were told the lawyer was in Aspen. We didn't know he was in Aspen when we set up the interview. Firewalls were put up in front of us," Harrell says.

Barbara Davis feels the defense did not attack aggressively enough the testimony of the nurses when they took the stand and gave damning testimony about Routier's demeanor. Their shift notes had described Routier as "frightened" and "very tearful.""He [Mulder] should have gone after the doctors and nurses like a maniac," Davis says. "He could have eaten them alive. There was something different about him at this trial."

Under questioning by defense attorney Richard Mosty, it was revealed that prosecutor Toby Shook had met with the medical staff as a group the day before, in Room 109 at the Kerrville Holiday Inn. He showed the group photos taken four days after the murders that showed severe bruising on Routier's arms. When the medical staff took the stand, they each stated that if the bruising had occurred in the alleged attack from an unknown intruder, they would have seen indications of it during Routier's hospital stay. Prosecutors would claim that Routier, or her husband, inflicted the injuries to bolster claims of an intruder.

Appellate attorney John Hagler, who was part of the defense team, made a motion for a mistrial, claiming that Shook had violated "the rule" by meeting with the medical professionals while the trial was in progress. The rule pertains to sequestration—a requirement that certain witnesses remain outside the presence of other testifying witnesses. Tolle denied the motion.

Though the meeting has fueled controversy, both Mulder and Cooper say Shook did nothing wrong by meeting with the nurses. Legal ethics expert Keith Hampton says that a person is under the rule only if they have been sworn and admonished about the rule. If they weren't, then there is no violation.

But the testimony of the nurses continues to be a key issue in the contro-versial conviction of Darlie Routier. There is suspicion that the witnesses were improperly coached. Barbara Davis believes she knows what likely happened, based upon her experience working in the prosecution side of the justice sys-tem. She said she does not blame the medical professionals for their puzzling testimony, because she does not believe they intended to be untruthful. She believes they bonded with the prosecutors and were led to believe that a guilty woman was going to walk free if they didn't help the state put her away. "It's easy for the state to bond with a witness," she says. "I think [the nurses] got on the bandwagon. It was a gang mentality, a we're-on-the-same-side kind of thing."

Of criminal cases in general, she states: "I've been in the prosecution, and I know what goes on. It's very subtle. There's trickery. Methods are used, and they're used to fool honest and good people to get them on the state's side."

The photos showing severe bruising on Routier's arms were part of what caused Barbara Davis to switch from believing the young mother had killed her children to becoming convinced that an innocent woman had been sent to death row.

"One of the things that juror Charlie Samford talked about—the injuries on her arms and hands not being shown to the jury—they absolutely were not," Davis says. "I was about three rows back, and I never saw them. And I saw every piece of evidence that was introduced. I did not even get up to go to the bathroom. In my eyes, if they weren't published to the jury, then the jury didn't see them."

Writer Anne Good, who wrote a half-dozen or so stories on the Routier case for the website *Justice Denied*, says she once spoke with remorseful juror Samford. "I talked to Charlie Samford several times and really tried to get a feel for what had gone on during those deliberations," says the Michigan resident. "And I recall how he told me how many times they watched that Silly String video. He does not recall ever having seen the photos of those injuries. I don't find anything in the transcripts that would indicate that they were shown. If Charlie does not recall having seen those photos, then he really didn't see them. I would have thought the defense would have had them blown up post-er-sized and would have had them on an easel the whole time Darlie testified."

Sandy Aitken, the only family member who could be in the courtroom since she was not on either side's witness list, agrees that the photos were not shown to the jury, though Shook showed photos to trauma surgeon Alejandro

Santos while he was on the stand. Barbara Davis surmises: "I think the photos were just marked into evidence and set aside. The jury could have looked through them, but I think the jury was so overwhelmed by the evidence." There was so much evidence, she says, that the judge allowed the jury to deliberate behind locked doors in the courtroom, while everyone else was ordered to wait downstairs.

Harrell says the bruisings shown in the photos are "girdle-like bruises." "They go around the arms as if someone is holding very tight against someone who is struggling," he says. "I do not think it would be possible for someone to bruise themselves in such a manner. The whole thing is so preposterous, it is hard to imagine that anyone could believe the bruising could have been self-inflicted." Renowned pathologist Dr. Vincent Di Maio, who at the time of Routier's trial was the medical examiner for Bexar County, testified for the defense that if Darlie had died, he would have ruled that her injuries were defensive wounds.

In 2002, the *Dallas Morning News* published an article by staff writer Ed Timms about children in Texas who die at the hands of their mothers. Tarrant County Medical Examiner Nizam Peerwani was quoted saying that back when he was an intern and doing his residency, those in the profession were taught that, based on the color changes of a bruise or "a tissue reaction," predictions could be made as to when the injury occurred. "We know now that this is absolutely bogus," Peerwani stated in the article. The medical examiner went on to explain that human tissues react differently and that color changes differ. Though the Baylor staff testified that they did not see the bruising on Routier's arms, some believe that a photo in state's evidence of Darlie lying in her hospital bed shows the beginning of bruises on her injured right arm.

The continued nagging suspicion about the testimony of the Baylor medical staff may be due in no small part to the testimony of two nurses, who took the stand one after the other. Each referred to their patient—a woman whose throat had been slashed and whose children had been murdered—as *whiny*.

Another controversy in the Routier case involves Dr. Kenneth Dekleva, a psychiatrist hired by the state who allegedly concluded that Routier posed no future danger in prison. Those involved in Routier's trial defense and appeals believe a *Brady* violation occurred when the Dallas County District Attorney's Office did not put Dekleva on the stand. Prosecutors also did not inform the defense about Dekleva's opinion. Posing a future danger is one of the criteria required for imposing a death sentence in Texas, and an expert opinion that a defendant would not pose a future danger is mitigating evidence that could prevent a death sentence.

Failure to reveal exculpatory evidence is a *Brady* rule violation. It comes from the 1963 case of *Brady v. Maryland,* in which the US Supreme Court determined that the Fifth and Fourteenth Amendments provide for the availability of all evidence in a case. To meet the criteria of a *Brady* violation, the evidence must have been favorable to the defense; the state must have withheld that information, even if unintentionally; and, as a result, the court was prejudiced against the accused.

Harrell says Dekleva's name was on the state's witness list, but without "Dr." in front of it, and with no indication of his relevance. (During the trial, attorney Richard Mosty commented to the judge that the state's witness list was "the Rowlett phone book.") The trial defense team, Harrell says, had assumed Dekleva was a member of law enforcement. Harrell tried to track down Dekleva, but with no success. In 1996, there was no such thing as Google searches. The defense was further hindered by the fact they were trying to beat the clock for a trial that was to begin just two months after the new defense team, chosen and led by the newly hired Doug Mulder, was assembled. The team included Curtis Glover, S. Preston Douglass Jr., John Hagler, and Kerrville attorney Richard C. Mosty.

It was after Routier's conviction that the Dekleva matter came to light, unearthed by the *Dallas Morning News.* In July 2002, Dr. J. Douglas Crowder, an assistant professor of psychiatry at the University of Texas Southwestern Medical School, signed an affidavit about what he claims his colleague Dekleva told him. At this point Dekleva himself has moved to Russia, and was not available to give a sworn testimony. According to Crowder: "During a lunchtime conversation that took place, to my best recollection, in the summer of 2000, Dr. Dekleva told me that he served as a psychiatric consultant for the State of Texas in the capital case of *Texas v. Routier.* I understood that Dr. Dekleva's duties as a consultant were to advise the prosecution on any psychiatric issues presented by the case, and possibly to serve as an expert witness. Dr. Dekleva informed me that he opined to the prosecution that, in his professional opinion, Darlie Lynn Routier is not likely to constitute a future danger in prison."

Prosecutor Toby Shook explained the Dekleva matter in his own affidavit. He stated the psychiatrist had been hired as a consultant in the Routier case, primarily so that the state would be prepared to cross-examine defense witness Dr. Lisa Clayton. The DA's office anticipated that Clayton, who had spent time interviewing the incarcerated Routier, would raise claims that the Rowlett homemaker had experienced traumatic amnesia. Shook said: "At some point, Dr. Dekleva and I discussed punishment issues (although we did not know at the time whether the defense would call a psychiatrist during the punishment phase). I personally selected the jury in Kerrville and, from questioning the jurors and reading their questionnaires, I did not feel that they were going to put a whole lot of stock in psychiatric testimony."

His affidavit further stated: "In Mrs. Routier's case, Dr. Dekleva indicated that risk factors showing her to be dangerous were, obviously, the brutality of the crime, her lack of remorse, and the innocence of the victims she had chosen. . . . Dr. Dekleva said that there was no evidence of her being violent while in jail awaiting trial. It should be noted, however, that any time a capital murder defendant has not had discipline problems in jail, the psychiatrist most always says under oath that this is a factor that weighs in the defendant's favor. It should be further noted that this is an obvious factor considered in any case, whether there is an expert involved or not. At no time did I ever tell Dr. Dekleva we were not calling him because he had an opinion that Mrs. Routier would not be violent in prison."

As for the state's witness list, Stephen Cooper points out: "Just giving a name on a witness list is not enough. The state must advise what the exculpatory evidence is, not just the name of the witness who has it."

Lubbock attorney Rick Wardroup, who conducts trainings throughout the state as a capital assistance attorney for the Texas Criminal Defense Lawyers Association, says: "I think that it would be a *Brady* violation if the state had consulted with an expert who said that the defendant was not a future danger [and did not disclose it]. I can imagine that the prosecutor would argue that it was work product and, therefore, didn't have to be disclosed. I think that the Michael Morton Act makes that type of evidence discoverable regardless of whether it was work product." The Michael Morton Act, which compels prosecutors to make their files available to defense attorneys, went into effect on January 1, 2013—too late to be of any help to Routier.

Legal ethics expert Keith Hampton, former president-elect of the Texas Criminal Defense Lawyers Association and the TCDLA's former legislative director, says if Dekleva did, indeed, make a determination that Routier posed no future danger, it was a violation for those in the Dallas County DA's office not to have made that known. "That is absolutely *Brady*. There's no question that's *Brady*," he says. "*Brady* doesn't just include evidence that exculpates you, it includes evidence that mitigates your punishment. A determination that you won't be a future danger—that's an issue that saves your life."

Harrell is suspicious that deliberate attempts may have been made by prosecutors to circumvent *Brady*, and Dekleva is but one example. He says instructing experts not to put their findings in writing can be a way to defeat the discovery process. Several state witnesses testified they had made no written reports.

Harrell points out that while Dekleva's professional relevance was not identified on the state's witness list, neither was Alan Brantley identified as an agent in the FBI's profiling and behavioral assessment unit. On the stand, Brantley noted that valuable items were not taken: a cluster of Darlie's jewelry was on a nearby countertop untouched (the same was true at the crime scenes of Michael Morton's wife Christine and Debra Masters Baker—another woman Mark Alan Norwood is believed to have murdered). Brantley, who also did not write a report, testified he believed the Routier boys were killed by someone they knew well, and that the crime scene was staged. Under cross-examination by lead defense attorney Mulder, however, Brantley acknowledged that he had not interviewed witnesses, but had relied on police interviews and police photos.

As for the "staged" crime scene, police photos documented that items at the crime scene had been moved. James Cron testified at trial that moving items is normal during an investigation, and in fact investigators would be guilty of "malpractice" if they failed to do so.

For Harrell, the crime scene photos and the moving of items were a major issue. He says he requested, but never received, contact sheets documenting the sequence in which the photos were taken and items moved. Contact sheets were important to those preparing Routier's defense. "To this day, we still don't know whether we have seen all the photos," Harrell says.

As for Brantley's alleged expertise at profiling, the FBI's profiling and behavioral assessment unit was the same unit that wrongly pinpointed Richard Jewell as the man who planted a backpack containing three pipe bombs at the 1996 Summer Olympics in Atlanta. The FBI agents believed Jewell, a police officer who was working as a security guard, had sounded the alarm and helped evacuate civilians because he wanted to be hailed as a hero. Ultimately, Jewell was exonerated, but he had already suffered from the undeserved national exposure.

East Coast blogger Melissa Higgins is an advocate for juveniles charged with serious crimes. She became concerned about the fairness of Darlie Routier's trial after a friend encouraged her to read the trial transcript. *Photo by Kay Anderson, courtesy of Melissa Higgins.*

East Coast blogger Melissa Higgins became involved in raising public awareness about troubling issues in the Routier case after she reviewed the trial transcript at the request of a friend. Higgins, who is primarily interested in how juveniles fare in the justice system, was among those who advocated for the "West Memphis Three." Damien Echols, Jessie Misskelley Jr., and Jason Baldwin were tried and convicted as teenagers for the 1993 murders of three eight-year-old boys in West Memphis, Arkansas. Prosecutors alleged that the boys had been killed as part of a satanic ritual. Echols received a death sentence. Misskelley got life, plus two twenty-year sentences. Baldwin was handed a life sentence. In the wake of new DNA evidence, the three were freed in August 2011, after they struck a deal with prosecutors and entered Alford pleas. The plea allows the accused to claim innocence while acknowledging that prosecutors have enough evidence to convict them. The three spent more than eighteen years in prison.

Melissa Higgins says that she became concerned—and suspicious— about the Routier trial when the trial transcript revealed that members of law enforcement and other witnesses for the state claimed they had either lost their reports or had not written reports. She believes officers followed Cron in lockstep when he determined within minutes that there had been no intruder. "It was the trial transcript that really convinced me that she was innocent—

the way the prosecution handled the case," Higgins says. "I really do believe that, from the beginning, they were only looking at Darlie and Darin, and then they decided that Darlie was probably the one that did it."

Not long after Michael Morton was set free, he spoke at a prosecutorial oversight panel discussion in Austin. He stated that his wrongful conviction had nothing to do with race or prior criminal record or "living in a bad part of town"—common assumptions about those who are profiled and cast under suspicion by law enforcement. "Look at me," he said, an apparent reference to the fact that he is white and, at the time of his wrongful conviction, lived in a "respectable" neighborhood. The prosecution's theory was that the mild-mannered pharmacy manager had beaten his wife to death because she had denied him sex on his birthday. DA Anderson had claimed that the "monster" described by the couple's three-year-old son, Eric, was actually Michael in a scuba suit. "Through innuendo and very salacious accusations, I was found guilty and got a life sentence," Morton told the panel.

He was luckier than Routier. She got death.

*   *   *

At Mountain View, Routier has often reached out to, or on behalf of, fellow death-row inmates. My interview with Coleman was at Routier's request. She had written to me expressing concern that Coleman's court-appointed lawyer was not keeping her informed of key appeal developments that were speeding her to an execution date. "She tries to help these women," says Darlie Kee. She and her daughter don't always agree on who is worthy of compassion.

Coleman's case involved the starvation and physical abuse of her female lover's nine-year-old son. Toni Knox, a mitigator who assisted Coleman's court-appointed attorneys at trial, told me that Coleman's codefendant, Marcella Williams, had previously come to the attention of Child Protective Services for allegedly abusing her son, Davontae. Yet it was Coleman—whom Knox came to believe had been "a victim for much of her life herself"—who ended up on death row. Williams received a life sentence, likely because she was savvy enough to be the first to cut a deal, the mitigator says.

Behind glass in the visitation room at Mountain View, Coleman's face softens and she smiles when the subject of Routier comes up. "Darlie," she says, "has been a real blessing to me."

While working on the *Routier Revisited* series for the Texas Center for Community Journalism, I submitted an Open Records request to the Texas Department of Criminal Justice for Routier's disciplinary reports. Shortly afterward, a manila envelope arrived in the mail. At the time the request was filed, Darlie had been on death row for sixteen years. During that time, she had received twelve write-ups for disciplinary infractions. None were for violent or dangerous offenses. The infractions were for such things as soliciting a prison staffer to make a phone call on behalf of another inmate and having in her cell items that are "not available at the prison commissary," such as magazines, tweezers, and cocoa mix.

A few of the infractions are perhaps the most telling. Darlie used an over-the-counter denture cleaner in a way "in which it was not intended"; violated prison rules by rolling her sleeves too high in the prison yard; and had a jar of petroleum jelly that had been mixed with an unknown pink substance. The woman prosecutors told the world was a psychopath wanted to dye her hair, get a tan, and wear lip gloss.

CHAPTER 19

Jezebel

This week has been very hard. Very long. It is hard to sit here and listen to all the lies and a lot of them are so obvious. Give Drake a lot of hugs and kisses for me. Tell him I love him and miss him. I am still trusting in God no matter what happens.

. . . .

—LETTER WRITTEN TO AUNT SANDY BY DARLIE ROUTIER
AS SHE SAT AT THE DEFENSE TABLE DURING TRIAL.

It was January 1997 and, in the Kerr County Courthouse, Dallas County Assistant District Attorney Greg Davis had Dr. Janis Townsend-Parchman on the stand. Davis was questioning Townsend-Parchman, a medical doctor and a Dallas County medical examiner, about the injuries she observed on Darlie Routier when the Rowlett homemaker was in Baylor Hospital with a slash across her throat and other injuries.

Townsend-Parchman had testified about the differences between "cut" and "stab" injuries. She had been quizzed about "rapid ooze" and about what types of wounds cause blood to gush as opposed to spurt. She had been asked to detail the depth of the slash on Routier's throat, and whether the injury could have been self-inflicted.

Then, Davis asked Townsend-Parchman this question: "At the time that you saw Mrs. Routier, did you know whether or not she had had breast implants?" It was not the only time during the trial that Davis would raise the issue of Routier's breast augmentation surgery. Routier's lead defense attorney, Doug Mulder, objected to the relevance of the implants. However, District Judge Mark Tolle overruled the objection after Davis explained that the implants were important in showing why Routier's injuries were not in her chest area.

Formidable opponent: Former Dallas County Assistant District Attorney Greg Davis. *Photo courtesy* Waco Tribune-Herald.

Also part of the line of questioning was Routier's habit of participating in occasional girls'-night-out events. During the punishment phase of the trial, when the jury was to determine whether to put the twenty-seven-year-old to death, Davis interrogated Melanie Waits about a Mother's Day weekend getaway that had involved a trip to LaBare, the only male strip club in Dallas. The line of questioning included this exchange:

Davis: "Where did y'all go to celebrate that night?"

Waits: "LaBare's."

Davis: "Okay. And LaBare is what?"

Waits: "A gentlemen's—or a ladies', where ladies go where gentlemen strip."

Davis: "Strip club for women?"

Waits: "Yeah, it's the only one in Dallas."

Davis: "And, after you finished there, did you stay the night there at the Anatole?"

Waits: "Yes."

Davis: "And I guess then, y'all wouldn't have gotten back home until what, about noon on Mother's Day?"

Waits: "Yes."

Davis: "And again, no children were invited to that party, were they?"

Waits: "No."

In his opening statements, Davis had detailed big-ticket purchases by both Darlie and Darin: a big house with a fountain, jewelry, a Jaguar, and a

Kathryn Kase, executive director,
Texas Defender Services.
Photo courtesy Kathryn Kase.

boat. But he characterized Darin as "a hard worker," while Darlie was "materialistic" and "self-centered." Darlie, he insinuated, was motivated to butcher her children out of frustration over not being able to lose weight from her recent pregnancy. At the time of her arrest, the five-foot-three Darlie weighed 134 pounds.

"This whole thing was just crazy to me," says family member Sandy Aitken. "Oh, their spin was bad." But "spin" may often be the name of the game when defense lawyers and prosecutors are competing to win in a courtroom. And, as with any game, there are losers.

"This is a troubling prosecution all the way around, and this opening encapsulates what's so troubling about it," says Kathryn Kase, executive director of Texas Defender Service. "It does not logically follow that a woman would kill her children because she has breast implants or because her husband doesn't make enough money. This opening statement seems calculated to demonize Darlie Routier in the jury's eyes as a vain, grasping woman—and, in the end, that doesn't tell us anything at all about whether Darlie Routier actually committed capital murder."

Brian Stull, senior staff attorney for the American Civil Liberties Union's Capital Punishment Project, also criticizes the courtroom portrayal of Routier, and the focus on things that were not related to evidence. "The stereo-

Brian Stull, senior staff attorney
for the American Civil Liberties
Union's Capital Punishment Project.
Photo Courtesy Brian Stull.

type here—that moms are more worried about their mummy tummy than the kids—that's offensive," he says. "And that's a male prosecutor making these comments about a woman. I don't think prosecutors are supposed to be in there appealing to the worst of us. They should be appealing to our better angels when we look at the facts. A lot of people harbor prejudices—even good people who wish they didn't. But I don't think prosecutors should try to appeal to that. Let's stick with the facts, especially when the prosecutor is asking for a death sentence."

But Mary Penrose, a professor at the Texas A&M University School of Law who teaches on gender discrimination, doesn't necessarily believe that Judge Tolle should have reined in Davis when he brought up breast implants and male strippers. Penrose, who is a court-appointed attorney on death penalty cases, says she does not particularly agree that sexism was at play in Routier's prosecution. "Death penalty cases have a very different flavor. You might see language that's very inflammatory and that, standing alone, could be considered classist and gender-biased," Penrose says. "The judge may give greater latitude, not only to the prosecution, but to the defense."

Penrose, who says she does not have an opinion as to whether Routier is guilty or innocent, said the prosecution's focus on the strip club outing likely fit into the overall theme of the case they were trying to make against her. It was a theme that helped send Darlie Routier to death row, despite claims from friends and family members that she was nothing like the picture painted by prosecutors who had never so much as spoken to her.

The American Bar Association's standards for prosecutors, however "specifically say that prosecutors should never appeal to prejudice of any kind—they flat-out say that," says Andrea Lyon, dean of Valparaiso University School of Law in Indiana. Lyon was the first woman in the United States to be lead counsel in a death penalty case and has written a memoir titled *Angel of Death Row*. Lyon says that one of the problems with the type of prosecutorial behavior exhibited in Routier's case is that courts often write it off as "harmless error" that has no effect on a trial's outcome. "The lesson to prosecutors," says Lyon, "is you can get away with it."

Melanie Waits feels that Davis's tactics were not "harmless"—especially in Kerrville, the seat of one of the most conservative counties in the state. "It was such a conservative town that they didn't like her from the beginning," says Waits. "It was not [a jury of] her peers, let's just put it that way."

Lyon says another hindrance to holding prosecutors accountable is that appellate courts do not name prosecutors when the courts agree with defense counsel that an error occurred. "There's no personal price to it," she says. "And I believe that if a prosecutor knew that if they crossed the line they would be named in an appellate opinion, they'd watch it because there would be a personal price to pay." Says Waits: "Their whole premise was that she had blonde hair, tattoos, and fake boobs. It was just slander."

Dallas attorney Richard Smith, a member of Routier's appellate team, states: "It was more than sexism. It was classism, too. She was portrayed as uppity white trash, though I don't think that phrase was ever used. She was living beyond her means and was not the type of person that you want to have in your community. The thing that struck me when I got closely involved in putting together the federal writ and the other pleadings that are involved in the various courts seeking to establish her innocence—the thing that really struck me is that the trial was much less about evidence than it was about character assassination—exactly the kind of evidence that isn't even supposed to be permitted in the courtroom at all when you're talking about a criminal prosecution. From virtually the first sentence in the state's opening statement, they were portraying her—I think the phrase was something like a cold and calculating woman who was so selfish that her desire for more financial secu-

Appellate team lawyer Richard Smith of Dallas.
Photo courtesy Richard Smith.

rity led her to stab her two children to death. That approach to a prosecution just inflames the jury. They were literally asking them to convict Darlie because they didn't like her, not because they had established that she had done anything wrong."

Greg Davis's opening statement at trial began with this: "The evidence will show you that the real Darlie Routier is, in fact, a self-centered woman, a materialistic woman, and a woman cold enough, in fact, to murder her own two children." As to how the Dallas prosecutors got away with tactics that should not have been allowed in the courtroom, Smith states: "Somebody has to object. And the overwhelming majority of the time, as far as I can tell, the defense didn't object."

Penrose says that sometimes zealousness becomes self-righteousness, and when that happens, justice suffers. Kerrville attorney Richard Mosty, who was a member of Routier's defense team, says of Davis: "I think he let his righteousness get in front of his professional responsibilities."

The fact that Routier's conviction continues to be widely debated may be due largely to hundreds of exonerations and differing opinions about what constitutes dirty pool in a courtroom. Mosty believed then—and still believes—the jury got it wrong, reaching a conclusion based on a deceptive image that prosecutors deliberately created of Routier. The defense lawyer was

Disillusioned: Kerrville attorney Richard Mosty, a member of the trial defense team, left private practice for a time after the Routier verdict. *Photo courtesy Richard Mosty.*

so disillusioned with the justice system after his client was sentenced to death that, for a time, he quit his law practice and went into the corporate world, working as in-house counsel for Gatti's Pizza.

Sandy Aitken and true-crime writer Anne Good believe the frumpy garments Routier wore during the trial likely backfired with the jury. "Doug Mulder putting her in that granny frock didn't fool anybody," says Good. "He should have put her in a stylish suit. There's nothing wrong with what she is. Instead, the jury could see right through that—that it was an effort to manipulate them." Says Aitken: "Mulder and [the defense team] didn't want her to look like she did when all this happened, so they dumbed her down really bad. They dyed her hair brown and put her in dowdy clothes so that she wouldn't look like she did before. Well, right off the bat, it screams liar. She had things that weren't suggestive. Why would they change her?"

Of Routier's visit to a male strip club, Lyon says there is still often a double standard in the justice system regarding what is acceptable behavior for a man and what is acceptable behavior for a woman. "Sexual behavior unnoticed or unimportant in a man becomes extremely important in a woman," she says. LaBare, which opened in 1978, continues to do a thriving business. The club's website advertises party packages, private parties, bachelorette/birthday parties—and girls' nights out.

* * *

I arrive at the cafe on Lake Austin Boulevard fourteen minutes early on a wintry gray Friday in February. Linda Guadarrama and I had planned to meet at five that evening at Sullivan's Steakhouse, but the Great Winter Storm That Wasn't has caused a realignment of our plans. Local news stations had made much ado about a winter storm that was likely going to make the streets of the state capital icy and dangerous before morning's end. Several school districts, including Austin's, reacted by shutting down for the entire day. So, too, did many government offices.

This turn of events means that I will not be able to progress with my death-row research at the Court of Criminal Appeals, where I want to continue examining the length of time between indictment and conviction, as well as the individual prosecutors and defense attorneys involved in each case. I had arrived in town Wednesday evening, just after the execution in Huntsville of Suzanne Basso—the fourteenth woman to be executed in the United States since the Supreme Court reinstated the death penalty in 1976. Her death brings the number of women on Texas's death row down to eight. Coincidentally, it is the second time I have arrived in Austin to do research on the same night a female Texas death-row inmate is executed. The other time was on a summer night eight months earlier, when Kimberly LaGayle McCarthy became the five hundredth person to be executed in Texas since the death penalty was reinstated. McCarthy, convicted of killing her elderly neighbor during a robbery, had been prosecuted by Greg Davis.

The idea to do the research was prompted by Davis's reported track record of twenty death penalty convictions. It was a number that alarmed a representative of the ACLU when I mentioned it in a phone conversation. Tracking the specific lawyers involved in death penalty cases has been tedious and slow, the days ending with a quick dinner at the Texas Chili Parlor around the corner, between the CCA and my hotel.

Early this Friday morning, I had watched in frustration as the closures scrolled across the bottom of my hotel room's TV screen while reporters and weather forecasters breathlessly gave dire warnings. I texted my publisher, who had footed the bill for this two-day trip, telling him that I would use vacation time for the next trip to make up for the wasted day. Community newspapers don't exactly operate on big budgets, and rare is the publisher who supports a research project such as this one.

Guadarrama, a defense attorney with offices in Austin and Dallas, was supposed to be in court this morning but that, too, got cancelled. So we have shifted from plan A to plan B, and that is why I am scootching into a booth in one of the two dining rooms at the Magnolia Cafe, where big windows afford a view of trees, shrubbery, and ice-free streets. The tablecloth is decorated with pink skulls—a clash of femininity and aggression. Just as a waiter sets a glass of orange juice before me, the door opens and in blows a puff of winter chill and Linda Guadarrama—the woman who once sued Dallas County District Attorney John Vance and his first assistant Norman "Norm" Kinne for sexual discrimination.

Though it was years ago, women in Dallas's political and justice systems still remember how Guadarrama took on the district attorney and his hatchet man. Some also recall the article about her lawsuit that was in the *Dallas Observer* back in September 1999. Felicia McCarthy wrote that former Assistant District Attorneys Linda Guadarrama and Terry Moore could only come up with one reason to explain why their careers in that office had not been more successful: "Neither of them has a penis."

Though records from the county auditor's office proved that male prosecutors were being paid more than their female counterparts, a federal jury determined that Guadarrama and Moore had no legal standing over their firings because, by law, they worked at the pleasure of the elected district attorney. But before it was all said and done, Guadarrama got her pound of flesh from the two men she believes cultivated an atmosphere of male domination. Over coffee and eggs Benedict, she details her views of the atmosphere inside the Dallas DA's office during the era when male prosecutors used breast implants and a male stripper called Master Blaster to help convince a jury that Darlie Routier deserved to die.

Our conversation starts with the lawsuit. In 1992, Guadarrama says, she went to the county auditor and requested the salaries of everyone working in the DA's office. The records, which are public, showed what she had suspected. Though the Dallas County Commissioners Court sets the budget for that office, Guadarrama tells me that Vance boosted the pay of his male prosecutors through a hot check fund, which she refers to as a "slush fund." "It's totally discretionary with the elected DA. It's really to use for equipment for the DA's office, but he used it for salary. And it was always men. When I would go to him and ask for a raise, he would say, 'We don't have the money. . . . County Commissioners, et cetera.' I said, 'That's not true, Mr. Vance, you have the slush fund.'"

Guadarrama confronted Vance with the names of male prosecutors who were earning more than she was—some of whom had not been there as long as she had and did not have a track record as impressive as hers. She had even trained some of them. "I said, 'They're making $500 more a month than I am—and that's a car payment to me.' And he would say, 'Well, so-and-so, he has a family to support' and 'So-and-so, he just got married.'"

It was just a few months later that Kinne phoned the DA workroom and summoned Guadarrama to his office. She took her time getting there. "I knew I was going to get fired," she says. "They escort you out, like you're a criminal. 'Give me your badge,' and da-da-da." Kinne told her she "didn't fit the mold." Guadarrama says she was among seven assistant DAs who were given the ax. Of the seven, five were women.

Terry Moore, a thirteen-and-a-half-year veteran who had been hired and promoted by Vance's predecessor, Henry Wade, was fired two years later. She would join the lawsuit that Guadarrama filed after finally finding a lawyer brave enough to take on the powerful DA.

Guadarrama says that during the Vance era, one male assistant DA was known for grabbing the breasts and buttocks of women in the office. A male prosecutor and a female prosecutor each had affairs with judges, she says, but the man was allowed to keep his job, while the woman was fired. She says that when interviewing women for assistant DA positions, Vance would ask personal questions, such as whether they intended to have a family.

Guadarrama recalls a time when seven women in the office were pregnant at the same time. Someone made a comment to Kinne that there must be "something in the air.""Yeah," he replied. "Their heels."

"He was just a good ol' boy country bumpkin who said stuff like that all the time—and thought there was nothing wrong with it," says Guadarrama, as a waiter replenishes her coffee and the cafe fills with the sound of laughter coming from a back table. I notice, apropos of nothing, really, that all of the wait staff on the pink skull side of the cafe are of the penile variety. Guadarrama continues: "The women were always complaining. They said, 'Hey, we want to do death penalty cases. Why is it always Toby [Shook]?'" One assistant DA had even been named Prosecutor of the Year, Guadarrama says, yet she was never allowed to handle a death penalty case. Guadarrama says she was surprised at Greg Davis's appointment over Shook as lead prosecutor in the

Routier case. Assistant DA Sherri Wallace also was part of the prosecutorial team, though there were whispers she was merely a token. A woman prosecutor on the team might help sway a jury to send another woman to death row.

During the time of her lawsuit, Guadarrama says that she instructed her attorney, the now-deceased Doug Larson, to refer to Vance in depositions as "the defend*ant*." It was the same way that he would typically refer to accused criminals. Forcing Vance and Kinne to sit for depositions and respond to accusations is a cherished memory. "He [Vance] was just so red. He gave me the worst look I have ever seen, like he wanted to kill me. But I wanted it to be just like they do when they arrest people. They don't care if they ruin somebody's career or business; they're law enforcement. It's heavy-handed sometimes, you know?"

Vance was district attorney from 1986 to 1998. Guadarrama says it was "a moral victory" the day she picked up a newspaper to read that Vance had decided not to run for reelection. Guadarrama believes his decision was tied, at least in part, to her pending lawsuit and the fact that she and other members of the county's Republican women groups intended to mount a campaign denouncing his treatment of women. And there was another moral victory as well. "I have heard that women *are* getting equal pay," she says.

As a waiter removes our plates, exposing more pink skulls, I think of how similar Guadarrama is to another woman who had the backbone to stand up to Norm Kinne. Darlie Kee had brazenly interrupted Kinne as he was being interviewed by television news reporters outside the Kerr County Courthouse, accusing him of lying about her daughter. "Do I have to interview in front of this trailer trash?" Kinne had sputtered.

Kee believes that the "trailer trash" comment likely dashed Kinne's dreams of becoming the next Dallas County district attorney. The footage, of course, was aired. *Texas Monthly* detailed the incident under the headline "Revoltin'." In Dallas, the name Norm Kinne became virtually synonymous with "trailer trash." "*He* was really the trailer trash," says Guadarrama. She adds that she doesn't believe Routier got a fair trial.

After a new regime eventually took over the DA's office and the years passed, Kinne met his end through pancreatic cancer. Vance died of complications from diabetes and heart disease. As Guadarrama and I gather our things to leave—the ice still not having made an appearance—I think back to a time when I was exchanging text messages with Kee regarding questions of alleged sexism in her daughter's trial. After several exchanges, I think we are done, but then, a minute or two later, another message shoots across the screen of my iPhone. It is one final, defiant comment from Kee: "And I loved every single minute at LaBare."

As Guadarrama and I head into the cold and part ways on the parking lot of the Magnolia Cafe, I smile over two strong women who never met, but have much in common. In the South, women like them are called steel magnolias.

CHAPTER 20

Thunder Rolls

The skies above Dallas were becoming increasingly turbulent, as was the atmosphere inside the chambers of State District Judge Robert Francis. At the center of the storm was Sandra Halsey, the court reporter responsible for the official record of the Darlie Routier capital murder trial. The date was Thursday, November 12, 1998.

Both the record and Halsey's longstanding career were in serious jeopardy. So, too, was the state's conviction of "Dallas's Susan Smith." Halsey had been late filing the trial transcript with the Court of Criminal Appeals (CCA). She had been granted several extensions, but still there were problems. In February, one year after Routier's conviction, Halsey finally filed the official record with the CCA, but the court returned it as not being sufficient. In March, the CCA issued an order of contempt against Halsey because she had failed to produce the trial transcript, impeding the appeals process. She filed the transcript again in April, but by October, Routier's attorneys began disputing the record's accuracy. There were discrepancies, they said, between what had been read to the deliberating jury and what was reflected in the corresponding portion of the transcript. There were also discrepancies over who was present, and when, during trial proceedings. "I've known Sandy for years and she was always competent and nice—one of the courthouse people," says appellate lawyer Stephen Cooper. "I was taken aback when she started saying things that didn't make sense."

The CCA ordered Halsey to prepare a supplemental record and ordered the trial court to resolve any disputes in order to ensure a transcript that was a true reflection of what had occurred at trial. Judge Francis determined the entire record needed to be reviewed. At a hearing on October 30, Halsey testified that the audiotape recorder had worked only during jury selection. Francis ordered her to produce her notes, disks, and tapes and to conduct her own review of the record. At a hearing a few days later, on November 4, he appointed three certified court reporters—Tommy Mullins, Judy Miller, and Jerry Calloway—to review Halsey's record and determine whether it could be certified.

The meeting in Francis's chambers on the blustery night of November 12 was a prehearing conference in preparation for yet another hearing that was to be held the next day, on Friday the thirteenth. Halsey was going to be asked tough questions during that hearing, and the three experts appointed to review her record also were to testify.

Gathered in Francis's office that night inside the Frank Crowley Courts Building were Cooper and Dallas County Assistant District Attorney Lindsey Roberts. Halsey, too, was summoned to the meeting by the agitated judge, but she had to call upon her daughter, Suzy Crowley, to give her a ride. It seemed Halsey was again plagued by a battery problem, but this time it was the one in her car. She had claimed that a battery issue with a microphone was to blame for there being no audiotapes of the five-week trial in Kerrville.

There was strong suspicion Halsey was lying about the tapes. Francis had ordered her to report to his chambers in Criminal District Court Number 3 in hopes of finally getting to the bottom of what was fast becoming a royal mess. According to Cooper, Francis had ordered that no one involved in the case was to talk to Halsey outside of the courtroom unless all parties were included in the conversation. But that night in Francis's chambers, Assistant DA Roberts asked the judge for permission to speak privately with Halsey in hopes of getting to the truth. "The judge grants permission to do this and so he leaves," recalls Cooper. "Forty-five minutes later, he comes in and says, 'Judge, there *are* tapes. She's told me.'

"It was stormy and getting nasty. It was lightning and thundering. He [Roberts] said the tapes were in a storage unit. Bobby [Judge Francis] said, 'All right, I want you as an officer of the court to go with her and don't go anywhere except to get her key to the storage unit and go straight there and pick up the tapes and bring them back.' So he leaves and we break up. I didn't care. I wasn't suspicious. It was in the [DA's] interest to have these tapes."

But what Cooper didn't know was that the group assembled in Criminal District Court Number 3 was not alone that night in the eleven-story courts building as the thunder rolled. And what he didn't know—until it was too late—was that a DA "super chief" with a vested interest in not having to retry the case would cut a deal with Halsey, protecting her from being prosecuted for a felony.

* * *

The next day at the hearing, Sandra Halsey—like investigators Patterson and Frosch during the trial—asserted her Fifth Amendment privilege against self-incrimination. In essence, this left Cooper all dressed up with no place to go. "She would have been eviscerated by me if she had testified," the lawyer says. "I would have put her in jail if anybody was inclined to prosecute her because I had so many contradictory things and so many things to hit her with."

It would be a couple of months later that Cooper would find out that no one was "inclined to prosecute" Halsey anyway. The night before the hearing, when Roberts left the judge's chambers with Halsey for a private talk, they met up with Assistant District Attorney Toby Shook—something Cooper found out about long after the fact. "I blew a gasket," Cooper says, recalling his anger over being kept in the dark about the discussion in which Halsey was given immunity. "It was just another backhanded deal. First of all, [Shook] was part of the prosecution team of Darlie. Second of all, he was very high ranking in that office. And to me, his being present was in essence a threat that [Halsey] was going to be prosecuted if she didn't [give] up the tapes. If that was the method of getting to the truth, some would argue, so what? Well, I never did get to question Sandy Halsey because she took the Fifth and those tapes are unverified."

Assistant DA Roberts would later state in sworn testimony before the Court Reporters Certification Board that he had encountered Shook as if by chance, after allowing Halsey and Crowley to talk privately inside the courtroom. Crowley—Halsey's daughter—had been one of two scopists who had helped Halsey with the transcript. Scopists receive rough copies of transcripts made by court reporters using stenotype machines or voice mask equipment. They compare the rough copies to audiotapes to help create the official record. "I stepped out of the room, left them alone in the courtroom for a little while," Roberts testified. "And I think at this time, I was joined by, actually one of the trial prosecutors on the case, Toby Shook."

Halsey conferred with her daughter, then approached Roberts and Shook. "What would happen," she asked, "if there were audiotapes?"

Roberts testified: "At that point in time, we were prepared to offer 'use

Re-created record: Court reporter Sandra Halsey's trial transcript—with thousands of errors marked in red ink—is stored in the basement of the Court of Criminal Appeals in Austin. Many in the legal profession are stunned that the epically flawed record did not result in a new trial for Darlie Routier. *Photo by the author.*

immunity' for her prior testimony—her prior statement that there were no [tapes]—just in order to secure audiotapes, because the audiotapes, at this point, were going to be the way we could verify this record, if at all. . . . So we told her that she wouldn't be prosecuted for her perjury if she would just give us those tapes."

"Use immunity," Roberts later explained to the certification board, is a limited type of immunity that protected Halsey from having wrongfully claimed that there were no audiotapes. Halsey now told Shook and Roberts that the tapes might be in a storage unit in Plano, although she wasn't certain. She and Roberts then joined Cooper and Francis in the judge's chambers, where Halsey—who had heard that Francis had a fiery temper—would face a bigger storm than the one raging outside.

* * *

Halsey later stated that there *were* tapes, but that she had listened to a

couple of them and heard nothing but static, leading her to believe the equipment had malfunctioned and there were no audiotapes that were usable. In
sworn testimony before the Court Reporters Certification Board, however, she
admitted she lied to Francis. "I was so scared of Judge Francis," she stated. "I had
already heard what a temper he has. I didn't want anything to upset this appeal."

Expert Susan Simmons was appointed to reconstruct Halsey's trial record. It was Simmons who ultimately revealed that there were thirty-three
thousand errors in the transcript.

Cooper says that at the time, he was not aware that the Halsey record was
going to be "a major issue in Darlie's appeal. I thought we were going to get a
good record. As an appellate lawyer, I want a good record." Trial transcripts are
extremely important, *Austin American-Statesman* staff writer Eric Dexheimer
explained in a July 2011 article, because a person's freedom can depend on
"precisely what was said." Of the thirty-three thousand errors in Halsey's transcript—a rate that hasn't been seen in the industry before or since—forty to
fifty percent of them were "substantive." On June 6, 1999, the third anniversary
of the murders of Devon and Damon Routier, the Court Reporters Certification Board voted to revoke the certification Halsey had held for more than
twenty-five years.

As with Halsey, Cooper says he was never allowed to question Simmons.
"The hearings where Simmons testified about her work were unlike any I have
experienced in my career," says Cooper. "The judge's rules included that only he
could question Simmons, that we had to write questions out and he would ask
them, if he deemed them worthy. I've had judges ask a witness a few questions
for clarification occasionally, but never act as the sole questioner, plus being
the gatekeeper of which of the proposed written questions he would even ask.
Another 'rule' was that no one could object to any question or answer."

The Simmons record was accepted by Francis and by the Court of Criminal Appeals—a fact that angers Cooper and astounds many to this day. "There
was a lot of sneaky business about it. Ultimately, it led to this bogus record
that's sitting on the floor over there that her appeal is based off of," Cooper
says as we sit in his office on Gaston Avenue. "The judge's rulings kept me from
demonstrating that [the record] is still no good—and there are fifty-four pages
that no one will swear to."

Cooper says Francis promised him that before the reconstructed record
was filed with the Court of Criminal Appeals, there would be another hearing
about the transcript—a hearing in which he could get on the record all of his

objections to the transcript and its reconstruction. "I had always been promised I could make global, specific objections to the record in what would have been the biggest hearing that would have ever occurred in Darlie's case. And he cancelled it at four o'clock in the afternoon the day before the hearing," Cooper says. "I was going to blow up his efforts to have this record reconstructed. Because I was not allowed to have that hearing, I wouldn't get into the record the things that were necessary to get into the record. And then the Court of Criminal Appeals just whitewashed it and said it was fine.

"I complained loudly and frequently and repeatedly that the manner in which he [Francis] was reconstructing this record [through Simmons] was not in accordance with the law and was unfair and in denial of due process—including keeping the witness, Susan Simmons, at bay. And he promised me, 'You can have a hearing when we're done.' We were friends and I trusted his word. Cameras were going to be there. Reporters from all over. The whole world was watching, and he bailed. He never called me to say why."

Cooper says that the essence of due process is the opportunity to be heard. "The quality of both the 'opportunity' and 'being heard' is critical," he says. "The opportunity must be real and someone must actually listen. This opportunity must include allowing the party to put objections and evidence into the record, with a court reporter taking notes, in order that an appeals court can have the pertinent objections and supporting evidence on which to base its rulings. In short, the proceeding must be fair. And, in Darlie's case, to deny her, through her lawyers, the opportunity to challenge the Simmons transcript with evidence and legal argument *before* accepting the record as true, was certainly not fair. In fact, it was shameful."

At the time of this writing, Francis, no longer with Dallas County Criminal District Court Number 3, is a judge in the Dallas Reentry Court, a probation-based custodial program. He states in an e-mail to me that he cannot ethically comment on Cooper's claims, since the case is still pending. However, an explanation of sorts was detailed in a document filed by the CCA. It states: "The trial court found that the appellant's objections were clear and concise and would apprise the Court of Criminal Appeals of the appellant's concerns about the record. . . . It also found that an evidentiary hearing as requested by the appellant was not necessary to comply with the orders of the Court of Criminal Appeals, the orders had been complied with, and that it would not hold any other hearings unless the Court of Criminal Appeals so ordered."

Those stunned by the piecing together of a trial record that contained thirty-three thousand errors might be just as astonished at what had started the whole mess to begin with.

* * *

It was when Halsey, her daughter, and the other scopist were working to construct the official trial record that an alarming mistake was discovered. When the jury had twice sent out a note asking about a portion of Darin Routier's testimony, Halsey had sent back the wrong answer. The discrepancy would also be discovered later by Routier's appeals lawyers.

The first note asked: "Did Darin lock the utility room door before he went to bed?" The second note said this: "Some of us 'remember' hearing Darrin [sic] say that he did not lock the door from the utility room to the garage before he went to bed 6/5/96—the rest of us 'remember' that Darrin said that he locked this door. Which is right??"

Halsey's response to the question from the jury was that Darin stated he had locked the door. What would later come to light—after Darlie Routier had been convicted and sent to death row—was that Darin had said the roll-down garage door had been locked, but the door leading from the garage to the utility room had not. When the jury determined Darlie Routier was guilty of killing her children and staging a crime scene, they did so under the belief that there would have been signs of forced entry through the utility room door had an intruder entered through the cut window screen in the garage. Of Halsey, Cooper says: "She was supposed to listen to her tapes to confirm what her notes said before transcribing the notes for the jury."

On Saturday, February 1, 1997, as the jury deliberated inside the cold courtroom, friends and family members were clustered on the courthouse lawn. Darlie Routier looked down at them from the room on the second floor where she was being held while the jury determined her fate. Those on the courthouse lawn could barely see the top of Darlie's head, but Darin Routier could tell she was crying. She held up her arm and gave them a thumbs down. Minutes later, it was announced that the jury had reached a verdict. Everyone scrambled to get to the courtroom. Darlie Routier already knew what the pronouncement was going to be because she had heard it from the court reporter.

"I was back in the holdover. It's where they put you outside of the courtroom when you're waiting to go back into court," she tells me during one of our interviews at Mountain View. She says the room was "horrible" and that it

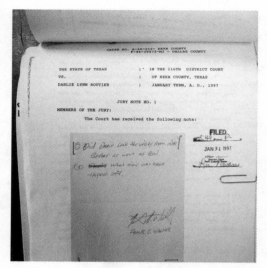

Alarming error: This key question was sent from the jury room as the jury deliberated. The court reporter sent back the wrong answer, telling the jury Darin Routier testified that he had locked the door leading from the garage into the house before going to bed. He testified that he had not done so. When the jury found Darlie Routier guilty, it did so believing there should have been signs of forced entry at that door. *Photo courtesy Nick Nelson.*

was littered with dead bugs, which she assumed was because of the courthouse renovation. Routier says Halsey was calling out to someone. She realized after hearing the other woman's voice that it was Norm Kinne's wife, an investigator who was present at the trial. "I guess they didn't know that I was in that holding area because it had a solid door. They were standing right in front of it. Sandra Halsey said something like, 'Did you hear?' And [Mrs. Kinne] said, 'What?' And Sandra Halsey said, 'It's a guilty verdict, so get your people together for the sentencing phase.'

"When I came back out and sat at the table, I told [the lawyers]. I explained to them what I had heard, what had been said. I don't think she did it intentionally for me to hear, but she never should have been the one to say it. How was she even privileged to that information before it was announced?"

Darlie Kee was among the group on the courthouse lawn that afternoon. She recalls: "We were talking to a photographer from the *Dallas Morning News*.

He had a camera with a long lens. We saw Darlie at the window. She kept trying to get our attention. She was drawing something on the window. Darin asked if he could look through the photographer's lens. She was drawing a "G" for guilty. Darin and I looked at each other. I didn't want to tell my sisters and daughters.

"When we got into the courtroom, we gathered together to shield each other from the blow. Darlie and Darin were crying and so were Darlie's sisters, Danelle and Dana. When the judge said "Guilty," Danelle—who was only thirteen—screamed, 'You will go to hell for lying!'" Darin's mother, Sarilda, who was also in the courtroom, imparted the same message, but specifically to lead prosecutor Greg Davis. "I looked him in the eye and mouthed, 'You will go to hell for this,'" she told me.

The conversation about Halsey causes Routier to remember something else about the court reporter's behavior in Kerrville. "During the trial, she and the bailiff that came down from Dallas for the trial, they took pictures with me. They asked me, but I just didn't question it. These are things you go back later and think, 'What was that about?' I wish I [had been] like I am now—stronger—to have said no. It makes me wonder, what were those pictures for? It was her personal camera and it was in the courtroom." Routier says the photos were snapped as she sat at the defense table in the otherwise empty courtroom. She was always brought in first before others were allowed in.

During the hearing in Austin, before the Court Reporters Certification Board, Halsey's testimony shed light on the possible reasons for her uncharacteristic behavior. She told the board she had begged Judge Mark Tolle not to make her go to Kerrville for the lengthy jury selection and trial because she had discovered that her husband, a judge, was allegedly having an affair with a younger, married woman who also worked in the courts building. She stated she took the female bailiff with her when she went to talk to Tolle.

The court reporter's plea, however, fell on deaf ears. Tolle said he wanted his staff intact for the high-profile criminal trial. Halsey was forced to spend a month in the Hill Country town during jury selection, and then another five weeks for the trial and punishment phase, leaving her husband behind in Dallas with his alleged mistress. During the time Halsey was dealing with the Routier trial transcript, her father suffered a stroke. She witnessed him throwing up blood. A short time later, he died.

Ultimately, Halsey and her husband of seventeen years divorced. She said she came home one day from a trip to Austin to find he had moved out of their home, leaving behind a note stating that he just wasn't happy. The audiotapes from the Routier trial had been stored in their garage, Halsey told the Court Reporters Certification Board. Unbeknownst to her, they had been moved by her husband to the storage unit in Plano.

Susan Simmons also testified before the Court Reporters Certification Board during the Halsey hearing. She said that Halsey's transcript contained misspellings, typographical errors, and incorrect words. She also stated that some words were omitted and that Halsey had at times misidentified speakers.

I sent Halsey a certified letter seeking her comment about that stressful period in her life, when she was shouldering responsibility for the official record of a criminal trial that had captured the nation's attention. She never responded. Had Halsey spoken with me, I would have asked whether antidepressants or antianxiety medication might have played a role in the fiasco that ended her career of more than a quarter of a century.

* * *

A court reporter raised the subject of the Darlie Routier trial record in a casual conversation with legal ethics expert Keith Hampton just a couple of days before he and I are scheduled to speak by phone about the controversial case. The court reporter asked him: "How did they let that case stand?" Hampton had no answer. "We were just chatting and it came up," he tells me. "I think everybody has heard about it. It definitely is known among court reporters."

According to Suzi Kelly, a court reporter for more than thirty years, the disaster cast a dark cloud over the court reporting profession and changed the industry. I meet with Kelly in her twelfth floor office on West 7th Street in Fort Worth on a Sunday afternoon in January. Kelly says that after the embarrassment with Halsey, the Court Reporters Certification Board "worked feverishly" to institute a uniform format manual. It dictates every margin, every font size, rules for documenting nonverbal communications, and more. Even now, she says, many court reporters harbor anger towards Halsey. "We court reporters really took it on the chin when this happened," says the softspoken Kelly. "It really impugned the integrity of court reporting in general. To this day, it's probably the most impactful trial for criminal trials that affect the way court reporters see their role.

"Everything in all my training led me to believe that if you make errors that had to do with the facts and particularly what was presented to the jury

and what wasn't, you were just about guaranteed that the case would be reversed and that hundreds of thousands of dollars would have to be spent to
have another go at it. Of course, the cost does not compare to somebody's lib-
erty. No appeals court ever hears the case again, other than what the reporter
puts down as the record. It lives on forevermore in that record, and when it's
flawed, it's not like they can go to the appeals court and retry it." The longtime
court reporter compares the challenges Susan Simmons faced to having to
rebuild an exotic car that had been taken apart by someone who disposed of
some of the parts.

Although Kelly does not excuse Halsey's mistakes with the record or her
lies to Judge Francis, she says culpability on the part of Judge Tolle for not
having heeded Halsey's plea may have been why the Court Reporters Certification Board "treated her mercifully." The vote to pull Halsey's certification
was 5-4. "She probably does have some excuses. Is anybody interested in them?
Probably not. But people who knew her said they didn't know what happened
to her. She was a nice lady."

Regarding the wrong answer Halsey sent to the jury deliberation room,
Kelly says: "She should have checked her audio and gone over it with a fine-
tooth comb to make sure, because reading back to a jury is even more important than a statement of facts. The jury is going to base their decision on that.
She probably knew there was a problem. But there is sort of a pressure to look
like you know what you're doing. I still hold out hope that there's a chance the
Darlie Routier case will be tried again because of errors in the transcript."

A few days after my meeting with Kelly, I speak by phone with John Clark
Long IV, an assistant district attorney in Kaufman County. Long was head
of the Dallas County DA's civil division back when the Dallas County Commissioners Court was seeing red over having to pay Susan Simmons to fix
a transcript for which the county had already paid Halsey. Although taking
responsibility for a voluminous trial transcript is "a huge undertaking," Long
says, it is also "very lucrative." Court reporters are paid a salary by the county,
but are paid separately for copies that are required when cases are appealed.
The transcript for the lengthy Routier trial was 53 volumes.

"It comes up that Sandra Halsey had emotional problems and whatever
else and that she had made a ton of mistakes," Long says. "The county had
paid for the transcript—$74,000, or something like that. In Commissioners
Court, they were livid that the county had paid her a salary and they had paid
her an additional $70,000 or $74,000 for a transcript that was so bad it had to

be redone and they effectively had to pay twice for it. They were so upset and they were saying, 'We need to sue her for what we paid her because we didn't get anything for it.' And I didn't know whether that had ever been done before." In today's dollars, the $74,000 would be about $107,000.

Though Halsey tried to claim judicial immunity, Long sued her under the premise that she had breached a contract with the county. He took heat from other county employees who resented him for suing one of their own. Some of the pressure came from within the DA's office. There was a fear that Long's attempts to recoup the county's money would impeach the conviction of Routier. Long's response was that a court had already determined that the record was unacceptable.

Long also faced opposition in the Court of Appeals in Dallas when he attempted to recoup the county's money. "The Court of Appeals was upset that anyone would ever sue a court reporter. We went to the Texas Supreme Court, and the Texas Supreme Court, without hearing arguments, ruled in our favor and said *of course* it's a contract and they can sue for it."

Long says that, to the best of his knowledge, the money was never repaid. "It [the lawsuit] was more to push a point and say, 'We're not going to sit still. Just because we're the county and we're paying for it doesn't mean we're going to accept something crappy.'" Long states that the majority of court reporters are professional and take pride in their work. "Most of them are the silent party in the courtroom that gets it all correct," he says.

The Halsey record that allegedly contained thirty-three thousand errors is "amazing," Long says. "A death penalty case by definition would be the most important work a court reporter would ever do. In something where someone's life is on the line—a life or death decision—you should have the best, most alert professional court reporter. I would be very concerned at trying to reconstruct a record. I would think that there might be some exceptional cases—for example a court reporter dies—but their rough draft of what they did would usually be good enough that some other court reporter could read it and you could have some degree of comfort. But the number of errors [in the Routier trial record] was so astounding."

Appellate team member Richard Smith says he is shocked that the jerry-rigging of the trial record was allowed. "The level of re-creation that they had to go to in order to create something that purports to be an accurate, contemporary record of that trial is ridiculous. It should never have been permitted," he says. "It was a fantastic appellate point that should have entitled

Darlie to a new trial all on its own, and I think the Court of Criminal Appeals departed from its own precedent when it decided that the process of re-creating it from notes and from audio tapes, by a court reporter who wasn't even present at the trial, was acceptable." Smith says nonverbal communications such as head nodding, or 'uh-huhs' and 'uh-uhs,' would be problematic in the reconstruction of a record by someone who was not present at trial.

In one of my meetings with Cooper, I ask him how the reconstruction with the uncertified pages can be considered a true record. "Well, it's not. It's just simply not," he says. "I've never been an appellate judge, but occasionally you get cases that are just flat, smooth, crazy wrong. They're wrong when they were decided and they're wrong ever since."

According to Cooper, when Halsey's epic failure came to light, the state offered to take death off the table for Darlie Routier, giving her life in prison instead. All she had to do was give up her appeals and admit she had killed her children. She refused.

CHAPTER 21

A Matter of Integrity

D allas County District Attorney Craig Watkins is running late on a mild Friday morning in January. I am to meet with him, along with Russell Wilson, head of the Conviction Integrity Unit, and First Assistant DA Heath Harris, at 10:00 a.m. The topic of the discussion will be Darlie Routier.

Watkins, the first black DA in Texas history, is towering, charismatic, and in demand. The spring primaries are just over four weeks away, and he is seeking reelection for a third term. Though he is unopposed on the Democratic ticket, two Republicans are on the March ballot. This means Watkins will spend the next nine months fighting to keep from being a casualty in the November elections.

A graduate of Texas Wesleyan Univesity School of Law in Fort Worth (now Texas A&M University School of Law), Watkins had tried three times to get hired on as a prosecutor in the Dallas County DA's office, but was rejected every time. In 2002, he attempted to unseat incumbent Bill Hill, a Republican, but was unsuccessful. His luck changed when he tried again in 2006. Watkins was swept into office by a Democratic tidal wave, besting Hill's heir apparent, Toby Shook.

After taking office, Watkins made national headlines when he created the nation's first Conviction Integrity Unit. The role the Dallas DA's office played in DNA exonerations led to a six-episode television series called *Dallas DNA*. The show first aired on the Investigation Discovery channel in April 2009. Not everyone was happy about Watkins's newfound fame, or the fact that he didn't fit the mold of an old-school district attorney. He was called a rogue prosecutor, and there were snide jokes with "hug a thug" as the punchline. His relationship with the Dallas media was sometimes rocky, and there were accusations that he encouraged his prosecutors to run against judges who had crossed him.

Watkins had been the Dallas County district attorney for six years when he stunned the media with the revelation that he is the great-grandson of an executed man. Richard Johnson, the father of Watkins's grandmother, was thirty-one when he was strapped into the electric chair on August 10, 1932. Johnson and twenty-year-old Richard Brown allegedly confessed to the Wichita Falls robbery of Fort Worth oil man Ted Nodurft and the robbery and rape of his fiance. Each said it was the other who pulled the trigger on Nodurft, who later died of his injuries. The state settled the matter by executing both men, on the same day.

To what extent Watkins has been influenced by his great-grandfather's execution is unknown. He is a complex man whose beliefs and behaviors at times appear incongruent. It is unusual for a district attorney to publicly state that he is against the death penalty, but Watkins has done exactly that. He has also pledged, however, to continue seeking death sentences—and he has certainly done so. Between the time Watkins took the reins in 2007 to the end of 2013, his office won more death sentences than any other district attorney's office in the state. The twelve defendants sentenced to death in Dallas County during that time had collectively killed twenty people, many of them children.

Nothing appears to have changed in the fifteen months since I was here to interview Russell Wilson for a newspaper series I was writing for the Texas Center for Community Journalism. The phones ring continually, and the women who work behind the glass windows in the foyer are still answering questions from callers, some of whom seem to have little knowledge about the workings of a district attorney's office. "Our attorneys are not for hire, sir," one of them explains to a caller in need of legal representation.

On this day in January, it is less than a month after the *Dallas Morning News* reported on Watkins's death-row numbers and how they contrast with a national decline. I pass the time by reflecting upon that October day when I met first Wilson and then Stephen Cooper. Russell Wilson had talked about the growing number of exonerations from Dallas County: at that point thirty-three people convicted in Dallas County had been exonerated since 2001. Those who had been freed were all male and mostly black, but this was for valid reason. Statistically, males commit more crimes than females, and historically, America's racist roots had penetrated law enforcement.

My conversation with Wilson had touched only briefly upon Darlie Routier. He had explained that, despite many advocates pushing for a review of her case, the Conviction Integrity Unit must have something solid to act

Russell Wilson of the Dallas County District
Attorney's Conviction Integrity Unit. *Photo by the author.*

upon, such as a constitutional violation, before it commits taxpayer resources
to overturning a jury's verdict.

While we were talking, Wilson's cell phone buzzed. "Big Tex is on fire?" he
asked, his voice incredulous. He turned the cell phone to show me an image of
flames and smoke billowing around the fifty-two-foot icon that had welcomed
visitors to the State Fair of Texas for sixty years. For a few seconds, Wilson
did not seem like the head of one of the most groundbreaking, justice-related
endeavors in the country, but rather just another helpless observer watching as
something beloved was consumed and destroyed.

Later that same day I met Stephen Cooper at a two-story house-turned-
office-building on Gaston Avenue in East Dallas, between the skyscrapers of
downtown and the Lakewood neighborhood where a Dixie House restaurant
serves a bustling lunch crowd. The woman who answered the doorbell led me
to a room at the top of a flight of stairs. There, amid a clutter of boxes that bore
testament to the years-long battle between the state and Darlie Routier, was
Stephen Cooper. Autumn sunlight streamed through window blinds onto a
scattering of framed photos of grandchildren. One bore a striking resemblance
to the iconic photo of toddler Caroline Kennedy kissing her newborn brother. Cooper talked for three hours that day about the woman he began representing back in 1997, after a jury in Kerrville had found her guilty of capital
murder. At first, during the direct appeal process, he was court appointed and

compensated by taxpayers. But for years now, he has worked pro bono to free a woman he believes is innocent.

Cooper said he became convinced of Routier's innocence the first time he went to see her. After she had been sentenced to die by lethal injection, he went to the jail expecting to stay a few minutes. He ended up staying two hours. "I thought, 'This is not the woman people think she is,'" Cooper recalled. "She was intelligent. There was linear, progressive thought. And there was this God-awful, bright red, still-healing slash across her neck. It was clear to me that the public image was false and, as she relayed the facts, it was more im-probable that the state's version was true."

Cooper spoke of the DNA test results that still had not come in and about the advances in DNA technology that have occurred since Routier's conviction. Attempts to reverse that conviction have taken years, and there is no end in sight. "It's just bullshit," Cooper says of the state's case against his client. "And it leads to a lot of people's lives being ruined."

As Dallas rush hour was hitting its peak that day, Cooper carried a large white cardboard box marked "Darlie" down the stairs to the backseat of my car. Darkness had fallen by the time I pulled into a garage seventy miles away, in a neighborhood where pumpkins and orange lights decorated front porches. For the time being, I left the box on the backseat where Cooper had placed it. The car had been silhouetted in the dark against the garage windows as I closed and locked the utility room door, shutting out the box full of bloody crime scene photos. The photos documented in horrific detail a crime that had involved a different garage window and utility room door.

Later that night, an e-mail appeared in my inbox from Darlie Kee. Her sister from Pennsylvania was in town, and the previous day they had spent four hours at the Mountain View prison unit in Gatesville. But on this day, the sisters had put their cares aside long enough to visit the State Fair. They had been among a crowd of onlookers that watched as Big Tex fell victim to an electrical malfunction and went up in flames.

Kee wrote that supporters were participating in a three-day prayer vigil in hopes that Dallas DA Craig Watkins's heart would open and he would call for a review of the Darlie Routier case. When Watkins ushered in a new era by creating the Conviction Integrity Unit, Routier's supporters hoped he would be the answer to their prayers. I didn't respond that night to Kee's e-mail, be-cause Wilson's comments about the Routier case had not been promising, and I wanted to avoid the subject of the DA's office. There is a fine line that separates hope and despair, and Kee has had more anguish than many people experience in a lifetime.

* * *

Now, all these months later, the time has finally come for me to ask Watkins himself whether he has any intention of reviewing the troublesome prosecution of a blonde homemaker whose life could not have been more different from the lives of the men who have been exonerated. Sitting in the foyer, my reflections are interrupted by a young man who has walked from the back offices to summon me.

"They're ready for you now."

In Watkins's corner office eleven stories high, the digital recorder is once again called into service. It is placed on a round table near the window, just as it has been placed on so many other tables for more than a year and a half now. Watkins, who is wearing cowboy boots, settles into a chair, as do Wilson and Harris. A bulletproof vest is propped against the wall near the door. It was purchased for Dallas County's top prosecutor after the 2013 assassinations of Kaufman County District Attorney Mike McLelland, his wife, and Chief Deputy Mark Hasse. Former Justice of the Peace Eric Williams and his wife, Kim, were charged with capital murder in the crimes. Toby Shook is one of the special prosecutors who will be taking the two to trial.

We start the interview with Watkins going back to the time, seven years earlier, when he had first moved into this office. Almost immediately, he began hearing about Darlie Routier.

"I thought, 'What *is* it about the Darlie Routier case?' I would hear about it at least once or twice a week. When I first came into office, it was pretty heavy. It's slowed down some since then. I would get an e-mail or a letter, something of that nature. I have also seen some petitions," Watkins says. "When I took office, we had about forty people on death row. Because of the exonerations, we said, 'Let's take a look at all of the cases that have been prosecuted that are pending execution and present those to the panel to make sure that we were not going to execute someone that didn't commit the crime.' We ended up taking two of them off death row. They are now serving life in prison."

The "panel" is a death penalty review team. The assistant DA who will be responsible for the prosecution of a capital murder case presents the case to the panel, and the group decides whether the death penalty should be sought.

Watkins has the final say. The practice is not uncommon today in district attorney offices. In former DA John Vance's administration, one person—First Assistant Norm Kinne—made that call, according to a February 1995 article in the *New York Times*. Kinne was quoted as saying that his office sought the death penalty only in cases where he felt virtually certain the jury would impose the ultimate punishment.

Watkins says that at the time Vance's office was handling the Routier case, he was a defense attorney "watching from afar." "I think from the outset the question became, 'Why would a mother kill her two kids?' As the case developed, that question lingered. It just didn't gel with certain individuals. Before that, there had been no indications of violence or mental illness, or something that would cause this defendant to commit this type of crime. From the outside looking in, it was just hard to accept. Darlie, she got the death penalty. Not that many women do. That makes it more interesting, and that's why people are still talking about it. Law enforcement has evolved since then. We've learned a lot from twenty years ago to now. We don't want to be critical of them back then, because that's how law enforcement worked. But we've learned that maybe some things weren't the best way to do things back then."

I bring up the courtroom testimony of crime scene investigator James Cron in which he stated he determined within minutes during his intitial walk-through of the crime scene that the killings of Devon and Damon Routier had been an inside job. Some believe that the Rowlett Police Department put so much faith in Cron's assessment that they never seriously considered other possibilities. The fact that the statement made by Cron continues to be a point of controversy was the point I made when I e-mailed Cron about his statement. Cron, though polite and professional in his response, declined an interview.

Watkins, Wilson, and Harris believe it is unfair to judge Cron for that statement, especially since he was on the scene at 5801 Eagle Drive for hours. "The twenty-minute thing is a soundbite," says Wilson. "The reality is that the information presented to the jury was much more than what was known within the first twenty minutes. Ultimately, it was pretty expansive information that was evaluated by the jury. It wasn't like it was a twenty-minute investigation. But it will always be a matter of conversation."

First Assistant DA Heath Harris points out that law enforcement officers receive training in how to spot a crime scene that is contrived. "They go to that scene with the notion in mind that this could potentially be staged," he says. He notes a recent case in the Dallas area involving a twenty-five-year-old woman who is suspected of suffocating her ex-fiancé's two-year-old daughter and then staging a crime scene, claiming she had been sexually assaulted. When the woman's story didn't add up, investigators found surveillance video showing her taking the child with her earlier that day to a dollar store, where she purchased items used in the staging—including duct tape. The child was found unconcious in her crib with duct tape over her mouth. She later died. One year earlier, a Keller woman was arrested in the death of her husband after she allegedly staged a home invasion. She alledgedly struck herself in the head with a wrench and then called 911, claiming that she and her husband had been attacked.

Watkins and Harris say that if a crime like the Routier case were to happen on their watch, they would handle it according to their plan for any crime that carries potential for the death penalty. "If a capital murder happens and we think it may be a potential death penalty case, our people immediately start pulling information on the defendant," says Harris, a Lubbock native who in 2008 received the DA's Above and Beyond Award. "We immediately start our own investigation. We don't just accept the information that the police give us."

Says Watkins: "We start pulling school records to see if there have been any instances of mental illness, that kind of stuff—future danger issues." Adds Harris: "We're going to get those family members in as quickly as we can so they can start telling us stuff about the defendant's history."

But though the current-era DA's office might handle a case like Routier's a bit differently from the way it was handled in the John Vance era, Watkins is inclined to believe that those who investigated and prosecuted Routier got it right. He gets to the heart of the reason for the interview. "We have a responsibility not just to protect the jury verdict, but we're of the opinion that she did commit the crime. We believe she committed the crime, so we're defending the conviction." Watkins says he had also asked Mike Ware, Wilson's predecessor as head of the Conviction Integrity Unit, to review the case. Ware, too, believes the conviction should stand.

The state's lengthy *Statement of Facts* about the case details alleged inconsistencies in Routier's story, both in her oral and written accounts. For instance, Routier allegedly stated in one account that she had been awakened by an intruder; in another, she said she awoke when Damon called out to her and poked her on the shoulder. The *Statement of Facts* also states that Routier gave differing accounts of a struggle with the intruder. She reported grappling with him while she was on the couch, but also stated they engaged in a struggle in the kitchen. As well, the *Statement of Facts* claims that the garage window screen had been cut from the inside; an intruder should have left a bloody trail, but didn't; there was no physical evidence of a third party's presence in the house; the Routiers were experiencing financial problems; a housekeeper claimed Routier had wrapped baby Drake so tightly in a blanket that his lips were blue; and many other details.

Watkins says that, although it will be difficult to sign the required paperwork when the time comes for Routier's execution, it will not be any more difficult than the other times he has had to follow the protocol. Each time has been hard. "Every one of them impact me. . . . You lose sleep over it."

I note that when Routier is executed, there may be no family members representing Devon and Damon in the room reserved for victims' family members. To this day, no one in Darlie's family or in Darin's family believe she killed her children. I also add that it is likely, considering the public interest in the case, that Routier's eventual execution will create a firestorm similar to when Karla Faye Tucker was put to death in 1998, almost exactly one year after Routier walked onto death row.

Tucker was convicted in the June 1983 pickax killings of Jerry Lynn Dean and his companion, Deborah Thornton, in Dean's Houston apartment. She became the first woman since 1984 to be executed in the United States. Tucker's widely publicized conversion to Christianity, and her feelings of remorse, contributed to the controversy surrounding her execution. Tucker admitted her guilt, while Routier has always proclaimed her innocence.

I mention a comment made by Mike Ware a few months earlier, during a session of the Actual Innocence class he teaches at Texas A&M University School of Law. Ware had allowed me to sit in on the class, which met on Saturdays. Regarding those convicted of crimes, Ware had said: "My experience has been that ninety-nine percent of them 'fess up and say, 'Yeah, I did it.' There's not that many of them that maintain their innocence. To me, that perception that everybody in prison says they're innocent—that just hasn't been my experience." Harris replies that Routier fits into the smaller category of those who are guilty, but never admit it. "It's not that unusual for people on the gurney to be adamently saying, 'I didn't do it,'" he says. "But on the flip side, you have several that accept responsibility and ask forgiveness." Karla Faye Tucker fit into the latter category. In her final words, she apologized to the family members of Dean and Thornton and said that she hoped God would give them peace.

I leave the interview thinking of the last words of another well-known death-row inmate—a man who proclaimed his innocence right up to the end: Cameron Todd Willingham.

* * *

Months after my meeting with Watkins, Harris and Wilson, I schedule a phone interview with Assistant District Attorney Lisa Smith. She is responsible for representing the state in Routier's appeals. Smith has worked in that office since 1994. She was there when Greg Davis, Toby Shook, and Sherri Wallace prosecuted Routier.

I state to Smith that those who support Routier or who feel a lack of confidence in her conviction have been waiting and hoping that Watkins's Conviction Integrity Unit will reopen the Routier file. Smith responds that the office *has* reexamined the case, along with many other cases, but sees no need to do anything further. "When Mr. Watkins took office, he wanted cases looked at closely, so if a case was examined, it was examined from beginning to end. When we looked at [the Routier case], we looked at it from the offense investigation all the way through all of the appeals that had occurred and the claims that had been raised and the results of the appellate litigation. We looked at it from beginning to end," she says.

"A lot of claims have been litigated. There were some things at trial [that were litigated] through cross [examination] and the appellate and writ process, and now DNA litigation. We haven't turned a blind eye to them. If anything, we've actually focused our efforts on addressing them. We're very open to hearing any arguments or claims that an opposing counsel might have to present to us. Our door is open. The process is alive and well.

"I think the attacks that have been made on the trial attorneys have all been examined. And the trial court has collected evidence on those issues and reviewed the claims and decided to deny them. Trials are human events, so they're never going to be 100 percent perfect. But we do have a constitutional standard, and her counsel was held to that. The trial court reviewed the claims, the CCA reviewed the claims, and they felt that she had counsel that met the standard."

I tell Smith that the testimony of Tom Bevel was key in Routier's conviction, but a 2009 report on forensic science funded by the US Department of Justice states that bloodstain pattern analysis is highly subjective and prone to misinterpretation. Did the report cause the state to have any concerns about Bevel's testimony in the trial of Darlie Routier?

"I can say I know he was very thoroughly cross-examined on his opinion about the bloodstain evidence in this case and actually made some concessions," Smith says. "He acknowledged that it was just his opinion and that there's more than one interpretation. My view of that evidence is that it's highly credible. I haven't seen anything in his testimony that gives me great concern. I thought he was pretty evenhanded."

I ask Smith why some people are so vocal in their belief that the state got it wrong with Routier. She replies: "I think they're sincere. But we are just as sincerely proponents of the jury's verdict. We very strongly feel that the jury got it right. We have a lot of confidence in that decision."

At the time of this writing, there have been 1,536 exonerations nationwide—150 of which were from death row, according to the California Innocence Project. Of the 185 exonerations in Texas, forty-seven are from Dallas County. Twenty-eight of them occurred after Watkins took office. All of the twenty-eight are men. All but five are black.

Several months before I met with Watkins, Harris, and Wilson to discuss the Routier case, I spoke with the DA in his office about the history he made, both by being the state's first black district attorney and in his work to exonerate those wrongfully convicted. His first appearance before the Dallas County Commissioners Court was to request funding to hire staff for the Conviction Integrity Unit. "There were two Democrats and three Republicans. It was a screaming match. They tried to embarass me in Commissioners Court, but they voted for it," he recalled. On the paperwork to approve the funding, one of the commissioners had written "No, no, no!" above his signature.

The idea to form the Conviction Integrity Unit did not come from Watkins, but rather from his former first assistant, Terri Moore. "I'm as green as the grass on a spring day," Watkins recalls. "Terri Moore said, 'Craig, this is your opportunity. This is your legacy. This is a chance to make a difference.' I said, 'I'm the first black DA in the state, hardly won the election, and you want me to do *what?*!' Watkins has a different attitude now, and he doesn't regret having followed Moore's visionary advice. "I'm here for a reason," he says. "I regret the fear and the hesitation I had with Terri. I will never, ever be afraid to do what's right again."

A year after Watkins was elected to his first term, the groundbreaking DA was featured on a segment of *60 Minutes*. The segment led with election night footage of Watkins thanking supporters and proclaiming: "It's a new Day in Dallas County!" Watkins discussed with correspondent Scott Pelley his ambivalence about the death penalty. "When I walk out of church on Sunday morning, I am strictly against the death penalty. But when I come in here on Monday morning and I'm reviewing autopsy photos of a child that's been murdered—that's when the gray area starts."

Among the viewing audience that Sunday night was Stephen Cooper, watching from his home east of Dallas County. When he heard Watkins's comment about looking at autopsy photos of a murdered child, he had a feeling that it wasn't really a new day in Dallas County at all—at least, not for Darlie Routier.

CHAPTER 22

The Hanging Capital

One of the most controversial issues in the *State of Texas v. Darlie Lynn Routier* is the change of venue to Kerr County. Darlie Kee says her daughter's court-appointed lawyers, Doug Parks and Wayne Huff, suggested a venue change because of the publicity that swirled around the case. The family trusted that the attorneys knew what would be in Darlie's best interest, so when the attorneys encouraged a venue change, the family readily agreed. "I just remember asking them why we were losing so much," recounts Darlie Kee, referring to pretrial hearings, such as the one in which Darlie was denied bond. "I knew nothing about Kerrville or its conviction rate. It's not like I knew, or any of us knew, what we were doing. None of us were familiar with trials, criminals, courtrooms, prosecutors, or lawyers.

"They [Parks and Huff] thought Darin could be involved, and since he was living at my house in Plano—and I wouldn't have believed them—they didn't share much. They convinced me and Darlie that a change of venue was needed because of the bad media coverage at that time."

In an interview at Mountain View, Routier says this about the venue change: "I didn't even know about the system, much less change of venue. A year or so after my conviction, I received a lot of letters from people telling me that they have a name for Kerrville, like 'the Hanging Capital.' If you want to get a conviction, take them to Kerrville."

Mulder gives this account of what he had heard, pertaining to the change of venue, before he was hired as Routier's lead defense attorney: "[Mark] Tolle and I had always been friendly from the time that he was a prosecutor down in the DA's office. He was on the bench and the case had been moved to Kerrville, which just astounded me. I visited with him and talked to him about it. He told me, in essence, that inasmuch as the case happened on his watch, he wanted to try it. Apparently, Bobby Francis would not agree to let him try

Cold justice: Though other courthouses in the state reportedly could have handled the five-week trial and the media contingent, State District Judge Mark Tolle determined the trial would take place in Kerr County. At that time, the courthouse was under renovation and had little or no heat. Conservative Kerr County is known for its death penalty convictions. *Photo by the author.*

it. He [Tolle] knew it couldn't be tried before the end of the year. Mark had apparently taken it upon himself to kind of feel around and see if there was someplace it could be moved on a change of venue. He said Parks and Huff thought it ought to be moved on a change of venue. He talked with Steve Ables, who was the administrative judge for that district. It was agreed to appoint Tolle to hear the case.

"It was no stretch to believe that they would move it to a place like Kerrville, one of the most conservative areas in Texas. It was obviously advantageous to the state. It was upper middle class, a lot of retired military, [an] ultra-conservative, pro-prosecution, pro-state venue. So it was no surprise that the state would readily agree to move it there. I said, why would any defense lawyer in his right mind agree to move a case from a jurisdiction like Dallas, which has probably five or six hundred thousand eligible jurors, to a place like

Kerrville that's ultra-conservative and has probably fifteen thousand eligible jurors, on a change of venue where the sole purpose for moving the case is publicity? There are tens of thousands, maybe hundreds of thousands, of people in the jurisdiction of Dallas that maybe hadn't formed opinions and hadn't read that much about it, but once the case was moved to Kerrville, literally everybody in town knew about it.

"I asked Tolle, why would the defense, under any circumstance, agree to move it there? And he told me at that time, it was either Huff or Parks, but I think it was Huff's aunt had a condo down there and they could stay down there, in effect, free and draw their per diem from the state. Everybody agreed to move it down there. And the change of venue benefited everyone except the person whom it was designed to benefit—and that was Darlie. Everybody benefited except Darlie.

"The first thing I did was file a motion to move it back to Dallas. And that would be the logical place to try it. All the witnesses were in Dallas. It would be a tremendous savings for the state to move it back there. Of course, there was no incentive for [the prosecutors] to move it back. They had won the lottery by moving it down there. I've always said, and I've always believed, that had the case been tried in Dallas, we would have won."

Parks and Huff were in Kerrville in October 1996 for jury selection. Mulder was substituted as counsel on October 21. Darlie Kee says that Parks, Huff, and Tolle chatted in the courtroom about hunting in Kerr County. "It was during *voir dire*. The judge was talking in between interviews with prospective jurors about how he and his wife had been hunting there," Kee says. "They didn't care that I was in the courtroom. I also heard Parks talking about Huff's hunting cabin—or maybe it was a relative's—that saved them hotel fees. Kerr County is a big hunting area."

Whitetail deer season began during jury selection and ended the first Sunday in January, just before the trial started. "I swear, I felt like I was in the Twilight Zone, with the judge and the defense and the prosecutors joking and talking about hunting, and I was there fighting for Darlie's life and for the truth about what happened to my murdered grandsons," says Kee. "A man who ended up being picked for the jury—I will never forget how, under oath, he said he could never sentence anyone to death unless there was an eyewitness. I'm not kidding."

Kenneth Waits, the husband of Darlie Routier's closest friend, Melanie, says he had strongly advised the family not to agree to a change of venue. "I said, 'Whatever you do, don't move the trial. Darin, don't move the trial.' Parks said, 'Yeah, we want a change of venue.' The judge asked, 'Anywhere in the state of Texas?" Parks said, 'Anywhere.'

"Greg Davis literally craned his neck. He said, 'Anywhere?!' He might as well have jumped up and down doing jumping jacks that day whenever they announced they could go anywhere. It was like he had just won the lottery. I mean, literally, that was the look on his face—like he had just won the lottery. That's when I walked out of the courtroom and never had anything to do with them after that."

Kenneth says that Peter Lesser—the defense attorney he had wanted the family to hire—had warned about changing the venue. "Lesser said, 'Don't change the venue. If you do, maybe Houston or somewhere like that. It has to be a big city. It has to be a big city.'" The 2000 US Census put Kerr County's population at just 43,653. By contrast, Dallas County's population was more than 2.2 million.

"I told Darin, 'You're just playing into the state's hands. I just remember Darin sitting there [in the courtroom] almost praying, 'This is the right thing to do. Lord, I know this is right.' Well, if you're looking for signs, you might want to look at the guy who's calling all the shots right. If Darlie had had Lesser, she'd be out on the street. There's no doubt in my mind."

In an obituary for Tolle written by Joe Simnacher for the *Dallas Morning News*, Tolle's widow Tammy denied rumors that her husband had deliberately moved the trial to Kerrville to ensure a guilty verdict or to look for ranch property. Tolle died in September 2007, of complications of frontal temporal dementia. "It [the trial] was put down in Kerrville because it was the only county in Texas that had an opening in its court docket for a trial of that magnitude," Tammy Tolle said, according to Simnacher.

But there are those who challenge that claim. Kee says that she phoned county courthouses throughout the state pretending to be Mulder's assistant, asking about the availability of courtrooms. There were several available from among Texas's 254 counties, she says. "I called El Paso, Galveston, and San Antonio and acted like I worked for Mulder," Kee says. "All three agreed they could do it. Tolle lied. He wanted it in Kerrville."

Richard Mosty, the Kerrville lawyer whom Mulder enlisted to be part of the defense team, says: "I cannot give you a good and valid reason why Kerr County was where the case was tried. Number one, the courthouse was under renovation, so why in the world would somebody move a big trial out of Dallas to a small town where the courthouse was under renovation? We didn't have facilities for the press. We barely had facilities for the lawyers. At that time, there was not [adequate] space at the courthouse. There was the one courtroom. It was just not conducive to a trial with lots of out-of-town witnesses. When you have a case like that, my experience is, you need a motel for the jury, you need a motel for the prosecution team and their witnesses. You need court space. You need court personnel. We obviously don't have the kind of personnel that you have in Dallas.

"It was always told to me that [the venue change] had been decided and when Doug got hired, one of the things [stipulated by the court] was that he wouldn't be substituted in unless we stuck with the current schedule, which was really breakneck speed. Doug's motion for a continuance was denied. There were DNA samples that were coming in just sort of randomly. It took a significant period of time to even get DNA results."

Mulder feels there was no valid reason to move the trial from larger Dallas County, where more liberal jurors likely would have been less inclined to let character judgments determine their verdict. "I think she would have been acquitted, had the trial been held in Dallas. Most of my clients get acquitted. No one has a record of more wins in murder cases than I do. It should have been moved back to Dallas. That would have been in her best interest."

Says Cooper: "Judge Tolle had already announced he wasn't going to run for another term, and the Darlie case ended up in his court and he wanted to keep it. It was *the* reason why this was a June offense and they're picking a goddamn jury in four months on a change of venue—just so he can stay on it. Then, having them go to trial in January—six months—it was unheard of before or since. This is a blood evidence case. This was intricate work."

Attorney Peter Lesser says that Tolle's reputation with the defense bar "was not very good." He adds: "I would have been kicking and screaming not to go to Kerrville. I would rather have waited to let Francis hear the case, then we would maybe have had a reversible error. I would rather have had a novice than an experienced judge. Death is different. We're playing for high stakes here."

Lesser says he would have requested a continuance, but would have raised hell when it was denied. "The judge could have held me in contempt, and then he would get [negative] publicity about a rush to trial," the lawyer said. Lesser states, however, that he is not critical of Mulder, whom he calls "an excellent lawyer." "It's easy to second-guess lawyers in capital cases. In capital cases, [alleged mistakes] become magnified."

There are some who criticize Mulder for a vacation trip to Hawaii that he took after being hired to represent Routier. He says he spent the time preparing for the trial. "It really allowed me to prepare without the distractions that you ordinarily would have if you were in your office daily. That was an advantage, not a disadvantage."

Rick Wardroup, with the Texas Criminal Defense Lawyers Association, said attorneys who handle death penalty cases make "hundreds of decisions on the fly" and do the best they can at the time. He is shocked at how little time Routier's trial defense team had to prepare. "It is incredible to me that Ms. Routier was tried in such a short period," he says. "We tell trial teams all the time that they shouldn't go to trial in anything under eighteen months."

Legal ethics expert Keith Hampton says the problem with requesting a change of venue is that defense attorneys don't get to pick the location—the judge does. "Here's the remedy, though," he says. "There should have been an objection when he picked Kerr County. I will tell you that Kerr County is so infamous that judges all around the state—it happens today, but it was very common back in the '90s—would look at you and smile and say, 'You really want to go to Kerrville?' to make you back off your motion."

A strange and tragic twist of fate would befall Tolle's family after his death, ten years after the trial in Kerrville. Police say Tolle's daughter, Jeanmarie Geis, shot and killed herself just days after reporting three alleged incidents that involved a robbery, a home invasion, and her own abduction and subsequent escape. Geis told dubious officers she believed she was being targeted because of her father's role in the Darlie Routier case. Authorities say that before turning the gun on herself, Geis, a blonde with breast implants, shot to death her adopted children, ages eight and four.

CHAPTER 23

A Hand to Hold

"Guilty."

The pronouncement from Judge Mark Tolle reverberated through the courtroom. Sandy Aitken locked eyes with lead prosecutor Greg Davis. Danelle, Darlie Routier's thirteen-year-old sister, screamed and wept, as did Sherry Moses's twelve-year-old daughter, Shana. "You're going to burn in hell for lying!" the girls shouted at the man who had led the state's charge.

But to the twelve-member jury—and to most of those in the court-room—Greg Davis was not a liar, but a man who had spoken the truth, bringing justice for Devon and Damon Routier. The state had won its case, and it did so through the testimony of investigators, police officers, medical and forensic experts, and others.

Even though her daughter's signal from a second floor window of the courthouse had given her forewarning, the verdict was nevertheless a knife through the heart for Darlie Kee. She refused, though, to let them see her cry. In the courtroom's circus-like atmosphere, Kee glimpsed authors Barbara Davis and Patricia Springer turning to look at her, no doubt for the purpose of describing her reaction in the books they were writing. Holding her head high, Kee gave the women no fodder for their colorful prose.

For LuAnn Mauk Black, everything seemed to be happening in slow motion: the expressions of shock and disbelief washing over the family; the stares of those who believed Darlie to be guilty; a tearful Richard Mosty supporting Darin when Darin's legs collapsed from under him. As she stood numb, LuAnn felt a tug on her hand. Her sister Darlie began pulling her toward the courtroom door. "Just keep holding my hand," Darlie Kee said. With Kee leading the way, LuAnn, their sister Sherry, and the rest of the family fled from the courtroom and down flights of stairs, bursting through a door into the February air.

Kee wanted to get her family out of the courthouse that was as dead cold, in her view, as the hearts of the people who had taken her daughter and the killer who had taken her grandchildren. She recalls: "They had extra bailiffs in the courtroom, like we were going to kidnap Darlie. We were all on Paxil, a strong antidepressant. Darlie was sobbing the moment she came into the courtroom, because she had heard Sandra Halsey coming down the hall saying, 'We got a guilty verdict.' I can't believe that woman did that."

As television and print reporters scrambled to report on the verdict, the devastated family headed to Mosty's office to confer with the defense team about the punishment phase of the trial. Even there, they were not safe from the media. A newspaper reporter scaled a fence in hopes of getting quotes. What he got for his effort were quotes that were unprintable.

"He had been at the prayer service at the cemetery, and Mulder should have put his ass on the stand," Kee says. "I called him every bad name in the book. He later took a reporting job in New York. Years later, Stephen Cooper sent me an article about [the reporter] having been punched in the mouth by someone. It made our day. I think [the reporter] knew she was innocent, but he wouldn't help her, not even if it meant her life. I have nothing but contempt for people who are cowards."

Although the thought of Darlie being sent to death row was heartbreaking, the family believed a death sentence might be better than a life sentence spent in general population. Those convicted of crimes against children oftentimes are targeted for violence by other inmates. Later, when the jury imposed a death sentence upon Darlie, the family viewed that as God's way of protecting her.

"It was an emotional roller coaster," says Sherry Moses of the weeks spent in Kerrville. The family stayed together in a rented condominium. At times, Sarilda Routier stayed there as well. "Darlie, LuAnn, and I would kneel at the bed every night and pray together," Sherry says.

Recalls LuAnn: "The trial was like a nightmare you couldn't wake up from. We'd hear about people [allegedly] lying on the stand, and we couldn't say anything. When I testified, Norm Kinne and his wife sat there making faces at me. I had never been through anything like this in my life. I was so scared and nervous and the judge kept saying, 'You have to speak louder. You have to speak louder.' He wasn't very nice. And Norm Kinne and his wife would lean to the side and snarl and make faces. The judge would have to have seen that because he was sitting not far from me."

It wasn't the only shocking behavior the family claims to have witnessed. Says Sherry: "I was surprised that jurors were allowed to be out talking amongst each other and to other people. We'd actually run into them at restaurants. They'd be talking about the case with other people. We heard them in bathrooms [at the courthouse]. I was just flabbergasted that they weren't sequestered. It was just crazy."

Sandy Aitken claims that, during one break in the proceedings, a female juror was talking on a phone just feet from where Greg Davis was being interviewed by reporters. "She looked at me and asked, 'Am I supposed to be hearing this?' And I said, 'No, you're not,'" Sandy says. Sandy and others kept trying to get Davis's attention by saying, "Juror in the room! Juror in the room!" "But he just kept on talking," Sandy says.

The family felt as if everywhere they turned, there was judgment and hostility. "It was like, no matter what we did, the media tore at us. Darlie, LuAnn and I, the kids and Sarilda, we were sitting on the courthouse steps singing. We were praying and singing hymns. And somebody wrote that we were chanting and speaking in tongues," said Sherry. "We're just Christians, and we were singing regular hymns. That's what helped us get through it. You go in there believing the truth is going to set you free, but it was never about the truth in that trial—ever. It was a competition."

Relates LuAnn: "The trial was like a big act. It was just about winning, and that was it. And it didn't matter what you said. If you spoke from the heart, they would slam you and twist your words. We knew her. We *knew* her. They said she was this person that she wasn't. You go away from that trial thinking you can't trust policemen, you can't trust attorneys, you can't trust judges, you can't trust the system. That's how it was for me."

Darlie's conviction and death sentence has had a lasting impact on the family. For years, Darlie Kee has suffered from sleep difficulties and depression. She has been through a host of medications and dosage adjustments. Even during good times when the family shares laughter, Kee's sisters always see the sadness return to her eyes when the laughter stops.

Family members are concerned for Darlie's younger sister, Dana, who was just sixteen when she handed her sister a can of Silly String at Rest Haven Memorial Park. Dana has little contact with her older sister, and did not join her family members and members of the Routier family when they traveled

Refusing to be silent: Sarilda Routier stands on the steps of the Capitol in Austin to address a crowd gathered for the 2012 March to Abolish the Death Penalty. The family of Darin Routier, as well as Darlie's family members, continue to proclaim her innocence. *Photo by the author.*

to Austin in the fall of 2012 for the annual March to Abolish the Death Penalty. The reason Dana has pulled away is not because she believes her sister is guilty, family members say, but because she simply cannot cope with her feelings that she is responsible for her sister being on death row.

"I really worry about Dana," Sherry says. "She feels so much guilt because of the Silly String. Nobody in the family blames her for that, but she blames herself. She loved those boys and she was just doing what would have made them happy. She has distanced herself from everything."

LuAnn deals with her own self-blame. "I still think that I'm the one who gave her gum that day in the car. I was riding with them in Darlie's green Pathfinder. She was asking if anybody had a mint because of the bad taste in her mouth." The bad taste Darlie complained of might have been because of medication family members claim she was taking—dosages that were beyond the prescribed amount, or which had been prescribed to others.

The three sisters laugh at the memory of when an investigator for the Dallas County DA's office flew to Altoona before the trial to interview family members at Sherry's house. He sat in a chair at the kitchen table. "The chairs—you could lean back, but if you leaned too hard, you could almost fall," chuckles LuAnn. "And that's what happened. He almost fell on his butt. It was hysterical because he thought he was so cool and so tough. It couldn't have happened to a better person. It wasn't intentional. It just happened."

After the trial, the media went on to cover other stories and the lawyers focused on other cases. But for the family of Darlie Routier, there was no such thing as moving on. Sherry says: "After the trial, it was really bad. You just felt so weighted, like you couldn't breathe. I was in such depression, I slept for a week. I would feel guilty and start to cry whenever I would feel joy—like I just didn't have the right to feel happiness."

It was the same with LuAnn. "I worked at a bank. When I went back to work, I would be sitting there in my little cubicle and just crying and crying. It has never been the same. And it's so much worse for Darlie because that's her daughter. To this day, I hate to go into a courtroom. It makes me nervous and sick when I see a jury box."

Despite 6-6-6 and its aftermath, the close-knit sisters have held onto their faith. "If anything, it has brought me closer to Him," explains LuAnn. "I have depended more on God than ever before. Darlie [Kee], I know she has gone through times when she's mad at God, and I can understand. I mean, it's been so many years. It's okay to ask God why. He sees the big picture; we don't."

For Darlie Kee, her faith, her family, and her hometown of Altoona have offered respite as the fight to reclaim her daughter has gone on year after year. She makes regular trips to Altoona, where much of her family has continued to live. The scenic city, with its population of just under fifty thousand, is located at the base of Brush Mountain. The community was founded by the Pennsylvania Railroad in 1849, and flourished when the Civil War brought a demand for locomotives.

As far as LuAnn can tell, she has been permanently excused from jury duty in her hometown. She has never been asked to serve on a panel since she wrote a letter to the Blair County courts explaining why she has lost all faith in the justice system. Her letter detailed a different type of railroad than one typically thought of in Altoona.

CHAPTER 24

Hindsight

It is a foggy, drizzly day in late February when I pull up to the visitors parking area by one of the guard towers at Mountain View. For this interview, possibly our last, I intend to discreetly take note of Darlie Routier's body language and eye contact. Melanie Waits had said Routier's hands shake. It was something I had not noticed before, probably because of the barrier between me and the death-row inmate. Waits's remark makes me wonder what else I might have missed.

Inside the visitation room, Routier is seated in the same spot where she had been the first time I came here. After we greet each other, she tells me that, just twenty-four hours earlier, the US Supreme Court had denied Lisa Coleman's appeals. This means the state will soon set an execution date. Coleman heard the news by listening to the radio in her cell.

I have brought with me a list of topics to discuss, hoping a cheat sheet will help make the most of our brief time together. Media interviews, according to prison rules, can last only one hour. Sometimes the guards allow them to run longer, but you just never know.

We talk again about the night Devon and Damon were killed, when life was forever changed for Routier and her family. "I've been thinking about that whole night. It's really been heavy on me lately," she says. "After I had already been convicted and I had gotten a whole stack of crime scene photos, I noticed something strange about the front door. It had a real nice doorknob and a little key hole and a bolt to lock it. Everywhere I touched was bloody because I was bleeding so badly. I had opened the door and screamed for Karen [Neal, a neighbor across the street]. You can see my blood on the doorknob, on the light switch, on the phone—everywhere. But it was not on that bolt to open the door."

Though prosecutors might claim she had gone out the front door to deposit the bloodstained sock down the alley before inflicting injuries upon herself, it could be argued that Routier likely would have left blood on the bolt if she had been the one who had attacked the boys. Darin Routier said he had locked the front door before going to bed that night. The Routiers kept a spare key inside a ceramic frog on the front porch. Although neighbor William Gorsuch and Officer David Waddell would testify they saw Darin near the front door, it apparently was Darlie who first opened that door. During the almost six-minute 911 call, while Darin was administering CPR to Devon, she opened the front door and screamed for her neighbor, who was a nurse.

"That door was already [unlocked]," Routier says. "It had to have been because I could not have opened that door without turning the bolt. I didn't even think about it until I went back and started looking through the pictures. I was hysterical. It never registered to me until a year and a half later when I started going through all those pictures. That got me to thinking: What if the guy that Waddell saw was about to go out? There was a huge room right beside the door and it was dark in there. When I started screaming for Darin, he could have gone there."

Waddell had testified he saw Darin by the front door when he pulled up in his squad car. Neighbor William Gorsuch testified he had been semi-awakened by an unidentifiable noise, then became fully awake when he heard Darin shouting that someone had stabbed his children. He said he looked out the window and saw Darin dressed in jeans near the fountain in the front yard. A police car was by the curb, facing west, he said, and a police officer was walking toward Darin.

"You can hear Darin when Waddell walks in," Routier says. "The more I think about it and put all the facts, all the pieces, together, it makes perfect sense. I know I saw one leave through the utility room. I know that because I saw that with my own eyes."

But could there have been two intruders—one of whom went through the utility room to the garage, while the other hid in the dark living room or dining room near the front door when Darlie began screaming? Or could the man Routier saw walking toward the utility room have circled around to the front of the house when she turned to tell Damon to stay back?

"I don't remember going to the front door, to be honest with you," Darin told me at the Starbucks in Lubbock. "I never said I went to the front door, that I can remember. I went to the Neals' house after the cops had already arrived."

Former FBI special agent Lloyd Harrell believes there was so much chaos during those minutes that it is not surprising there are differing accounts from those involved. The mind, he says, oftentimes "sees" what it wants or expects to see. He has wondered whether Darin thought he saw a police officer in the entryway because that was who he expected to see, since he knew help was on the way. And he has considered the possibility that Waddell may have unwittingly let the perpetrator slip away because he had not expected to see the attacker walk out the front door. Harrell has wondered whether, in the seconds when Waddell parked his squad car and got out of the vehicle, the intruder slipped around the side of the house and Darin came out the front door. In the midst of the chaos and the rush of adrenalin, neither may have realized that they had seen the intruder.

The possibility that the intruder, or one of the intruders, was still in the house when all hell broke loose is one that Harrell had considered in the weeks leading up to Routier's trial. In an e-mail exchange after my visit with Routier, he wrote: "I posed this scenario in a 12/21 [December 21, 1996] memo after reviewing the various reports and testimonies prior to trial, noting their obvious inconsistencies."

His memo from that time states: "It would appear to me that Darin saw a man in the hallway who he thought was a police officer. . . . Darin was tending to Devon and shortly after the man in the hallway appeared, much confusion begins to occur. Darin is pissed off because he thinks the cop is not doing anything. He runs out to get help, and then Waddell drives up and sees him. The only conclusion is that Waddell is telling the truth, and so is Darin. Darin, expecting to see a cop, sees the intruder who is still in the house. He leaves via the front door, explaining the inconsistencies of the police. The light in the back yard does not come on because the intruder leaves via the front door.

"Darlie turns her back on the [utility room] and the guy goes into the living room. No one checks out the front room. Waddell comes and sees Darin, and they both go into the house. Darin does not realize Waddell is the first cop on the scene. . . . Waddell is confused, as is Darin. . . . The problem is the cops, knowing there were inconsistencies, never looked further. They knew the inconsistencies were a problem, but they did not consider that Darin had seen the intruder.

"Darin is convinced to this day the first person he saw was a cop. He was expecting a cop, and that is what he believes he saw. But it is possible that what Darin saw was the intruder. It's possible that the intruder heard the cops coming from the Dalrock side of the house [a major road], and ran around the house down the alley, dropping evidence on the way. He did not leave blood

Appellate team lawyer Lauren Schmidt
of Colorado. *Photo courtesy Lauren Schmidt.*

or hair or marks in the backyard, as he did not leave that way. The cops just blew it because they did not question Darin with sufficient specificity to figure out what he had seen." Harrell's theory that the intruder could hear sirens approaching via Dalrock Road could explain why he may have fled down the alley, rather than toward the main road, which leads to Interstate 30. The alleged intruder's flight down the alley instead of toward the main road is one of the things that caused some to doubt Routier's story of an intruder.

The state claims no evidence was found to indicate the presence of an intruder. However, a piece of evidence that might prove an intruder's presence that night is a bloody partial fingerprint taken from a glass sofa table between the family room where the attacks occurred and the kitchen where Darlie claims the intruder fled. The person who left the print had to have done so while the blood was still wet. At trial, crime scene investigator James Cron testified that he could not make a positive identification of the bloody fingerprint, but that it was "small" and "consistent with having been left by a five- or six-year-old child."

According to appellate team member Lauren Schmidt, the state changed its argument about the fingerprint in the postconviction proceedings. Richard

Jantz, a renowned forensic anthropologist, stated in an affidavit for the defense that the fingerprint belonged to an unidentified adult. "The state's new fingerprint expert then said that he excluded every adult who was present at the crime scene, except for Darlie," says Schmidt, a lawyer in Colorado. However, Robert Lohnes, a latent print consultant obtained by ABC News, stated in a January 2003 affidavit that his examination of State's Evidence 85-J showed that Darlie was not the source of the print. "Based on the evidence in the record now, the print was made by an unknown adult," says Schmidt.

Schmidt says there is debate as to whether the print is clear enough for an identification to be made. The easiest way to test the print, she says, would be to run it through the Federal Bureau of Investigation's Integrated Automated Fingerprint Identification System (IAFIS). "This has been a Herculean effort. Law enforcement has to make the request; the defense can't do it. The state has so far refused to do it. In November 2008, the federal court for the Western District of Texas granted the defense's request to test 85-J and some additional fingerprints in IAFIS. The state asked the FBI to run the prints, and the FBI responded that the request did not comply with FBI protocol, and the Texas Department of Public Safety should do it. To date, the print hasn't been tested. I have no doubt if this were a law enforcement effort, it would have been done immediately. But for the defense, it takes years of battling."

In our interview at Mountain View, Routier continues with what she remembers of that night: "I've told them [police and attorneys] this from the beginning, when we've gone through everything about that night. I remember a weight around my legs. I just remember a real heaviness. My panties were gone. I didn't even realize that until they took me to the ambulance. It's been a question, but there has never been an answer to it. They [Baylor officials] said they didn't actually do a rape kit, that it was just a visual."

Darin told me hypnosis was performed on Darlie after she had been convicted. He said she once again stated she had felt something heavy on her legs. And he said something else: the hypnosis indicated she may have witnessed Devon being stabbed as she was being held down. If true, this would mean there had to have been two intruders. Routier's lawyers have raised the possibility of traumatic amnesia to explain her confusion. Harrell, however, is more inclined to believe she had been rendered unconscious. The mind's tendency to try to fill in memory gaps might explain at least some of the variations in her story, he says. Also, she may have claimed having struggled with the intruder, not because she had a clear memory of having done so, but because the severe bruising on her arms indicated that there had been a struggle. Harrell also believes that possible theories presented to her by family members and others might have influenced her. Against advice from her lead defense attorney, Doug Mulder, Darlie wrote letters to friends and family members from jail, making claims that were used against her at trial. For instance, she accused Glenn Mize of being the perpetrator. Mize was the stepfather of a friend of the Routiers' teenaged babysitter.

Mulder says he warned Darlie about putting such thoughts in writing and advised her to send him the messages to forward on to others, since there was attorney-client privilege. "The letters were self-destructive," Mulder says. "I had cautioned her about that, and she knew they read her mail. I said, 'Hey, if you're going to write letters, send everything to *me*.' And she didn't, and that came back to haunt her, big time." On the stand, Darlie became angered when questioned about the letters by coprosecutor Toby Shook, asking him whether his reading of her mail was illegal. By some accounts, the jury did not seem to take it favorably when she bowed up to the prosecutor.

I ask Routier if she regrets speaking so freely to police without a lawyer. "Knowing everything I know now, I would tell anybody to get legal representation, even if [police] just want to question you. I would always have legal representation. If you know you're guilty of something and they're bringing you in to question you, I would think you would know to 'lawyer up' right away. But for me and Darin, that wasn't even a thought. Now, it's something I would think about. Now I tell everybody I know."

She talks about the lengthy interrogation by Bill Parker, without a lawyer present, just before she was booked on murder charges. "His style was more calm. He talked to me about the different pieces of evidence, but not in a way, like, 'You did this.' He was just casually talking about things. At some point— and this is what made me realize they were thinking that I had done this— he started talking about if you've ever been somewhere and had too much to drink, maybe you passed out and don't remember what you did—in other words, you could have done this and not remembered. But it was in a long, drawn-out type story. I said, 'But what about the man? I saw a man leaving my home. I know that just as sure as I know you're sitting there.' I said, 'I did not murder my children.'

"He goes and gets me a glass of water and that just went on and on and on like that. I guess he was trying to get me to say [I had done it]. Finally, after however many hours it was, I could tell they weren't believing me. It's like they were trying to convince me what they wanted me to say. Finally, I said, 'I want an attorney.' He left and came back with the arrest warrant and started reading it. I was just crying. I think I was in so much shock. I was still in shock over losing my children. I hadn't even dealt with *that* yet."

Parker testified at trial that he had made no audio or video recordings of the lengthy interrogation. He claimed he told Routier up to a dozen times that he believed she had killed her children and she never denied it. "She always had the same response: 'If I did it, I don't remember,'" he said on the stand. "One occasion, she just didn't respond at all. She just shrugged her shoulders." Routier claims she never made the statement. She also denies Parker's assertion that he had informed her at the outset of the interrogation that she was under arrest. Harrell believes Routier would have immediately demanded an attorney and refused to answer questions if she had been told she was under arrest.

At the time Routier talked with me about her interrogation by Parker, the Innocence Project of Texas was making plans for the upcoming 84th Legislature. The group determined it would push for a bill mandating that all custodial law enforcement interrogations be recorded. A bill calling for audio or audiovisual recordings of custodial interrogations had been sponsored by State Senator Rodney Ellis (D-Houston) and State Representative Terry Canales (D-Edinburgh) in the 83rd Legislature, but the measure failed to pass. The American Bar Association recommended recording all custodial interrogations in its 2013 report *Evaluating Fairness and Accuracy in State Death Penalty Systems: The Texas Capital Punishment Assessment Report*.

After discussing the interrogation by Parker, I ask Routier what her thoughts are today about the Silly String footage. "Judge me all you want to," she says, meaning the public in general. "The last thing I would do if [guilty] would be to go and spray Silly String so that there would be all this attention on me. It doesn't fit."

Routier says she has received letters in prison from sympathetic people who detailed unusual ways that they, too, have grieved a loved one. I tell her about a reality TV show called "Best Funeral Ever" that had debuted a year earlier. The focus of the show is the Golden Gate Funeral Home, where staffers help grieving families honor their dearly departed in bizarre ways. Golden Gate Funeral Home is in Dallas. "That whole thing was just completely misconstrued," Routier says of the June 1996 incident. "The Silly String was done in memory of Devon and Damon. They loved playing with it. To me, that was a gesture of love."

I tell her about my interview with Dallas County District Attorney Craig Watkins, and that he and those in his office believe she is guilty. I wonder if Darlie's polygraph examination had anything to do with it. A polygraph was administered to Routier when she was represented by court-appointed attorneys Parks and Huff. The results were not made public, which led the media to believe she must have failed it. Darlie acknowledged to Jerry Palace and Reggie Britt of the television series *The Wrong Man?* that the results were "inconclusive." I relay Harrell's theory about polygraphs administered to mothers of dead or missing children, and his suspicion that Watkins may have relied largely on the polygraph when he determined that the jury's verdict was correct. Harrell told me of two cases he worked involving missing children. He believed that neither mother had any knowledge of what had happened to their children, yet both were judged to be "deceptive" when polygraph tests were administered. Harrell believes that in cases involving missing or murdered children, polygraphs administered to their mothers might show them to be deceptive, or the results might be inconclusive, because many mothers feel somehow responsible for not having protected their children. In Darlie's case, feelings of guilt might be compounded by the fact that her children were just inches or feet away from her when the fatal attacks occurred. In addition, questions posed to her about Darin's possible involvement also might have skewed the results, he said.

In response, Routier says she not only feels guilty about not having prevented her children's deaths; she also harbors survivor guilt. "When I was in the ER, I remember the doctor coming in before they took me to surgery and he was asking about Damon, his age or something like that. And I thought that he was still alive and I was excited," she says. "I kept saying, 'Is he going to be okay?' And nobody would answer me." Her eyes well up, and her voice breaks. I notice that Waits is correct. Routier's hands do shake. "I guess there was part of me that knew then, even though nobody would answer me, that he was dead."

Before going on, Routier breaks eye contact. "There's other things, too, because at that time, there were some things that I had been told about Darin . . . and I don't really want to get into all that. . . . Some things that were being said to me about Darin by my defense team [Parks and Huff] . . . and, of course, I wasn't [willing to hear] that. But you're still hearing it and you're thinking about it. I know that the one thing that they kept asking me a lot, [including] the police, they asked me several times about Darin. A lot has come out since then.... Do I think Darin had anything to do with it? No, I don't. But is there a part of me that questions some of the things that have been brought to me because of his involvement with other people and the kind of people that they are? Could they have had something to do with it? Of course, I've wondered...."

One of those associates was Barry Fife, who owned an auto shop in Rowlett. It has been rumored that Darin solicited his help in staging the burglary. When Fife was confronted by investigators Palace and Britt—and a camera crew for *The Wrong Man?* series—he denied any involvement and said he believes that Darin "snapped" and committed the crime himself. When I watched the footage, I wondered whether Fife was sending a message to Darin that he'd best keep his mouth shut.

As Darlie's eyes avoid mine, I think about the anger she may feel toward Darin, the fear she may hold for the safety of her surviving son, and a letter she wrote to Sandy Aitken, dated July 11, 2000—three and a half years after her conviction. "Darin knows the marriage is over," she had written. I file away these thoughts as Routier continues: "These are things you go through, you think about, because you want answers. I've done this to myself for almost eighteen years now.... When all this stuff started coming out about [Darin's associates] and all those scams that they were doing.... If you stop and look at the actual evidence, it doesn't fit." When she says "it doesn't fit," she is referring to the state's claims that it was she who committed the crime.

The voice of the female guard at the far end of the room interrupts the interview. We have gone "way over" our time limit. However, she readily agrees when I request five more minutes to wrap up. When I look back at Routier, her eyes have filled with tears.

"It's been seventeen and a half, eighteen years, and I'm still sitting here," she says. "Have you ever been in a situation where you're telling the truth about something and it doesn't matter because people just don't believe you? I'm tired. But we just have to, I don't know, somehow believe that [the truth] will come out. I don't know how. I don't know when. But it just feels like it has to. It's just too big of a wrong not to be corrected. So, we'll just keep on fighting and try to be strong, even though I don't feel like it all the time. But God is faithful."

With that, she gets up from the chair and walks to the guard, who is just beyond my line of sight. The guard tells me that someone will be coming to escort me out. As I stand waiting, I hear the guard say, "Okay, let's get this over with." Since I continue to hear both Routier's voice and the guard's for a couple more minutes, I assume that Routier is being strip-searched before being taken back to her cell. It is a daily occurrence.

Within a few minutes, another guard comes for me. She is friendly and makes small talk as we walk out of the building and into the gray drizzle. The guard comments that she is tired of the long, cold winter. But surely it can't last forever, I tell her.

CHAPTER 25

Aunt Sandy's Letters

Twenty-two months after my visit to Aunt Sandy's house to examine her handwritten notes from the trial, I return—this time to read some of the approximately two hundred letters she received from Darlie from 1996, after her arrest, to sometime in 2000. Robert, who has heart problems, has been in ill health. He appears frail, and thinner than when I last saw him. Sandy is convinced prayer extended his life when heart surgeons saw no hope.

It is a Saturday. As Robert watches sports on TV, Sandy and I settle in at the kitchen table. The sun is out, but a text message from the National Weather Service alerts us that scattered thunderstorms are in the area. At times, we hear claps of thunder. Throughout the afternoon, the lights in the chandelier over the table blink on and off.

On the table is a large plastic tub full of letters. Other letters, sitting in piles, have yellow Post-it notes stuck to them with Sandy's handwritten annotations about their subject matter. Another large tub filled with letters is on the kitchen island. Before we start delving into them, we talk again about how Sandy and Darlie became close after Darlie's arrest. Sandy feels she had not been at her best on our first visit because she had buried her father just twenty-four hours earlier. Our discussion of Darlie includes Sandy's explanation of why the letters between the two stopped abruptly in 2000.

Prior to June 6, 1996, Sandy had only seen Darlie once. It was after the funeral of Darin's grandfather, who was Sandy's former father-in-law. Sandy would lose two husbands to premature death before marrying Robert. "She and Darin were there and all the teenagers had gotten into the swimming pool," Sandy recalls. "I had not spoken to her. The first time I really saw her was the night we did the visitation with the boys at the funeral home. She was by the casket, sitting in a chair and there were people around her. I just patted her on the back and moved on."

After Darlie's arrest, Darin phoned his aunt. As they began talking, Sandy was struck by a conviction. "I felt the Lord said three things just as plain as day to my heart. He said: 'I want you to love her and I want you to support her and I want you to stand by her.' So I wrote her a letter and gave her my phone number. She was in the Dallas jail. It was some time before she called. It was a Sunday afternoon."

When she answered the phone, Sandy was startled to hear a voice asking if she would accept a collect call. Then she realized it was Darlie calling from jail. She accepted the call. "She called back and forth for like an hour and a half that day. [The phone calls] will only go for a certain amount of time, and she kept calling back. I remember walking all over the house saying, 'God, tell me what to say.'" Sandy kept reassuring Darlie that God was in control. "She just clung to me," Sandy says.

The closeness between the two that grew through phone calls, letters, and visits at the Lew Sterrett Justice Center raised red flags on both sides of Darlie's family. "Darlie Kee and I had an immense amount of trouble because she was like, 'That's my daughter. Why is she talking to *you?*' Richard Mosty said he believed the reason was because I was just a slice away." In other words—family, but not close family. Sandy believes Darlie felt she could confide in her more than in other family members who might try to control her.

Sandy says it was during a jail visit that Darlie whispered to her that she had asked Darin for a divorce just hours before she was attacked and the boys were killed. Darlie put her face close to the glass and mouthed the words, speaking softly in case other ears were listening, she says. "I go, '*What?!*' And she said, 'You know, I'm just tired of the Daisy Duke outfits he wants me to wear.'"

Sandy says Darlie told her it was not the first time she had asked for a divorce. The times before, Darin would threaten in front of the boys to harm himself. Sandy asked Darlie how Darin had reacted that night when she again brought up the subject of ending the marriage. "She said, 'Oh, he just went upstairs and went to bed.' He had a totally different reaction that night. I think [the divorce] has been a whole big let's-keep-everything-a-big-secret from day one."

Sandy suspects the family was so sure Darlie would be acquitted that they tried to hide certain things—such as discord in the marriage—in an effort to keep the family's dirty laundry out of public view. "I think they thought 'There's no evidence that she did this, so let's cover up all our secrets because, in the end, she's going to come out [of jail].' She trusted me, and that's when she started telling me things."

Of the alleged divorce discussions between Darin and Darlie, Sandy says: "He was putting a lot of pressure on her to be the little Daisy Duke girl that he liked. She didn't feel comfortable with that any more. She was outgrowing that because she was the mother of their little boys and the boys were getting older and she didn't want to walk around with everything hanging out and shorts up to here, and Darin was still into that. That was one of the things they fought about. She didn't want to be like that. She said that it had become a real issue with them."

Darlie told Sandy her jewelry was lying out on a countertop that night because she had shown it to a girlfriend. But Sandy wonders if Darin was planning a break-in and told Darlie about it, which led her to again ask for a divorce. "She never said that to me; that's just my thinking," Sandy says. "I think maybe he said, 'Okay, I won't do it.' But I think it's funny because her precious jewelry was always upstairs." She notes that the couple had gotten behind on mortgage payments and she believes the two fought "a lot" about Darin's methods of coming up with quick cash.

Sandy says Darlie was medicated all the way through the trial, and that her letters in the months after her conviction indicate she was coming out of her altered state. "All of a sudden, the message in her letters was 'I'm thinking clearer. I'm thinking clearer.' These letters are extremely painful to me. Who knows the pressure her family was putting on her?"

When Sandy got Brian Pardo involved in the case and he came to believe Darin was connected to the crime, Darlie became angry along with other family members. The turmoil caused Sandy to feel a great deal of stress, as did Darlie's correspondence with other men who were writing to her in prison. Darin, she says, found out about it, and was upset that she was writing letters to other men.

"My mother was dying of Alzheimer's in Houston. My daughter had premature triplets. And I thought, maybe it's time I start taking care of my own family. Finally, one day I was in church and there was an altar call. I prayed and said, 'God, I'm asking you to please release me because I don't think I can go any farther.' You know, God sometimes asks you to do something just for a season." Sandy says that after she prayed, she immediately felt as if a weight had been lifted. She never sent Darlie another letter, and never again received one from her. From that day forward, Sandy no longer felt wrapped up in the case involving her nephew's wife—until the day her cell phone rang while she was in Walmart.

* * *

Darlie's letters are full of recurring themes: faith in God, pleas for God's help, love for her children, and claims that it was an intruder who killed Devon and Damon. In several letters, Darlie expresses guilt and remorse for not having stopped the man and for not being able to describe his face. In a letter dated August 22, 1996, she describes her questioning by Rowlett detectives after her surgery and then, later, by Bill Parker:

"I just kept crying and I hurt all over and so they gave me a shot of Demerol pain medicine and then I remember the detectives coming in and asking me all kinds of questions & I was telling them about the man and they kept saying was his hair like Darin's and was he Darin's height and it scared me that they thought it was Darin and I told them it didn't look like Darin & that he [Darin] came from upstairs and it was like they didn't listen to what I was saying and I started crying and the nurses made them leave.

"Aunt Sandy, I was in shock, traumatized, and recovering from surgery and they want to question me—what kind of detectives *are* these? Sounds to me like they had their minds made up from the beginning. I really don't understand what they all expect—I just saw my children die in front of me and watched the man that did it walk out the door! I hated myself for not going after him. I should have been more brave but I was afraid and wasn't sure what to do. . . .

"The worst part that they did to me was try to convince me that during my sleep I woke up, blacked out, murdered my children, tried to cut my own head off, and then went back to sleep! And then when I said to him, 'Have people really done that before?' he said sure they do and had, and I said I know I saw a man walk out my kitchen. I'm not crazy and I said I didn't kill my babies and he said well, we don't think that's what happened anyway. We think you just killed them because you were tired of them, and I told him he was sick.

"I had a bad dream last night. The boys were alive and with me & Darin but the police were still trying to say that I killed them & all my relatives were there and they were saying I was going to be put to death & I kept saying we have to find this man and then I woke up. God has to allow this nightmare to end. I know I must say the same things over and over, but I just feel so helpless at times. . . . Aunt Sandy, I dream of holding Drake again, the only thing that mattered to me were my babies—none of this makes any sense and I don't understand why they believe a mother would do this to her children. I really don't understand this world anymore."

The letters contain hints of childlike naïveté, such as references to the state having "pooh-pooh" on its hands. One message dryly states: "I guess the man should have left his business card for them." Sandy chuckles over a card featuring a handsome, muscular man in a swimming pool, his chin resting on his arms on the side of the pool. "This man comes fully equipped to make all your fondest dreams come true," it says. The message inside the card reads: "He drives a hot-fudge delivery truck!" The handwritten note inside is a stark contrast to the card's humorous printed message: "Please promise me if something happens and I am executed that Drake will know the truth and know I did not murder Devon and Damon or attack myself!"

On her first Christmas Day behind bars, Darlie wrote about finding out that Barbara "Basia" Jovell, a Testnec employee who had been the maid of honor at her wedding, was going to testify for the state. Jovell testified that Darlie had planned suicide and had become increasingly materialistic. "It hurts me so much to know that I helped her a lot in all the 8 years that I knew her," Darlie wrote. "I had been wanting to fire her for almost 2 years now. She took advantage of our friendship and we put up with it because we felt sorry for her."

The letters contain clues indicating truth about some of the things I had been told, such as Kee's claims that several courthouses, including the one in San Antonio, would have been available for the trial. In one letter written prior to the trial, Darlie wrote, "I think maybe we might get to try this in San Antonio! That would be much better than Kerrville, from what I understand." Another letter confirms the intimacy and trust Sandy says had developed between Darlie and her: "You know I consider you a mother to me in my heart."

In a message dated July 15, 1996, Darlie says she received a letter from a death-row inmate named Michael Blair. He told her he was innocent of the 1993 murder of seven-year-old Ashley Estell, who was abducted from a park in the Dallas suburb of Plano. Years later, Blair's sentence was vacated and the charges against him dropped when it was determined that he was innocent of the crime.

In October 1996, when the family was trying to replace the court-appointed attorneys with Mulder, Darlie wrote: "Mulder needs more money, so we are all trying to come up with more. Oh God, please help us. We need Mulder. We only get one chance at this fight, that's it. . . . I want to have more children and I want to be a grandmother some day. Aunt Sandy, I promise you that I didn't do this and I need for this to end. I can only take so much. I didn't do anything to deserve this. All I did was go to sleep and I woke up to a nightmare."

Just over a month after her arrival on death row, Darlie wrote: "I am not happy with Mulder at all, but I don't know what to do. Mulder thought because we had so much reasonable doubt we would win and we should have. But Mulder took a lot for granted. There were a lot more witnesses we could have used and there were a lot more things that should have been brought out. It almost makes me wonder about Mulder—maybe I will fire him—but I don't want to lose Hagler for my appeal because he is the best in Texas. I want to keep Mosty as well. How do they put a person to death with no motive, no confession, no eyewitnesses, and no solid evidence? Only in Texas."

Around the first anniversary of the crime and Darlie's arrest, her letters to Aunt Sandy begin to take on a different tone where Darin is concerned. There is this one from June 14, 1997: "Darin said something to me about Drake on our visit and I just can't get it out of my mind. I'm sure Darin told you his 'version' of our talk. Well, he told me if I lose him, I also lose Drake!!! I don't understand how he could say something so terrible. I've lost the two most important people in my life and then for him to tell me I'll lose Drake. . . . He better be careful with what he says. Sometimes you can say things that can never be taken back, and I saw a side to him I will never forget.

"It's hard on us both, but no matter what, I am Drake's mother and I am innocent and I just can't believe Darin could say that to me. You know, they never ask for my opinion about Drake—how to cut his hair, or activities. I'm never told what he's doing, saying, his shoe size, anything. It's like I have no say in anything any more. I can't stand it and Darin doesn't even realize. I just don't understand that anymore. It's pushing me away from him, Aunt Sandy. I'm tired of this. I've already lost so much and now it's getting worse. I didn't think that was possible. Boy, was I wrong. Drake is all I have left. He gives me reason to fight. Sometimes I feel Darin has no idea the hell I'm enduring every day. Does he not realize he could be sitting where I am? It could have been him they went after. I'm not sure he really realizes this."

The next month, on July 7, Darlie wrote: "I worry about Darin and I worry about Drake, yet I can't be out there for them and it really bothers me. It hurts. Everything seems so different now, so distant. I know it's mostly me, but it's just very hard." Darlie then refers to letters exchanged between her and another man. "[He and I] will remain friends and only friends and I can say I didn't do to Darin what he had done to me."

Eight months later came hints of unhappiness with her in-laws, who had obtained custody of Drake shortly after Darlie was arrested: "Darin is Drake's father, end of issue. And if I have to request a visit with Sarilda and Lenny together—I will in a heartbeat. . . . I will be putting an ultimatum about Drake this weekend. Darin needs to plan on getting him back and I will no longer take no for an answer. Drake will be with Darin by his 3rd birthday this year! Period."

Two years later, on March 7, 2000, Darlie wrote this letter: "I haven't seen Darin in three weeks now and he is saying some things I don't believe I will ever forgive him for, not concerning this case, but he's using Drake for manipulation again. He is pissed at me about our relationship—or lack of one, I should say."

Four months later, on July 6, she wrote: "Darin and I had an argument during our visit Saturday night and it was pretty bad. I don't want to hurt him. We've already lost so much, and I can't give him what he wants. It's hard to explain, but it's like every time I see him or think about him, I get upset because he let us down. He slept through someone attacking me and our boys. He didn't protect us. I know it's not really his fault, but I can't help how I feel. Such a big part of me died with my boys. I don't know how to get through these days."

Though Darlie's letters appear to confirm Pardo's suspicion that Darin used Drake as manipulation, her messages never point to his possible guilt in the deaths of Devon and Damon. The letters also bear no hint that she had wanted a divorce—a point I raise with Sandy. She offers two theories that might explain this. One theory is that Darlie became so lonely and frightened after her arrest and conviction that her despair caused her to minimize Darin's faults; the other is that, since her mail is read by prison staffers, she may have been following instructions from the family to steer clear of that topic.

Not all of the handwritten messages by Darlie that are in Sandy's possession are letters. One is a poem she wrote to her dead sons, titled "Mommy, we love you." The poem reads:

I thought of you today, as I always do
I thought of your smile, and your laughter, too

Your little hand, pressed gently in mine
No hurry or rush, no pressing of time
I thought I could hold you forever, but God took you home
to His kingdom in Heaven
There are so many words, I never got to say
So many games and silly things that we never got to play
I saw the rainbow, not just one, but two
I knew it was a gift, from your brother and you
My heart longs for you, and I cry out in pain
Nothing in my life will ever be the same.

At the top of the sheet of paper is this notation: "Double rainbow seen over our home 6-18-96. Most beautiful rainbow I have ever seen." It was written on Darlie Routier's last day of freedom. That night, she was arrested and charged with capital murder.

For Sandy, what happened to Darlie and the actions of those in law enforcement bring to mind Isaiah 5:20: "Woe unto them that call evil good, and good evil." She says she will begin preparing for the storm that will rage once the family finds out she has shared Darlie's secrets. She knows Darlie herself may feel betrayed, but she believes the letters shed light on her true character. I am struck by the fact that Darlie's letters from so long ago are filled with faith in God, even as she was pleading for His help. Even after almost two decades on death row, the faith is still there.

I finally gather my things to leave, having spent six and a half hours talking with Sandy and reading Darlie's letters. It is dusk, and black trees are outlined against a coal sky. Sandy and Robert stand on the front porch as I back out of their driveway and head into the gloom. I have not seen the rooster on this trip, but as I make my way through the spiderweb of country roads, my worries are not for the barnyard fowl with wanderlust. I fear that soon Sandy may be traversing her own perilous terrain.

CHAPTER 26

Bent

Barbara Davis was not the only author who attended the trial in Kerrville. Don Davis (no relation) was there as well. In his author's notes for *Hush Little Babies*, Don Davis stated that prosecutors "played to fear and emotion." He criticized prosecutors for focusing on things that had more to do with character judgments than criminal culpability.

"So when prosecutors had Darlie admit she didn't regularly go to church, watched male strippers on Mother's Day, bought jewelry at a pawn shop, and let her kids listen to African American rap music, the jurors were jolted, although none of that had anything to do with murder." The rap music in question was Coolio's "Gangsta's Paradise"—a song that was played at the funeral of the Routier boys because it was their favorite song. Davis wrote that repeated mentions of the rap song, which contains no obscenities and calls for an end to gang violence, smacked of racial prejudice.

The work of the Rowlett police was "very questionable," the author wrote, with photos not being logged and documents and rags collected "seemingly at random." In her book *Flesh and Blood*, author Patricia Springer wrote: "As Cron and Nabors headed for the utility room and garage, Mayne began picking up evidence and placed the items in brown grocery bags from the local Albertson's." David Mayne was the crime scene photographer for the Rowlett Police Department, and he managed its evidence section.

Unlike authors Barbara Davis, Don Davis, and Patricia Springer, crime writer Anne Good did not become involved in the case until after Routier's conviction. She said when she first interviewed the incarcerated young mother and listened to her story, she had no strong feelings one way or the other about her guilt or innocence. That quickly changed. "By the end of the first interview, I thought that there was a big, huge problem here. Part of it was my sense of Darlie. I always think she's her own best evidence. She was, I felt, an

Cause for concern: Retired New York City
Police Detective Jerry Palace of *The Wrong Man?*
series on Court TV believes the case was far too
circumstantial to put Darlie Routier on death row.
Photo by Miriam Clifford.

open book," Good says. "There weren't hesitations or pauses. She wasn't careful
with her words. You really got the sense of her being an open book and just
completely truthful. There was a quality about her. I think I got the idea by
the end of it that this had really gone awry. I had done a little bit of research
and I knew what the problems in the case were—and they were troubling. The
time line, the way they were able to no-bond her—all those little elements that
make you uncomfortable with a verdict."

As the years tick by and Routier and her appellate lawyers wait for results from DNA testing—which always takes a back seat to pending cases
that have not yet gone to trial—evidence is deteriorating, Cooper says. "We've
spent hours [at the evidence clerk's office] going through the rat-nasty evidence
that is all contaminated. If this isn't contamination, I don't know what is, because it's in grocery bags—the same ones from June of 1996," the lawyer says.
"And they've been transporting pillows and covers and everything else back
and forth through trials and hearings and it's all disintegrating. All of it should
have been vacuum sealed."

Just as Harrell believes Darin may have seen the intruder but was convinced he saw a police officer, there are many who suspect Cron's quick assessment that there had been no intruder may have caused Rowlett police to disregard other leads or to see only evidence that pointed to Routier. Retired New York City police detective Jerry Palace says he sticks by the comment he made in a 2007 episode of the *The Wrong Man?* series that the case was "far too circumstantial" to send someone to death row. "Things should have been tested that weren't," he says. "It was a big case, but it was a small town. They came out pretty early on Darlie, saying that she was the one that killed the kids. Texas, I'm sorry to say, is pretty quick to flip the switch or inject the needle."

Like author Barbara Davis, longtime court reporter Suzi Kelly believes that sometimes those in law enforcement get tunnel vision. "Police officers—they're not evil. You want them as your next door neighbor," she says. "But they get tunnel vision on what they're trying to accomplish, and they just can't help but feel that the ends justify the means."

June 6, 1996, was a Thursday. Appellate attorney Stephen Cooper remembers being on a golf course on the following Sunday and hearing comments about the crime from a young woman driving the refreshment cart. She said she had been partying the night before with Rowlett cops. At that time, Cooper had no idea he would one day become involved in the case. "They [the officers] were talking about how the mother did it," Cooper recalls the young woman saying. "I remember her saying that the primary reason they believed it was because she had fake boobs and none of the knife wounds were in her boobs."

Sherry Moses, Darlie Routier's aunt, says: "I just think it's so arrogant of [Cron] to think that he can tell what happened at a crime scene within minutes of being there. How can you determine *anything* from that crime scene? It was so messed up with people running through there, and they moved things."

Defense attorneys have claimed that the injured and bleeding Darlie used the vacuum cleaner as a crutch, and that it was likely moved by first responders whose first priority was to save lives. They are puzzled as to why anyone would surmise that the vacuum cleaner was somehow part of the staging.

Witnesses for the state disputed claims made by both Routiers that Darlie tried to assist her dying sons by wetting towels to place over their wounds while she was on the phone with 911. Yet, police video of the crime scene shows wet towels on the floor. Spots of Darlie's blood on the kitchen floor were determined to be "low-velocity"—seemingly incongruent with her claims of having pursued the intruder—but the blood evidence might be consistent with her coming to after having been rendered unconscious.

The material found on the bread knife that was determined by state's witness Charlie Linch to be consistent with the material from the cut window screen is also similar to the material in fingerprint brushes used by law enforcement. Linch, at that time a trace evidence analyst with the Southwestern Institute of Forensic Sciences (SWIFS) in Dallas, had been hospitalized for alcoholism and depression prior to testifying in the trial, but this did not become known until several years after Routier's conviction. Her defense attorneys question his competency as an expert witness.

Cooper's view of Cron's expertise is the same as his opinion of bloodstain pattern expert Bevel and "Dr. Death," James Grigson. "Cron was raised in the Henry Wade era of trial and punishment—an era that led to innumerable bad convictions," he says. "Remember, Cron is the one who said the fingerprint [State's Evidence 85-J] 'appeared to be that of a child' when the experts say you cannot make that determination from a partial print. Cron led [police] immediately to Darlie, and I have corroboration that the Rowlett cops were blaming Darlie by Saturday night after the Thursday morning offense."

As for lead prosecutor Greg Davis, he did not respond when I reached out to him via fax, e-mail, and US mail while working on the *Routier Revisited* newspaper series, nor did he respond when I sought his input for this book. During that time period, however, he spoke on camera about the case for a documentary called *On Death Row* by Werner Herzog, a well-known German film director, producer, and actor.

Davis told Herzog that Routier "went to great effort to stage a crime scene." When Herzog brought up the use of the Silly String footage at trial, Davis described how he had watched the birthday celebration on the news that night in June 1996 and was repulsed by it. He said the jurors in Kerrville appeared to have the same reaction when the video was played in court. Davis said he felt it was appropriate for the jury to observe the behavior she had displayed that day. Herzog disagreed. "It is not a criminal offense," he stated in challenge to the prosecutor.

Coprosecutor Toby Shook told me that the evidence "was overwhelming at trial." Routier's lawyers say the evidence was weak. Those who have worked both sides of the famous case continue to insist that their viewpoint is the correct one. But, of course, one side has to be wrong.

* * *

Months after my meeting with Darin and just days after my second meeting with Aunt Sandy, I speak by phone to Darin to ask the question I had not asked that day at the Starbucks in Lubbock. In the affidavit he had given years earlier admitting to the planned insurance scam, he said that on the night of June 5, Darlie had asked for a separation. But I want to ask him whether she had asked to permanently end the marriage. I decide to build up to it by asking a couple of other questions first. We talk a bit about the thoroughness of the Rowlett Police Department's investigation and the amount of damage done by police to the family's home.

Darin says that, to the best of his knowledge, phone records weren't checked, but cops did show up at Testnec with a warrant to look over the company's payables and receivables. He says they accused him of selling drugs because it was unusual for someone so young to live in such an expensive home.

He says Rowlett cops caused an estimated $17,000 damage to the family's home—damage that was not repaired by homeowners insurance because it had been done by police and had resulted in a conviction. "They took walls out. They took cabinets out. The whole house was destroyed. If it had blood on it, they took it. They took plumbing because of blood down the sink. The insurance wouldn't pay, so we just let the house go. I was trying to fund a capital murder defense."

When I finally ask if Darlie had asked that night for a divorce, I am surprised by Darin's answer. "I don't know, to tell you the truth," he says. "We talked about a lot of things that night. Every time Darlie would get upset with me, she would [bring up divorce] because she knew it would push my buttons. But she didn't mean it."

I ask him when he last visited Darlie. About two and a half years ago, he replies. Then he says: "I'm not sure she wants to see me. She let go of me a long time ago. She wanted me to move on and raise Drake and give him a new mom. We grew apart. My job is to take care of our son and to do the best job that I can. But no matter what, I still love her."

As we hang up, my head is filled with thoughts about what others have told me about Darin having had little to do with Darlie for years, and about the letters Darlie sent to Aunt Sandy filled with love and longing for her surviving son. Both Darin and Melanie Waits say Darlie has tried to be as involved in Drake's life as she can from her cell on death row, and even wrote to some of his teachers when he was in school. How likely is it, I wonder, that Darlie would have been eager for Darin to find another woman to raise her son?

* * *

According to Cooper, there is no way of knowing when Routier's appeals will have run their course. It's been one long waiting game since 2008, when she won the right in court to do additional DNA testing on a handful of items from the crime scene. In July 2014, State District Judge Gracie Lewis of Dallas County Criminal District Court Number 3 signed an order for additional DNA testing. The order allows for the following items from the crime scene to be taken to the Southwestern Institute of Forensic Sciences for more testing: sock, knife, cap, nightshirt, child's blue jeans, maroon pillowcase, green blanket, blue blanket, green rug, placemat/towel, and the bloody fingerprint lift from the coffee table. The Dallas County District Attorney's Office had agreed with Routier's counsel that the additional testing should be done.

In an interview for KRLD radio, former assistant prosecutor Toby Shook expressed the view that the additional testing would likely show nothing to indicate Routier's innocence. In a statement that might seem ironic considering the speed with which Routier was taken to trial, he stated: "No one's going to rush through this thing."

"It took us two or three years just to get a record together," Cooper says, referring to the Halsey debacle. "This is a complicated case. There are a lot of issues which really should have been done prior to the trial. The trial should have taken two years to get started—even longer than that, simply because of the science evidence."

In 2009, the National Research Council released a 350-page report titled *Strengthening Forensic Science in the United States: A Path Forward*. In the section "Bloodstain Pattern Analysis," the Committee on Identifying the Needs of the Forensic Sciences Community states that "many sources of variability arise with the production of bloodstain patterns, and their interpretation is not nearly as straightforward as the process implies. . . . Bloodstain patterns found at scenes can be complex, because although overlapping patterns may appear simple, in many cases their interpretations are difficult or impossible."

The report further states that an "emphasis on experience over scientific foundations seems misguided. . . . In general, the opinions of bloodstain pattern analysts are more subjective than scientific. In addition, many blood-stain-pattern analysis cases are prosecution driven or defense driven, with targeted requests that can lead to context bias. . . . For these reasons, extra care must be given to the way in which the analyses are presented in court. The uncertainties associated with bloodstain pattern analysis are enormous."

In December 2013, the Associated Press reported that a former Indiana state trooper who was acquitted after being tried three times for the murders of his wife and two young children will work as a case coordinator for the national nonprofit organization Investigating Innocence. The AP story said David Camm's first case would be that of Darlie Routier.

Like Routier, Camm was convicted in trials in which bloodstain pattern expert Tom Bevel provided key testimony. The first two convictions were overturned on appeal. When the state prosecuted Camm a third time, he was acquitted. Camm, who has always maintained his innocence, spent thirteen years in prison for the September 2000 slayings.

Bevel provided me a written statement about his determinations in the case against Darlie Routier. He stood by his trial testimony pointing to her guilt. Regarding his investigations in more than three thousand cases and his experience with trial testimony, he wrote: "In the end, every analysis has experts from both sides and it is the jury that is tasked with assigning what weight they will give to any expert's testimony."

But in Routier's case, there was no expert testimony to counter Bevel's, since the defense did not put Terry Laber or Bart Epstein on the stand. I comment to Stephen Cooper that the trial defense team's failure to put a blood-stain-pattern expert on the stand to challenge Bevel may have been a fatal error. Cooper pauses. "Not yet," he says.

Because the trial was held before all DNA test results had come back—and because the defense did not seek its own testing—postconviction DNA testing will take years. Houston-area attorney Richard Burr, who is a member of Routier's appellate team, says that Mulder "should have asked for the assistance of forensic experts who would have recommended further examination of the prosecution's DNA testing, but didn't." Says Burr, who has been involved in several high-profile cases, including that of Oklahoma City bomber Timothy McVeigh: "There was a lot he failed to do." At his Dallas office, Cooper tells me: "I've said many times that I think [Mulder] thought he could win it with his oratory. The evidence sucks."

For his part, Mulder is not without criticism of Cooper and the appellate

On the team: Since 1979, Houston appellate lawyer Richard "Dick" Burr has represented defendants sentenced to death. He is Darlie Routier's attorney of record, though it is Stephen Cooper who typically speaks with representatives of the media. *Photo by Mandy Welch.*

team. He says that neither he nor any members of the trial defense team were asked to review the reconstructed trial record before it was accepted by the Court of Criminal Appeals. He also takes issue with the accuracy of the *Statement of Facts*, and says no one on the trial defense team was consulted about that, either.

Although unknown DNA has been found on Routier's bloody nightshirt and the sock found down the alley, "it doesn't prove our case yet," Cooper says. "We need male DNA that is unrelated to the Routier family or any other person that is connected to the offense. [The DNA evidence] has to be connected to the offense, like in the blood or on the sock." .

If the postconviction DNA testing uncovers evidence of an intruder, what will follow are lengthy scientific briefs and additional testing on those items, says Cooper. He says Lauren Schmidt of Colorado is the appellate team lawyer most knowledgeable about DNA. "We have much haggling to do," Cooper explains. "There are money issues involved in getting other things tested. The UNT [University of North Texas] lab has federal funding, but there are

Voices from the past: Dallas attorney Nick Nelson of the Haynes and Boone law firm was representing the Hood County News, a community newspaper in Texas, when he shot this photo of the original reel-to-reel 911 tape. State District Judge Gracie Lewis had signed a court order granting the newspaper's request to get a copy of the original recording. Both Routier and her mother claim Routier can be heard in the recording stating that her throat was cut, yet the outcry is not on the state's transcript of the 911 call. Routier claims she did not know of the wound until she saw herself in a mirror while on the phone with 911, and that the exclamation is an indication of her innocence. *Photo by Nick Nelson.*

strings attached. It's extremely complicated. We don't get priority in this stuff. This is a postconviction case. The cases going to trial pretty much have priority."

Appellate team member Richard Smith says there is "a hard threshold to meet" in overturning a conviction. If Darlie's blood is found on the sock through a new round of DNA testing, it would "go a long way to reaching the threshold that you have to meet in these habeas corpus proceedings," he says. Smith also notes that according to state witness testimony at trial, Damon could not have survived for more than a few minutes after the stab wounds were inflicted, and he was still alive when first responders arrived on the scene. "The time frame to stage a murder scene like that just doesn't make a whole lot of sense," he says. "And when you put basic reality checks on what it is the state claimed and how they claim this all came together in a staged murder scene, it doesn't pass the smell test."

Routier and her mother, Darlie Kee, claim that in a recording of the 911 call played at Routier's no-bond hearing in July 1996, the frantic young mother could be heard saying that her throat was cut. The recording captures the moment when she first realized that her throat had been slit, and the exclamation is an indication of her innocence, both say. However, those words did not appear in the state's transcript of the call.

My publisher footed the bill for a court order to make a copy of the original 911 recording. Nick Nelson, an attorney for the Haynes and Boone law firm, which represents the *Hood County News*, obtained the court order and made a copy of a cassette recording of the 911 call that is in a cardboard evidence box in the custody of the Dallas County evidence clerk. Nelson was unable to copy the recording from the original reel-to-reel tape, because the tape at the front end of the spool had come loose.

After Nelson e-mailed the audio file to me, I forwarded it to Tommy Thomason, founding director of the Schieffer School of Journalism at Texas Christian University (TCU) and founding director of the TCU-based Texas Center for Community Journalism (TCCJ). Thomason forwarded the recording to Russell Scott, an instructor in the Department of Film, Television, and Digital Media at the university. Thomason asked Scott to hone in on an exclamation uttered twice by Routier near the end of the recording. He gave Scott no other information.

Scott was unable to clarify the recording enough to make out anything but the final word of the utterance, so he sent it to a friend in the business who has access to better technology. The results, though, were the same. The first words of Routier's twice-stated utterance were still undecipherable. In the recording, Routier follows the second exclamation with, "Oh, my God."

The money spent on the court order and the efforts made in cleaning up the audio didn't amount to much in the end. And even if the full utterance had been unmistakable, the state would still argue that Routier had been faking. The state had spent more than $10,000 for audio experts with Graffiti Productions, Incorporated, in Dallas to clarify the frenzied recording and create a transcript before the trial. The transcript is eleven pages, and was entered into evidence by the Dallas County DA's office as State's Exhibit 18E.

On page ten, the transcript shows this exchange between Routier and the dispatcher:

Routier: "—there's nothing touched—"
Dispatcher: "—ok ma'am—"
Routier: "—there's nothing touched—oh my God—"

Less than one minute earlier, Routier had told the dispatcher she had touched a bloody knife and picked it up, possibly ruining the chance to get the fingerprints of the intruder. Why, then, would she follow that statement with, "there's nothing touched"? Perhaps she didn't. Present-day technology wasn't able to bring perfect clarity to the cluttered 911 call from almost two decades ago, but clean-up efforts by two experts at least determined that the last word in Routier's exclamation does not sound like "touched." In the opinion of those who have heard the clarified audio, it sounds like "cut."

Attorney Smith says he has continued to assist with Routier's appeals pro bono since 2002 for one reason: "The woman is innocent, and I don't want to see her executed. It is my true and honest and personal belief, based upon the evidence of the case—the evidence submitted at trial, the evidence that wasn't presented at trial, my interactions with Darlie, and, frankly, the rush to judgment that she was subjected to in the media and in that trial."

Appellate lawyer Lauren Schmidt believes Routier's trial was "horribly unfair." She says: "My work on this case and my interactions with Darlie over the years have convinced me she is innocent. I have closely followed cases about women who kill their children since I began representing Darlie. I'm not aware of any other case where a convicted mother has maintained her innocence for so long. Generally, women confess right away, or in a matter of days at most. Or they confess, but raise a defense, like insanity. What strikes me about this case is how long Darlie has maintained her innocence. Her story has been consistent since day one, notwithstanding the state's attempt to poke holes in it. The state's time line of the crime is unsupportable. There is no way Darlie could have staged the elaborate crime scene the state portrayed in the two to three minutes between when the boys were stabbed and she called 911."

I ask Cooper if police examined cell and land-line phone records from that night. I ask because of Sandy's assertions that Darlie had asked for a divorce, and her theory that Darin might have assured Darlie when she demanded a divorce that he would call off plans to stage a burglary. "Not to my knowledge," Cooper replies of the phone records. "But remember, they knew before the sun came up who had done it. Their only investigation thereafter was to confirm the theory." He refers to a quote by Sherlock Holmes: "It is a capital mistake to theorize before one has data. Insensibly one begins to twist facts to suit theories, instead of theories to suit facts."

Through Open Records, I obtained a copy of Cron's personnel file from the Dallas County Sheriff's Department, where he worked from November 1964 through March 1993. It is full of glowing performance evaluations. John

Clark Long, IV, who sued court reporter Sandra Halsey when he was head of the Dallas County District Attorney's civil division, said that prosecutors Greg Davis and Toby Shook are good attorneys who behave ethically. After losing the election for Dallas County district attorney to Craig Watkins in 2006, Shook committed himself to becoming a sought-after defense attorney. "Toby is a great defense attorney," Long says, noting that Shook was once named Prosecutor of the Year by the Texas District & County Attorneys Association. "People tell me he's one of the best lawyers they've ever seen. And people have said he was one of the best prosecutors in the state." As for Davis, Long says: "I've seen Greg, and he's very persuasive."

But the accomplished prosecutors and the experienced crime-scene investigator have been criticized for their roles in the prosecution of Darlie Routier. "I'm angry that there wasn't more investigation on this case," says Joyce Ann Brown, who was convicted in Dallas County for the robbery and murder of a North Dallas fur store owner and exonerated in 1989 after spending more than nine years in prison. Brown says that First Assistant DA Norm Kinne and others in the DA's office knew she wasn't the same Joyce Ann Brown involved in the crime, but they took her to trial anyway during the brutal era of Henry Wade.

Richard Reyna, the licensed private investigator who got involved in the case when Pardo funded an investigation, says this of Cron: "The guy comes in and, twenty minutes later, he concludes that nobody did it but Darlie. This guy must be a goddamn genius." Reyna continues to work the case, and does so for free because he is convinced Darlie was unjustly convicted. "I wanted to find something sinister in her," he says of Darlie when he first got involved in the case. "I tried every which way I could, and I couldn't find anything." He says that Darlie told him she had asked Darin for a divorce in the hours before the attacks.

Doug Mulder, the lead defense attorney at trial, has been criticized for not having created reasonable doubt by pointing the finger at Darin. But Mulder says there was little he could do since his own client insisted that the man she saw that night was not her husband. Mulder has also been accused of having had a conflict of interest, since he had represented Darin when Darin and Darlie Kee were accused of having violated the gag order. Mulder denies there was any conflict of interest, and says the matter ended when he simply explained to Judge Mark Tolle that the pair could not be held in contempt because they had never been admonished about the gag order. "It lasted, literally, not sixty seconds. That was the extent of my representation of [Darin]. Tolle dropped the whole thing. We never had a [formal] hearing." Still, some find it troubling that Mulder barely mentioned the life insurance on Darlie during the trial, and only made the connection that Darin stood to benefit from her death during the punishment phase of the trial, after the jury had found her guilty and was going to determine whether she would live or die.

Richard Smith believes that Darlie's insistence that Darin was not the man she saw that night may have been why Rowlett police discounted him as a suspect early on and focused on her instead. "One of the things that has always bugged me is, she was arrested and jailed and then something like three or four months later, it comes out that the sock down the alleyway has the boys' blood on it." The sock was found within hours of the crime, but its significance was not made known to the public until months later "after the public had already made up its mind," Smith says. "I mean, it's just appalling. They recognized that it was part of the crime scene, but no word is ever mentioned of that sock for *months*."

Cooper notes that by the time most convicted criminals end up on death row, they have spent a long time "working their way towards that." For many, family and friends have deserted them by that time. But such has not been the case with Routier. He is hoping if the day comes that the state sets an execution date for her, there will be an outcry. "Public opinion *does* matter," he says.

Long recalls a comment made to him back when he was dealing with Sandra Halsey and the flap over the trial transcript. "They said, 'John, cases that get bent, stay bent,'" Long says. "And the Routier case got bent and stayed bent."

The case of Darlie Lynn Routier isn't just bent. It's hopelessly twisted.

* * *

It has been almost two decades since breaking news bulletins interrupted scheduled programming throughout the nation to announce that Darlie Routier had been found guilty of capital murder by a jury in Texas's Hill Country. Much has happened within the justice system since then—hundreds of exonerations, stronger discovery laws, the creation of Innocence Projects and more accountability for prosecutors. But so far, nothing has happened to loosen the state's hold on Routier. Says Kerrville defense attorney Mosty: "I was very disappointed and upset [over the verdict]. This one has so many warts on it that I really don't think she got a fair shot." Appellate team member Richard Smith categorizes the case this way: "It's not a shining example of the way that you

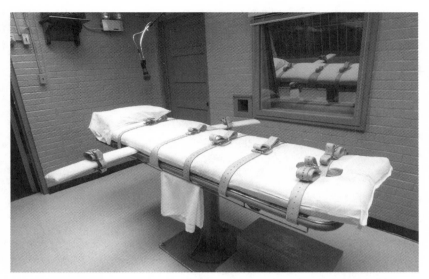

The results of DNA testing could determine whether Darlie Routier will die by lethal injection in the state's execution chamber in Huntsville. *Photo courtesy Texas Department of Criminal Justice.*

want the criminal justice system to work, that's for sure."

Over the years, Routier has written diaries from her cell on death row. The notebooks are in Cooper's custody, and not even Routier's family members have read them. If she is executed by the state, the journals will become the property of her sole surviving son, Drake. At the time of this writing, Drake is halfway through the three years of treatment he must undergo for leukemia. He is doing better than when he first began the treatments. He looks healthy, and the hair he lost because of chemotherapy has grown back, dark and curly. The only time he has ever been allowed to speak to his mother by telephone was the day he received his cancer diagnosis. "It was terrible," he says of the emotional conversation.

Drake says there were times in school when he suddenly began to cry. "Sometimes I would just have a random breakdown, crying out of nowhere, because I would start thinking about it," he says of the night his brothers died. "All the images would be going through my head of what happened." He has had dreams, he says, in which it is as if he is seeing his sleeping mother and

Surviving son: Drake Routier, nineteen and still under-
going treatment for leukemia at the time this photo
was taken, says he is convinced that his mother
is innocent in the murders of his older brothers.
Drake was just eight months old when his mother
was arrested and taken to trial. He has no
memories of her touch. *Photo by the author.*

brothers through the eyes of the killer.

Drake says he has never doubted his mother's innocence, and loves her
even though he was forced to spend his childhood without her. "It's never
enough time to talk to her," he says of the two-hour visits at Mountain View.
"Two hours is not long enough to make up for eighteen, nineteen years."

As this book was going into production, significant events occurred involving some of the players in the Darlie Routier story. Greg Davis abruptly
left his job as an assistant DA in the McLennan County District Attorney's
Office in Waco. According to media reports, he cleaned out his office over a
weekend, leaving at the same time as District Attorney Abel Reyna's office ad-
ministrator. The two were the sixth and seventh employees to leave that office
within a seven-month period. Davis did not publicly state a specific reason for
his departure.

Grant Jack, who had been a lieutenant with the Rowlett Police Department and commander of the department's investigative division at the time
Routier was arrested, was stripped of his gun and badge after Texas Rangers
searched his home as part of an investigation into allegations of bribery, official
oppression, and improperly taking videos and pictures. At the time of the raid
on his home, Jack was an investigator in the Dallas County DA's office, and was
assigned to a US Secret Service task force. A few months earlier, he had de-

clined my request for an interview about the Routier case, citing as his reason that the case is still pending since it is under appeal. Former federal prosecutor Jack Helms stated in media reports that the accusations against Jack suggest a possible willingness to break rules—and the law—in justice cases. Helms also stated that cases in which Jack was to be a key witness should be put on hold. A spokeswoman for Dallas County District Attorney Craig Watkins said many cases involving Jack had already been dismissed in light of the allegations. At the time of this writing, the investigation into Jack is continuing and he has not been arrested or charged. He has denied any wrongdoing.

Darlie's closest confidante on death row, Lisa Coleman, became the fifteenth woman to be executed in the United States since the Supreme Court reinstated the death penalty in 1976. In an article about Coleman's death by lethal injection, the *Washington Post* stated that Texas is "far and away" the leader in executions, carrying out five times as many as other states that have the death penalty. In her final words, Coleman, 38, sent her love to "the girls on the row," and said: "Tell Darlie I love her, hand in hand." She was pronounced dead twelve minutes after the lethal injection began.

Several weeks prior to Coleman's execution date, Darlie withdrew from the prison's work program in order to spend more time with Lisa in the days she had remaining. Their cells were side by side, though I don't know how long that had been the case. Previously, the cell of another death-row inmate had been between them, and the two friends communicated through vents. Darlie's withdrawal from the work program was a sacrifice. She would not be able to go back on the program for six months, meaning she would spend twenty-three hours a day in her cell, aside from showers, and meetings with attorneys and visitors.

Darlie saw redeeming qualities in Coleman that most people might not understand. A married couple who live in Gatesville and have been active for many years in prison ministry told me that Coleman changed considerably during her eight years on death row. Two days after Coleman's death, I received a letter from Routier. It was postmarked Tuesday—the day before the execution. "They took Lisa at 4 a.m.," she wrote. "We had stayed up all night because we knew they were going to take her. When she called my name, I could hear the fear in her voice, and it is haunting me. . . . By the time you get this, Lisa will either be back here with me or in the arms of Jesus. Either way, my faith in God is firm and I know *He* is in control—not man."

The man who many thought had control over what happens to Darlie

Routier no longer has that power. Craig Watkins, the groundbreaking district attorney that supporters of Routier had hoped would reopen her case, lost his bid for reelection to a third term. Watkins fell out of favor with constituents after alienating many within his own party, allegedly encouraging staffers to run against judges who had crossed him, and spending money from his office's asset forfeiture account to pay damages in a wreck he caused on the Dallas North Tollway after being distracted by a text message.

As for me, I realize I have not proven Routier innocent. If anything, I have merely given a voice to those who know her best and have held the justice system to the same harsh scrutiny to which she was held. Overturning a jury's verdict is no simple matter, and it would be naïve to think a new trial will miraculously happen for Routier. But there are those who believe she deserves it. Among them is Bruce Davis, the brother of lead prosecutor Greg Davis. Perhaps the only relief Darlie Routier will ever know will be through a jury system that will be less inclined to buy into far-fetched theories, questionable "science," and sexist character judgments.

It may never be revealed whether others besides juror Charlie Samford who were involved in Routier's conviction regret their role or secretly harbor doubts as to whether the state got it right. Samford says another juror allegedly has regrets about the verdict, but has been too afraid to speak out. One Sunday evening, I phoned the man. His wife answered, and immediately became suspicious when I asked to speak to him. When I identified myself and stated why I was calling, the woman's voice rose in agitation. "I *thought* so! Do you know we *still* get phone calls and letters about this case?! We've been through enough!" she said angrily. "I'm *sorry* she's on death row!" The woman then slammed down the phone as if the fires of hell had shot through the phone line.

Of those responsible for taking Routier to trial, private investigator Richard Reyna says: "I think there are some that honestly and secretly believe that they got it wrong, but they're never going to come out and say it. It's not going to happen."

In September 2013, the American Bar Association released a new study stating that, even though Texas has made improvements to its criminal justice system in the wake of dozens of exonerations, it still has a long way to go in terms of fairness and preventing executions of those who are innocent. The report states: "In many areas, Texas appears out of step with better practices implemented in other capital jurisdictions, fails to rely upon scientifically reliable methods and processes in the administration of the death penalty, and provides the public with inadequate information to understand and evaluate capital punishment in the state."

Barbara Davis believes that a way to reduce wrongful convictions is to institute a professional jury system. "The jury system doesn't work," says the former employee of the Tarrant County DA's office. "I believe a professional jury would have the disconnect. I've had a real problem with the jury system and the lay people who are involved. I know the process. You don't pick a jury; you delete the ones you don't want. And whoever's left, that's who your jury is. Prosecutors look for lambs—calm people who are easily led. The defense looks for rebels who will question an authority figure."

A commission similar to North Carolina's national model could arguably go a long way in putting to rest public debate over Routier's conviction. In 2006, the state's General Assembly established the North Carolina Innocence Inquiry Commission, the first of its kind in the United States.

The North Carolina commission consists of eight members selected by the chief justice of the North Carolina Supreme Court and the chief judge of the North Carolina Court of Appeals. Members include a Supreme Court judge, a prosecuting attorney, a defense attorney, a victim's advocate, a member of the public, a sheriff, and two discretionary members. Like Dallas County's Conviction Integrity Unit, the Commission has subpoena power. If Texas had a similar commission, its members could conceivably subpoena and question under oath those whose testimony—or lack of testimony—fueled unrest over the Rowlett homemaker's conviction.

Kendra Montgomery-Blinn, executive director for the North Carolina commission, says if Texas had a similar commission, it could issue subpoenas for depositions of witnesses. The commission could depose: the Baylor nurses, to determine whether they had been improperly coached; Dr. Kenneth Dekleva, to determine whether a *Brady* violation occurred when prosecutors did not relay to the defense his relevance; law enforcement and forensic witnesses, to determine whether they were instructed or encouraged not to create written reports that would have been made available to the defense; and court-appointed attorneys Parks and Huff, to probe whether private discussions had taken place with Judge Tolle about moving the trial to Kerrville.

Buried in case files in the basement of the Court of Criminal Appeals in Austin are notes written by Darlie Routier prior to June 6, 1996, detailing her wishes for her sons in the event she and Darin died. Darlie Kee was to share joint custody of the boys with Lenny and Sarilda Routier. Beloved possessions and pets were to accompany the boys to their new home, and money remaining after payment of funeral expenses was to be put into trusts for all three boys. Darlie further directed that if the boys did not go to college, they could not have access to the trusts until age twenty-five. She also took measures to protect the trust funds in the event the boys married. "Prenup for marriage for money in trust," she wrote. The young mother who wanted her sons to be surrounded by things they loved and for their financial futures to be safeguarded was the same young mother who prosecutors claimed murdered them because they threatened her lavish lifestyle.

PI Richard Reyna has seen Texas justice up close long enough to know how the game is often played. "It's a nasty, nasty business, because a prosecutor doesn't wear a white hat. He may not be the good guy. He may be doing whatever he can to win because he wants to be a judge." In Reyna's view, many convictions are won not only through overly ambitious prosecutors, but by questionable testimony from "experts" who value the money they are paid by the state more than they value the truth. He refers to such testimony as "the battle of the whores," though he acknowledges that not all experts who routinely testify in trials are worthy of such derision.

Though to date nothing has happened to exonerate Routier or to bring about a new trial, Cooper is right about public opinion: it does matter. But whether public opinion—or DNA—will turn the tide for Darlie Routier remains to be seen. As for my own reexamination of the long-ago case, I figure Waylon has probably earned a rest.

Near the end of my journey, after stopping by the office one night after a city council meeting, I impulsively do a Google search for "silver bullet." I learn that in folklore, a silver bullet was used to ward off evil. It was also used as a calling card—a symbol of justice—for the Lone Ranger.

I turn off the lights, set the alarm and get in my car. The moon is high in the sky. Somewhere in East Texas, a former FBI special agent known as Crimefighter is likely pacing the floor over a long-ago case that has refused to give him peace. In the wee hours, a Dallas appellate attorney may once again awaken hours ahead of the alarm clock.

As I start the engine and the dashboard begins to glow, I am struck with another impulse. Through the glass doors of the newspaper office, I see the silhouette of Hiram B. Granbury, a brigadier general in the Confederate States Army during the Civil War. At times, the life-size wooden figure of the man for whom the town of Granbury was named has been forced to suffer indignities. Bunny ears have been placed on his head in the spring and, during the summer months, he often sports a Hawaiian shirt and straw hat. But on this night, the silent sentinel is dressed only in his military garb, though two newspaper delivery bags are hanging from his squared shoulders.

I get out of the car, unlock the door, deactivate the alarm, turn on the back lights, and return to my cubicle for one more computer task before finally calling it a day. A Google search for Biblical references to the month of April pops up Exodus 13:4.

"On this day, in the month of April, you have been set free."

EPILOGUE

Standing at the door of my closet, I could see there was plenty of black apparel appropriate for a funeral. Yet, my eye kept falling on a sky-blue boucle suit with a matching flower pin.

I laid out on the bed the collection of black, but chose the blue.

The next day, arriving at the funeral chapel with my two sons, ages ten and thirteen, I walked into a sea of judgment and black. The blue suit stuck out like a scarlet letter on a forehead. Most of those in attendance were Dallas media. Few spoke to me.

It was much later that I realized my likely reason for choosing the blue suit for the funeral of the man who had been my ex-husband for only six weeks. It had to do with true colors. So many people thought they knew me, but didn't. When the spouse one leaves is soon after diagnosed with cancer and dies within months, the result is scorn and judgment—doubly so when the deceased was well-liked and well-respected.

The funeral coincided with Flag Day. The sight of hundreds, if not thousands, of American flags waving under the brilliant blue sky at the Dallas-Fort Worth National Cemetery was surreal. In a pavilion, with the flag-draped coffin just feet away and sunglasses providing some measure of insulation, I did my best to stand erect as, one by one, mourners filed past. The sky-blue suit hung on a frame that had grown alarmingly thin, but I'm not sure anyone noticed.

When I was working on the *Routier Revisited* newspaper series for the Texas Center for Community Journalism, Darlie Kee and Doug Mulder told me that I should contact Lloyd Harrell. I made excuses. I don't need him just yet, I reasoned, but will get around to phoning him eventually. But I knew the real reason—I was simply avoiding him. I didn't know how he would treat me, since he had known my ex-husband.

But then late one afternoon, while working in my cubicle, Crimefighter called *me*. Toward the end of our three-hour conversation about Darlie Routier, he brought up my ex-husband and told me something I hadn't known. He had been pursuing the Darlie Routier story when he became ill. He also reminded me of something I had somehow forgotten. He had been one of the few people who had hugged me that awful day in the summer of 2004.

When I became immersed in the Routier case, I sensed there was something more to my dogged obsession than an interest in the justice system. It would be well after the newspaper series had turned into a book project that I discovered I had more of a connection to Darlie than our sons having been close in age—the first born in June, the second born in February. We were both judged by the public, and by Dallas media, while we had stood at the grave of a loved one.

Darlie's day of judgment was June 14, 1996, the day of the Silly String episode. For me, it was June 14, 2004.

While there are many lessons to be learned from the Darlie Routier case regarding how our justice system should operate, there are other lessons that reporters typically don't write about. The lessons have to do with forgiveness and non-judgment, and the power in both.

Whether Darlie is guilty or innocent, she granted forgiveness to author Barbara Davis and juror Charlie Samford the minute they requested it. I wonder how many of us would have done the same. It is my hope that *Dateline: Purgatory* helps readers see more of Routier's true colors, as well as the true colors of our justice system.

Crimefighter's kindness opened the door for a collaboration that helped bring this book to fruition. He provided constant assistance and encouragement. As a result, I have written the book that a good man named Howard Swindle would have written, though I wrote it differently than he would have.

Like the plucky rooster on the road near Aunt Sandy's house, I have crossed the perilous terrain of my own purgatory, arriving safely on the other side. For that, I have an infamous death-row inmate and a former FBI special agent to thank.

Photo by Mary Vinson.

Kathy Cruz is a former reporter for the *Dallas Morning News*, now working as a staff writer at the *Hood County News* in Granbury, thirty-five miles southwest of Fort Worth. She has won numerous Journalist of the Year honors from Texas press associations, as well as many other awards from regional, state, and national press associations. She is the coauthor of *You Might Want to Carry a Gun: Community Newspapers Expose Big Problems in Small Towns*. Cruz is the recipient of five awards for excellence in legal reporting, including a Texas Gavel Award and four Stephen Philbin Awards from the Dallas Bar Association—two of which were grand prizes.